Mimi, 2009

We love you + miss you this Christmas! Enjoy the beauty of Colorado with us,

Craig, Terri, Lance, Kyle, Whitney

a COLORADO EXPRESSION book

Christmas in Colorado

COLORADO expression

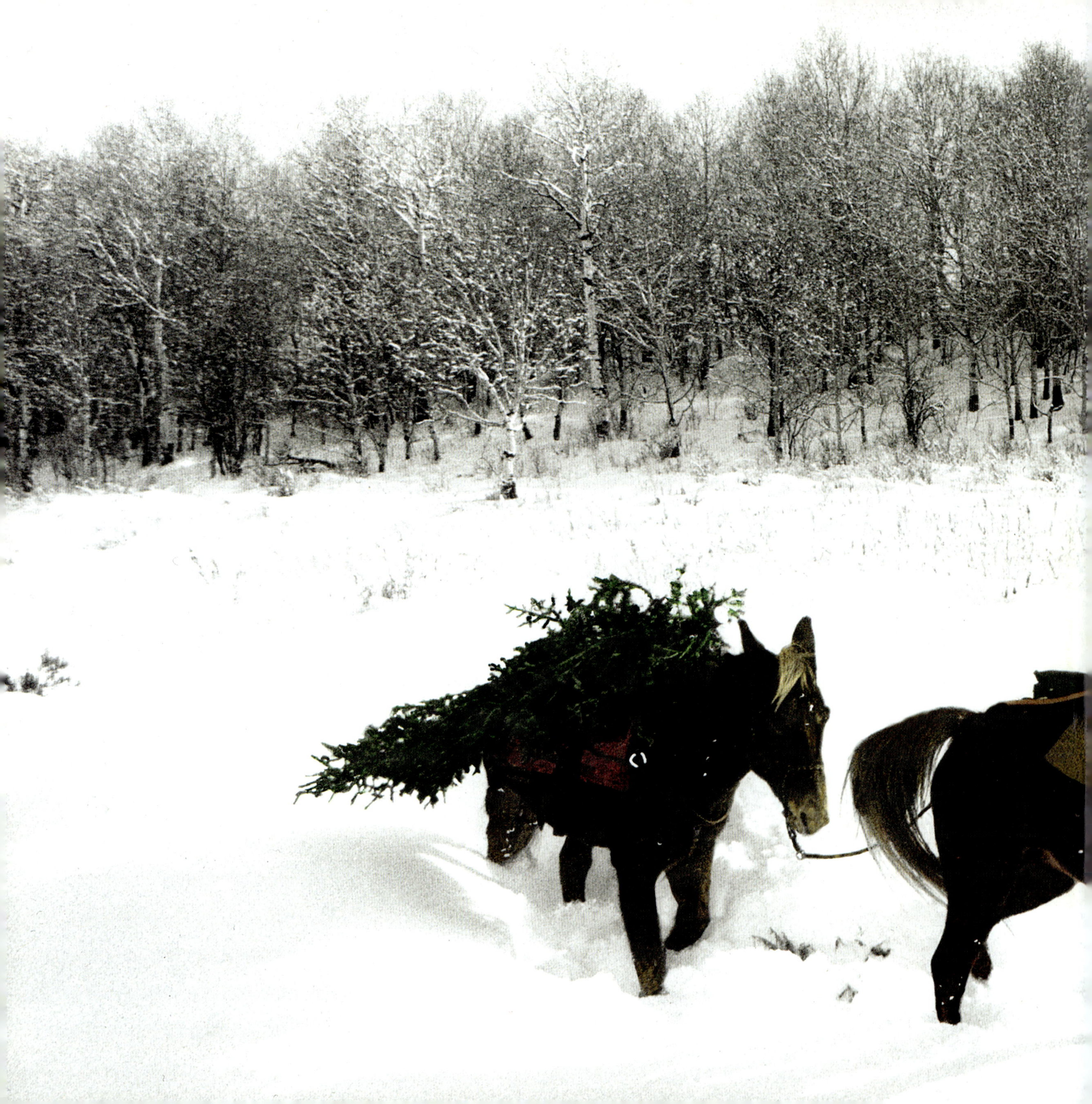

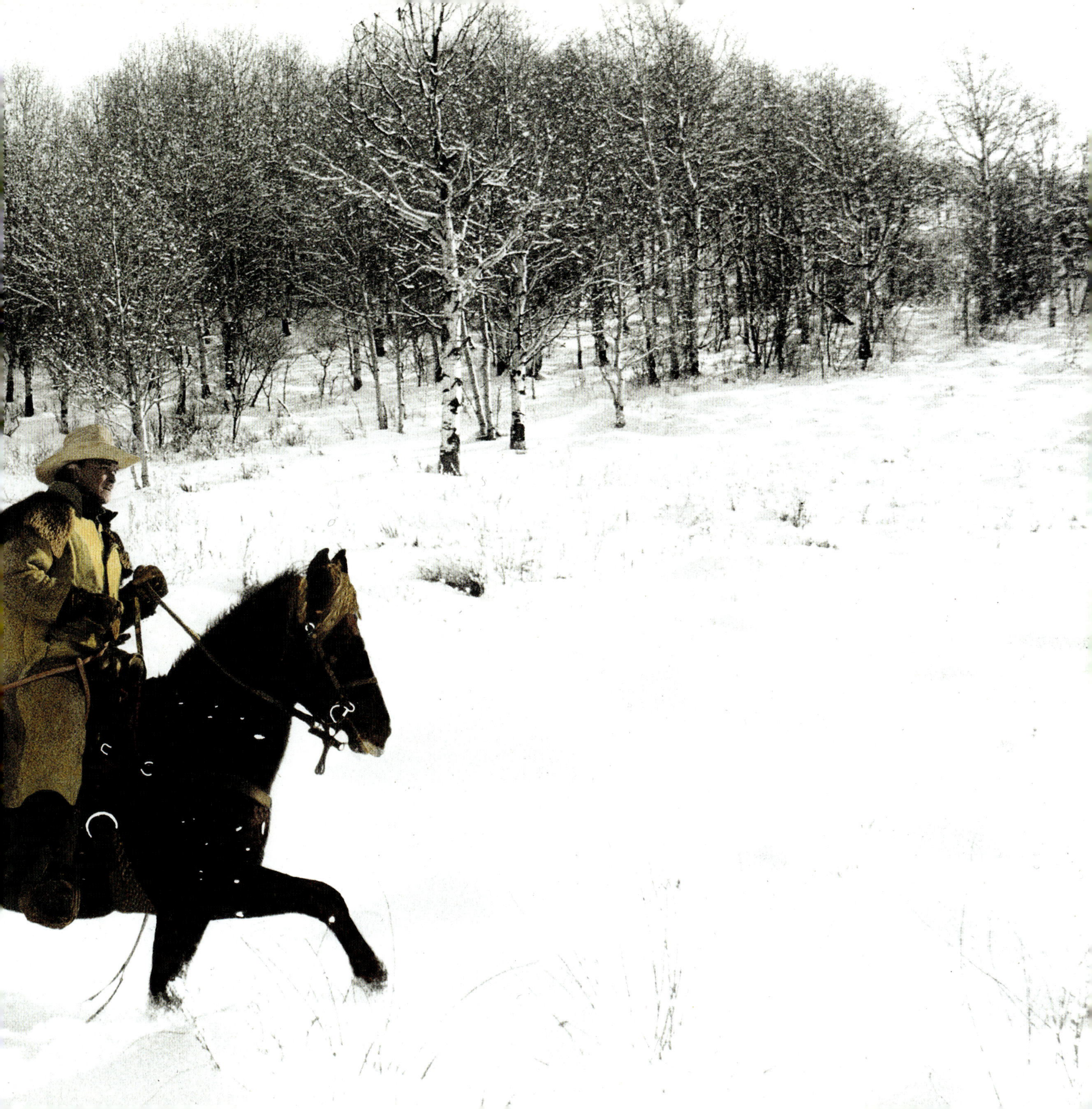

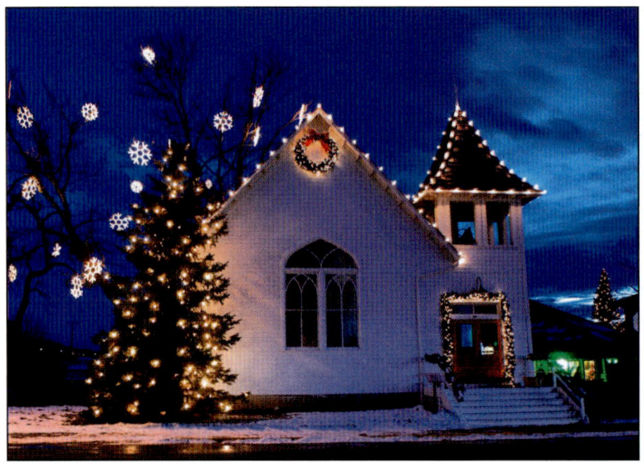

Parker Chapel, Main Street, downtown Parker

Previous page: Rowan Heid, of Triangle Ranch in Clark, Colorado, brings in a Christmas tree for a customer on his mule, Jerry

Dedication

TO MY CHILDREN,

TODD AND PIPER,

WHO MADE EVERY

CHRISTMAS IN COLORADO

A PIECE OF HEAVEN.

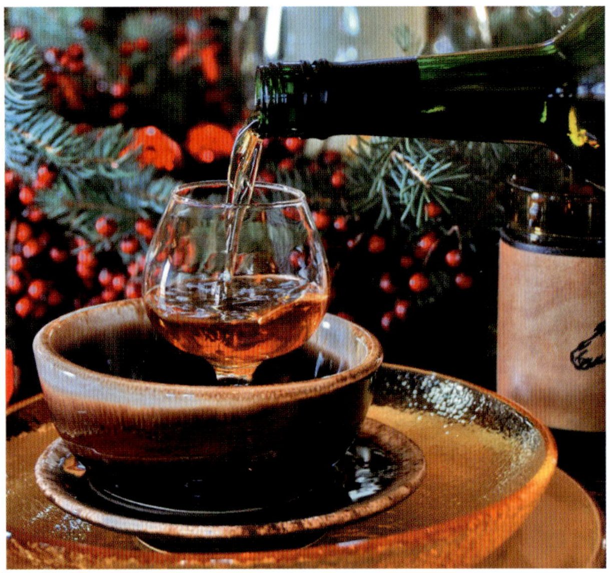

Above: Brandy snifter at Clinger Ranch house, Aspen
Right: L'Esprit de Noel Holiday Home Tour, Denver

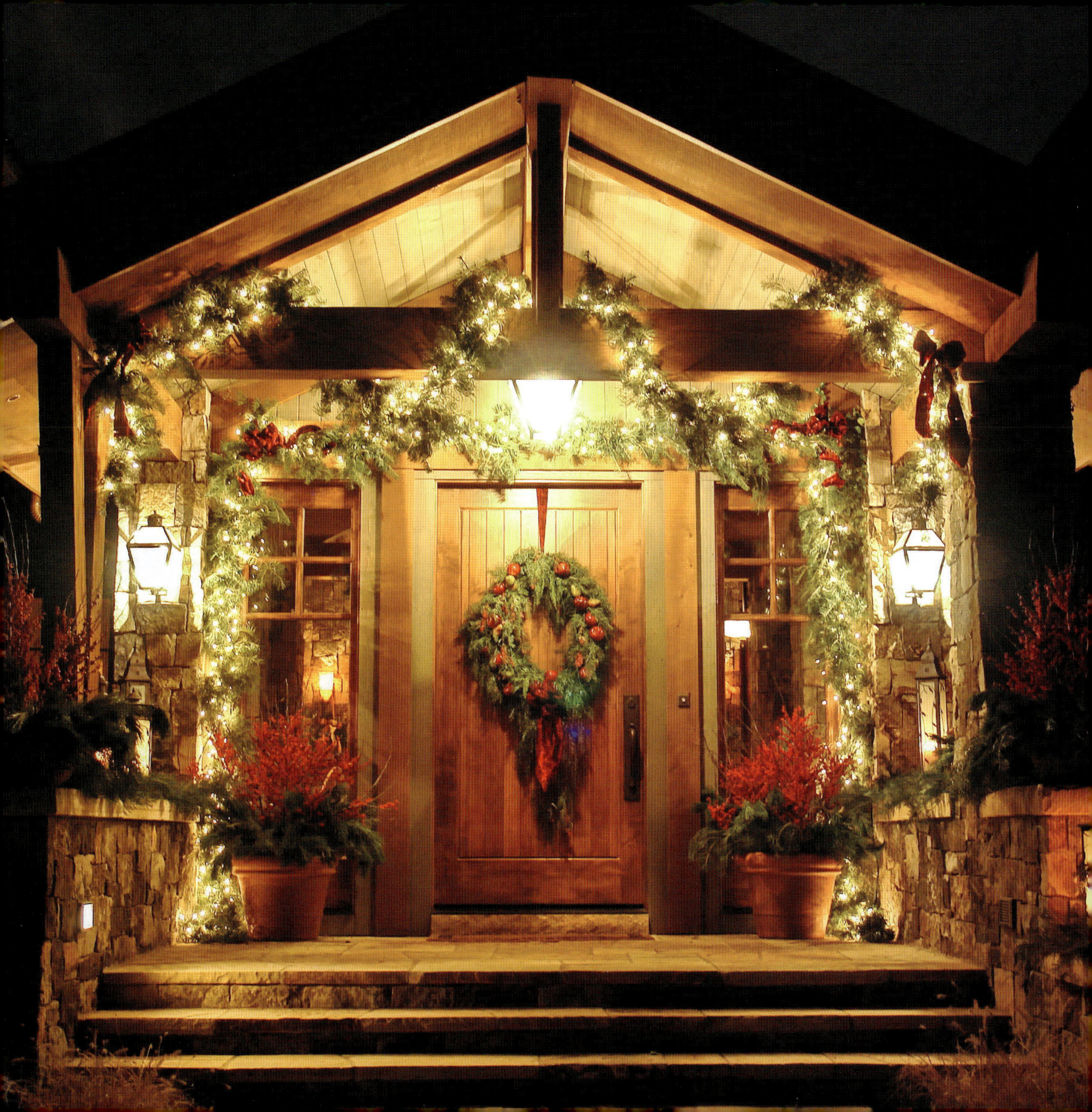

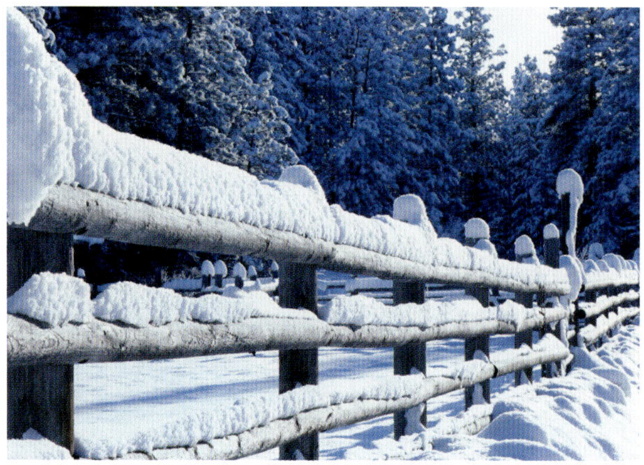

Introduction

COLORADO HAS ALWAYS HAD A PIECE OF MY HEART, but at no other time does it fill my heart more than at Christmastime. The skies are bluer, the snowflakes are fluffier, and the backdrop more magical than any other place on earth.

I have traveled throughout Colorado to share with you some of its most magical places, and I hope it will capture your heart as it did mine so many years ago.

Wrap your arms around this special place and enjoy Christmas in Colorado as I have, year after year.

—TERRY VITALE

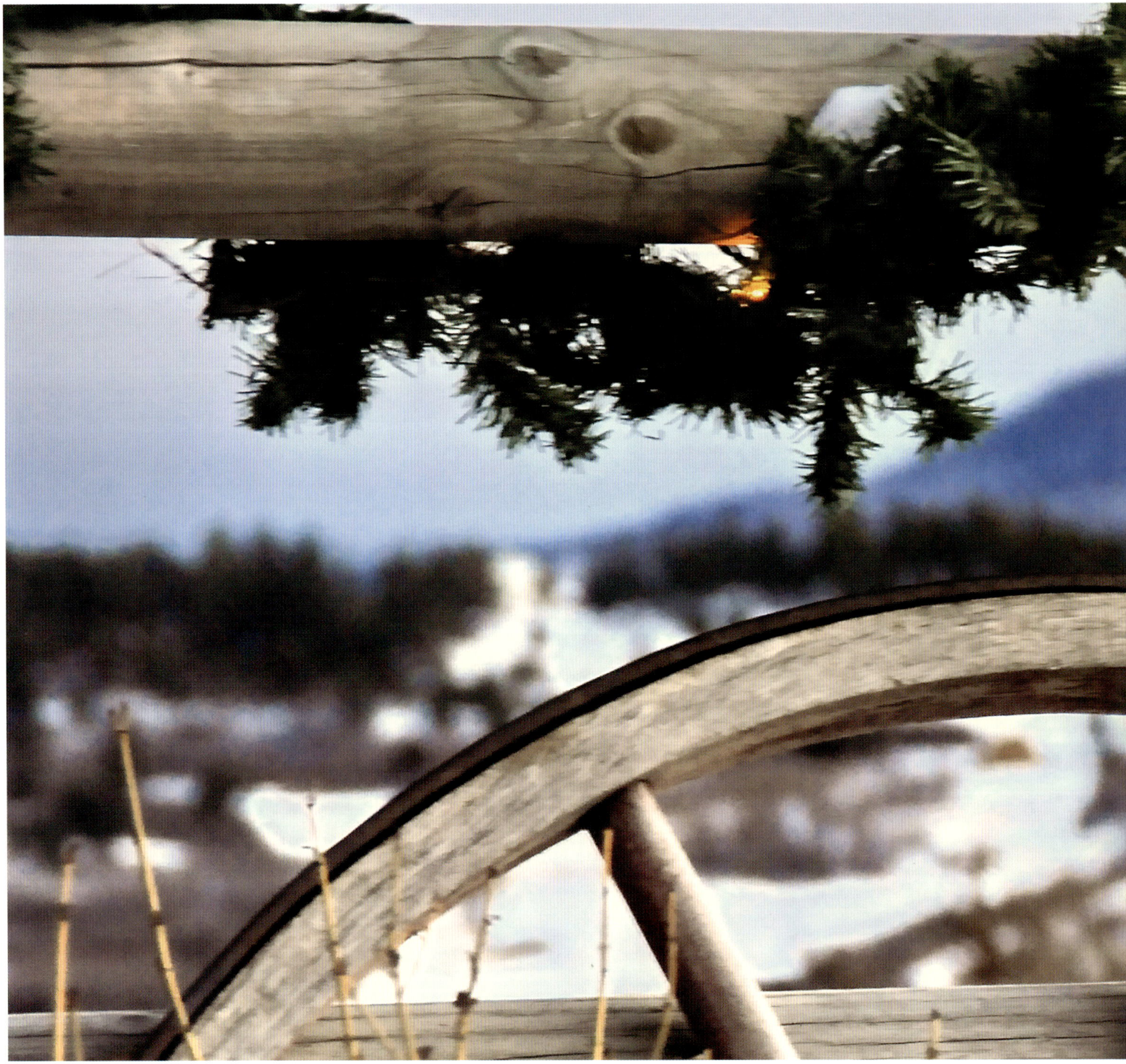

Wagon wheel and fence, Rock-A-Billy Ranch, Sedalia

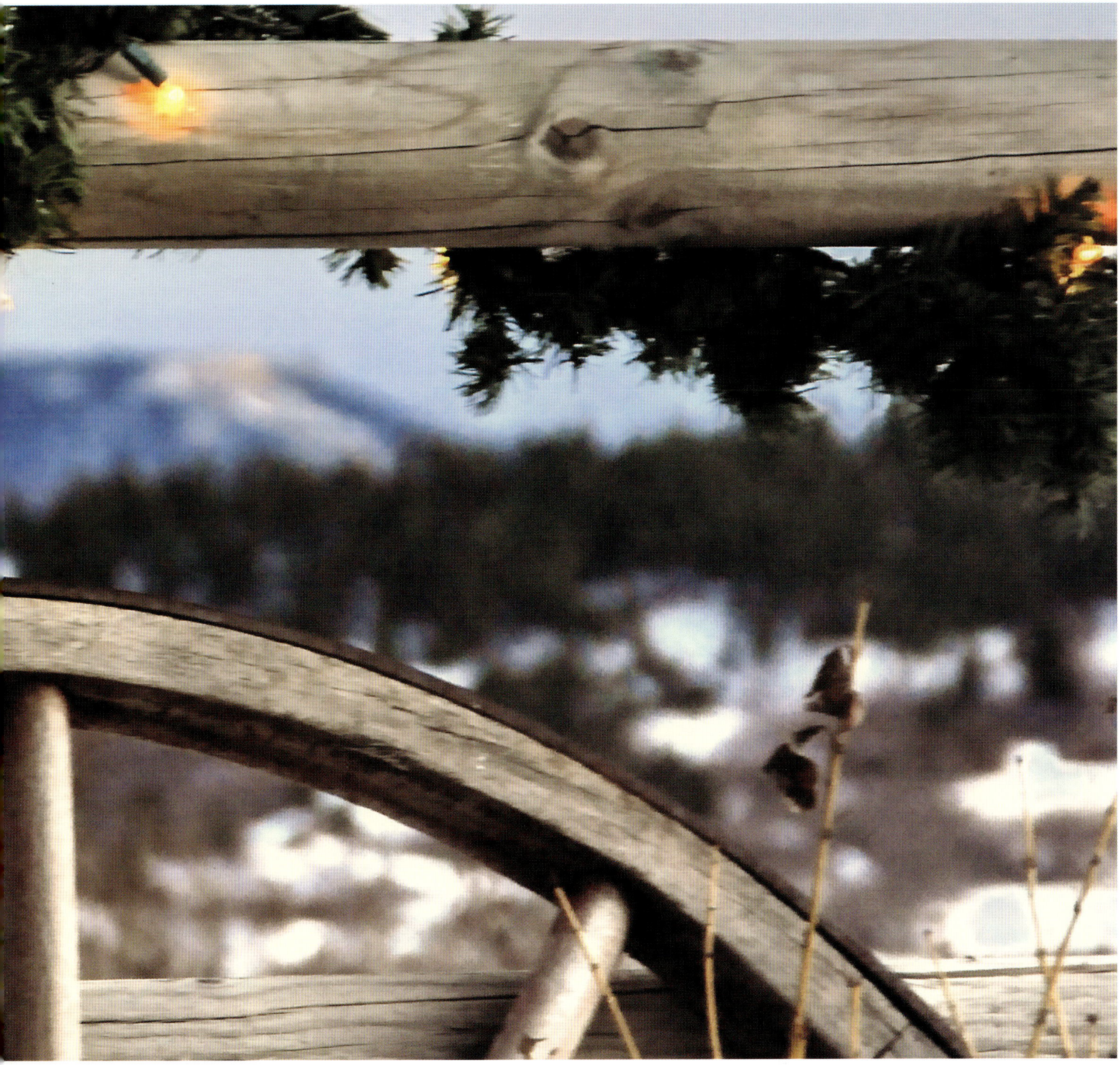

Contents

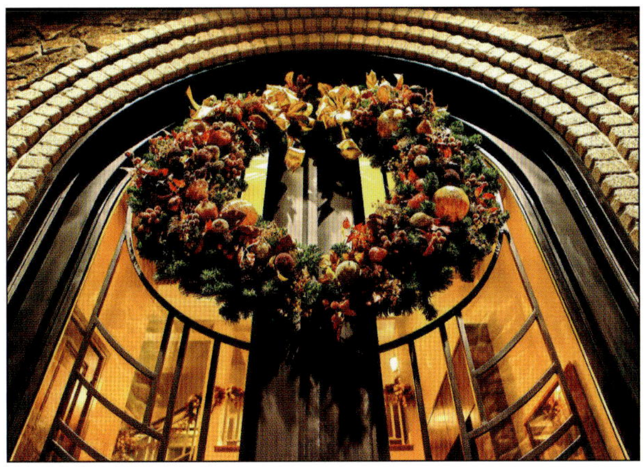

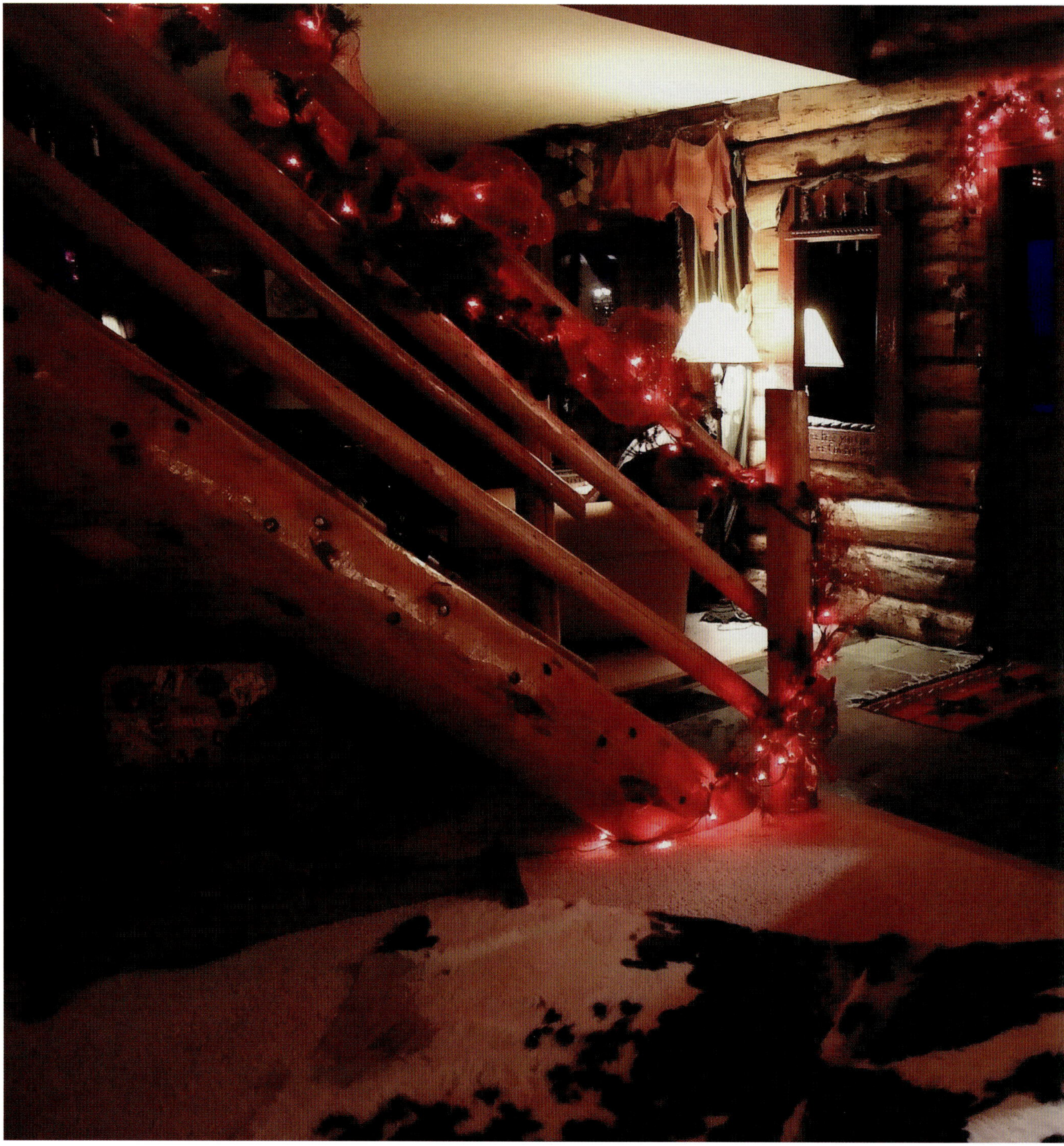

Living room, Rock-A-Billy Ranch, Sedalia

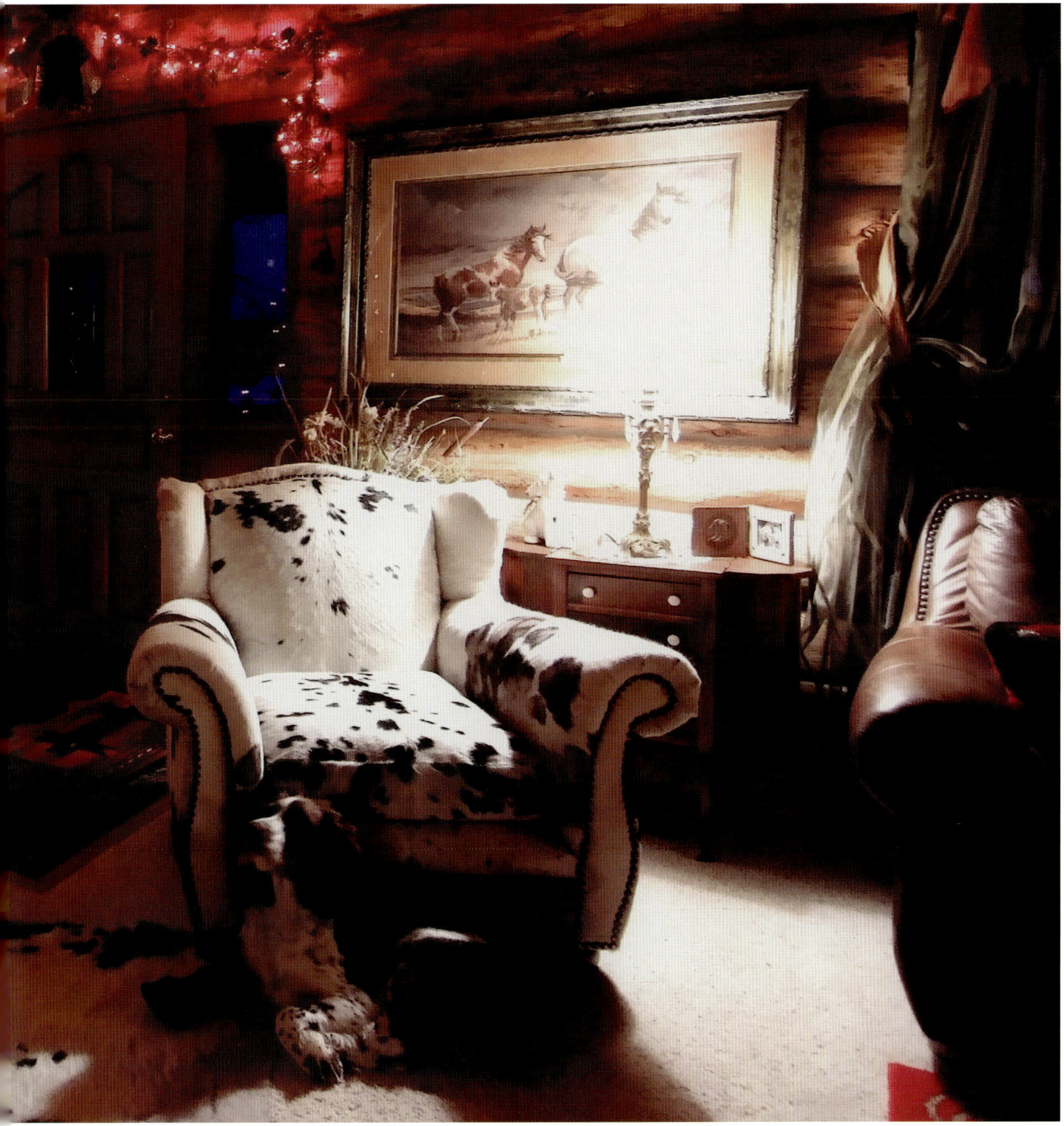

Aspen

& SNOWMASS

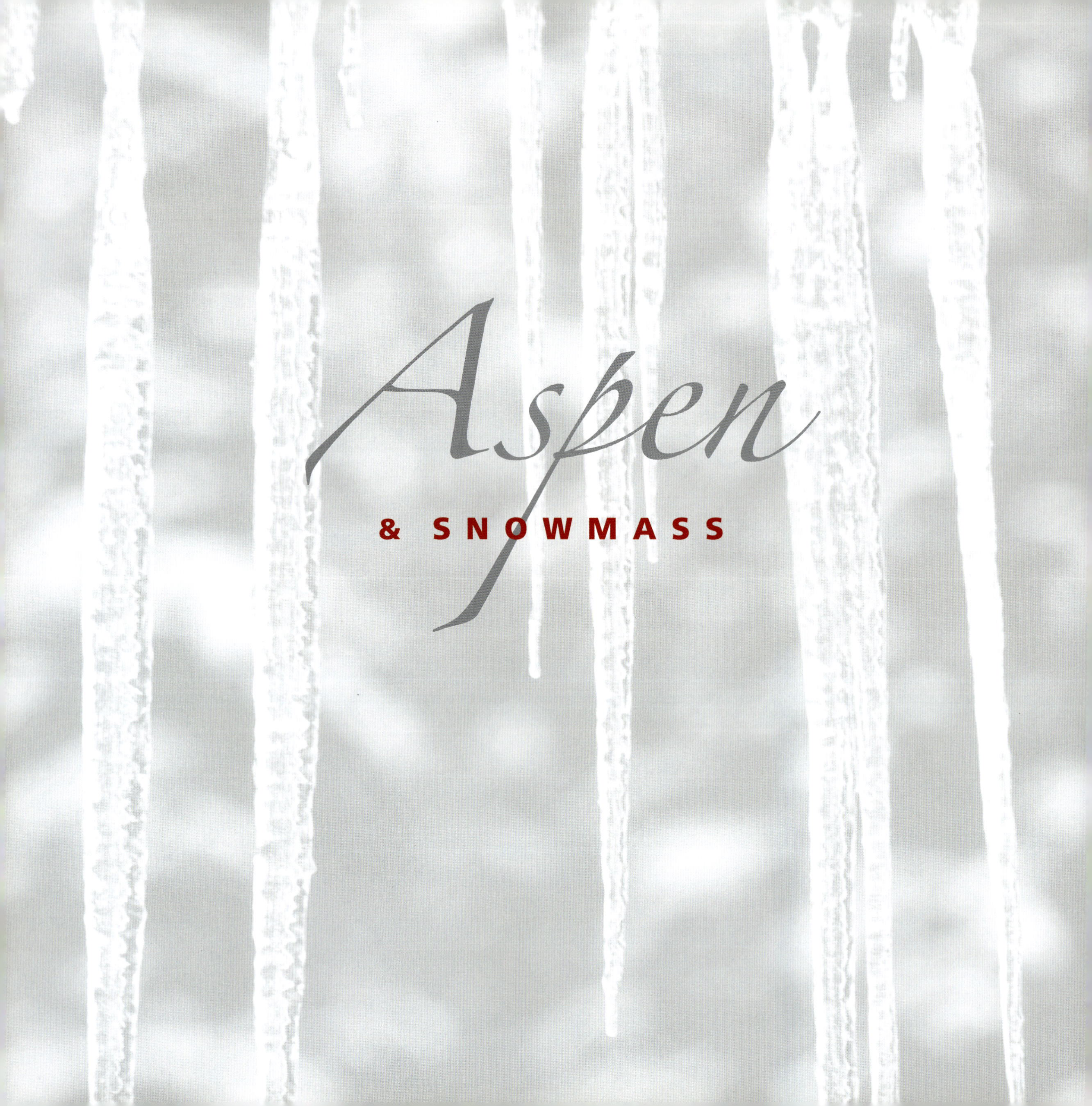

There has been
only one Christmas–
the rest are
anniversaries.

—W.J. CAMERON

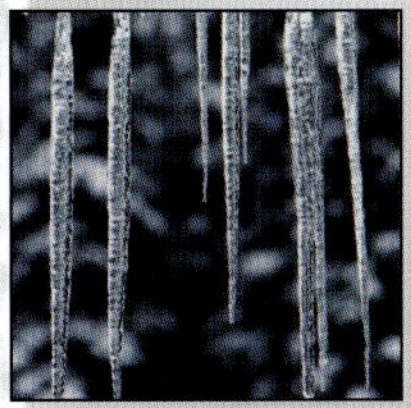

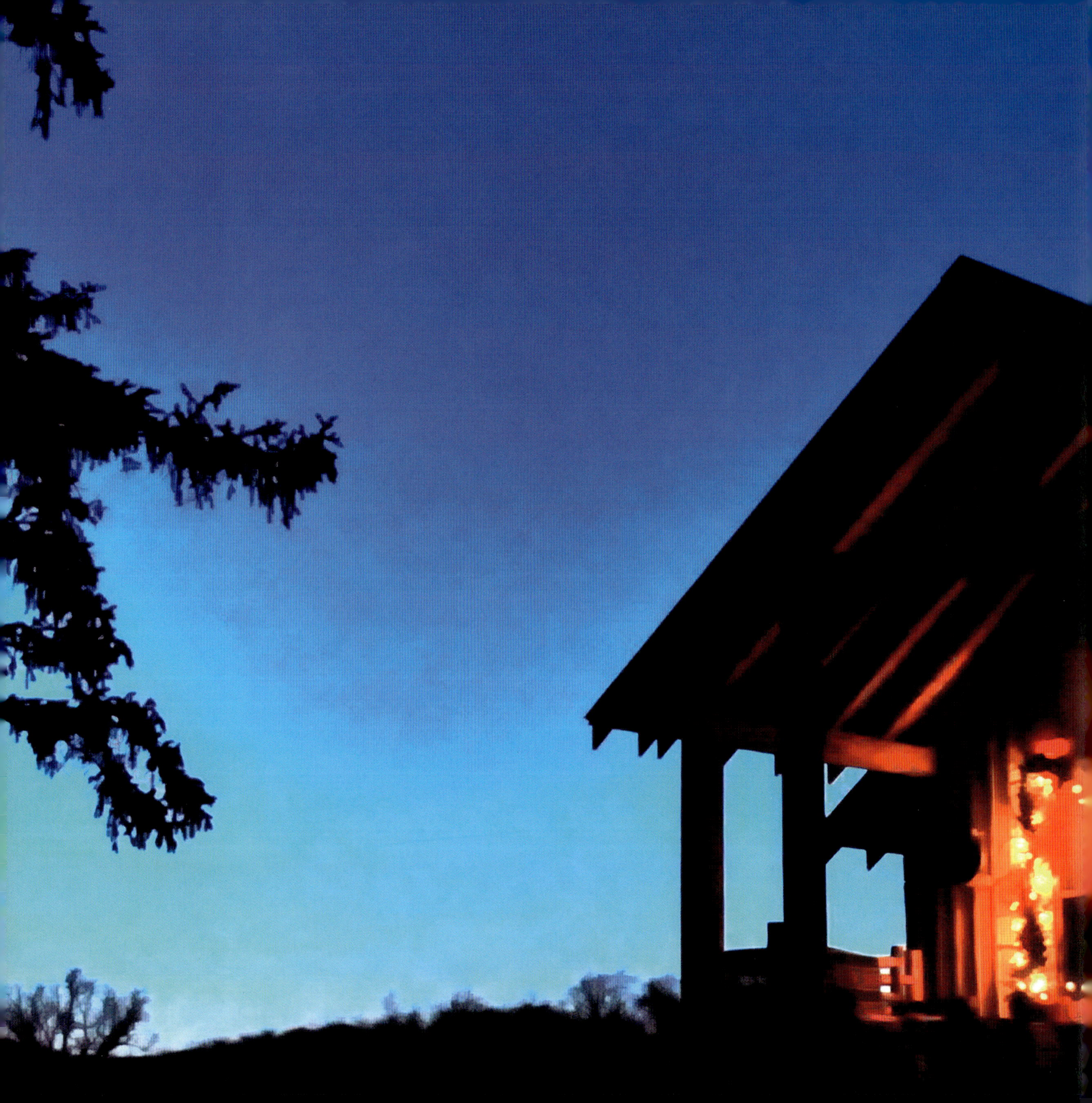

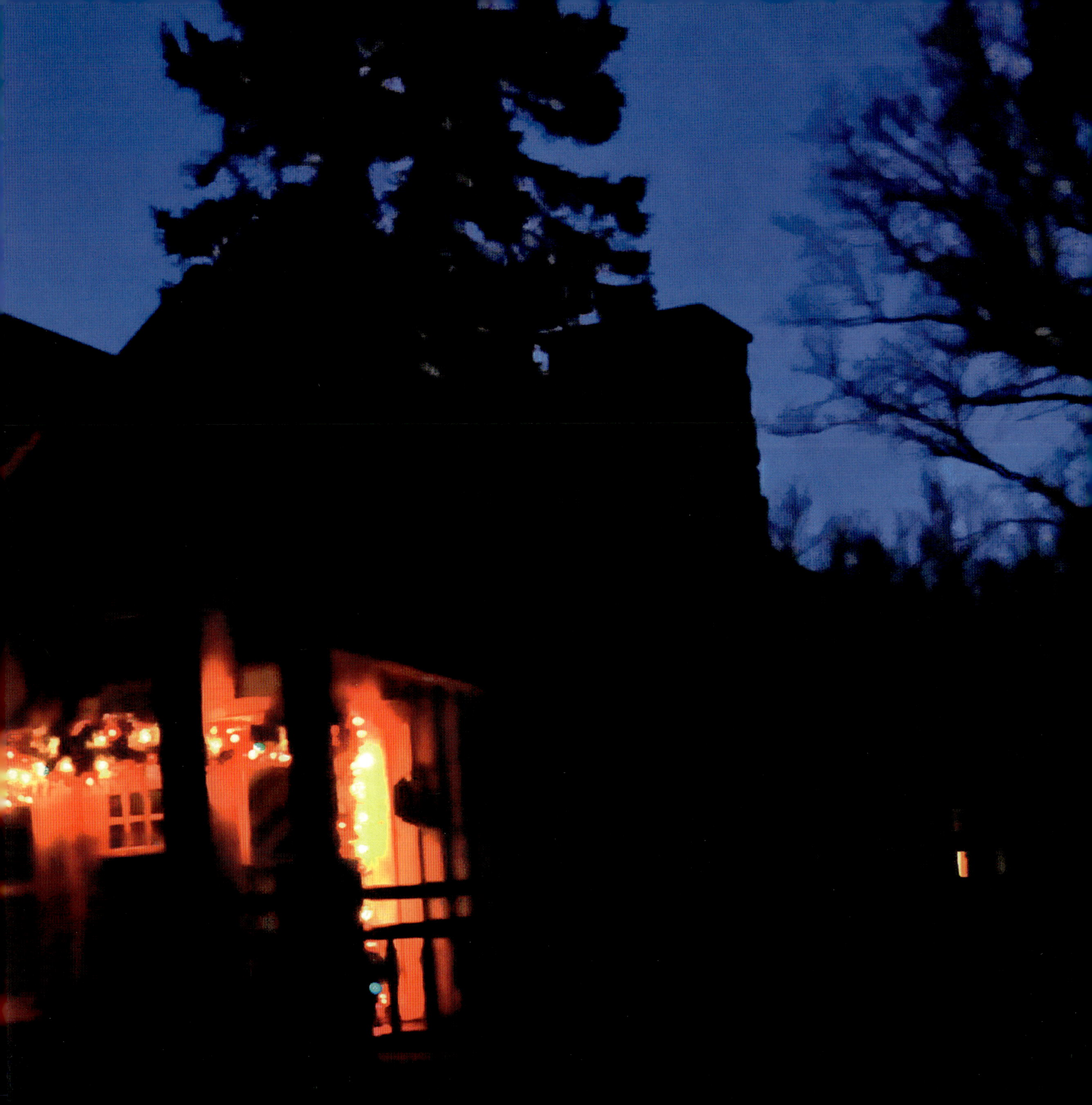

SURROUNDED BY CASCADING snow-peaked mountains, Christmas in Aspen/Snowmass is nothing short of enchanting. From perfectly powdered slopes to an active nightlife and hotels designed to pamper, Aspen shines with holiday spirit. To open the magical season, head down Snowmass' famed Fanny Hill in the annual Snowmass Torchlight Parade. Participation in this event is free and open to the public. Viewers watch in awe and the mountains flow with holiday cheer as illuminated skiers and snowboarders float down the slopes in a trail of light. After the parade, watch as Snowmass Village becomes Santa's Village and lights up to the sounds of carolers.

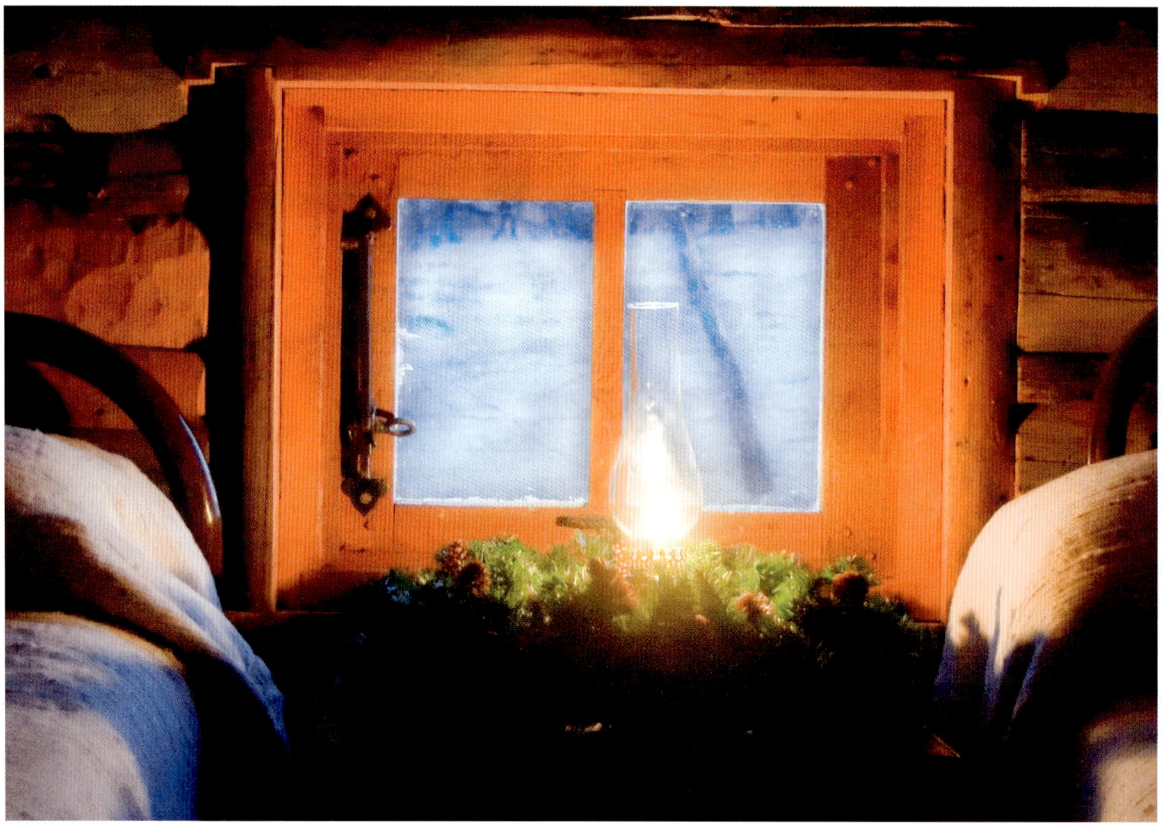

Above: A candle warms up the Clinger Ranch house, Aspen

Previous page: The Clinger Ranch house glowing from within, Aspen

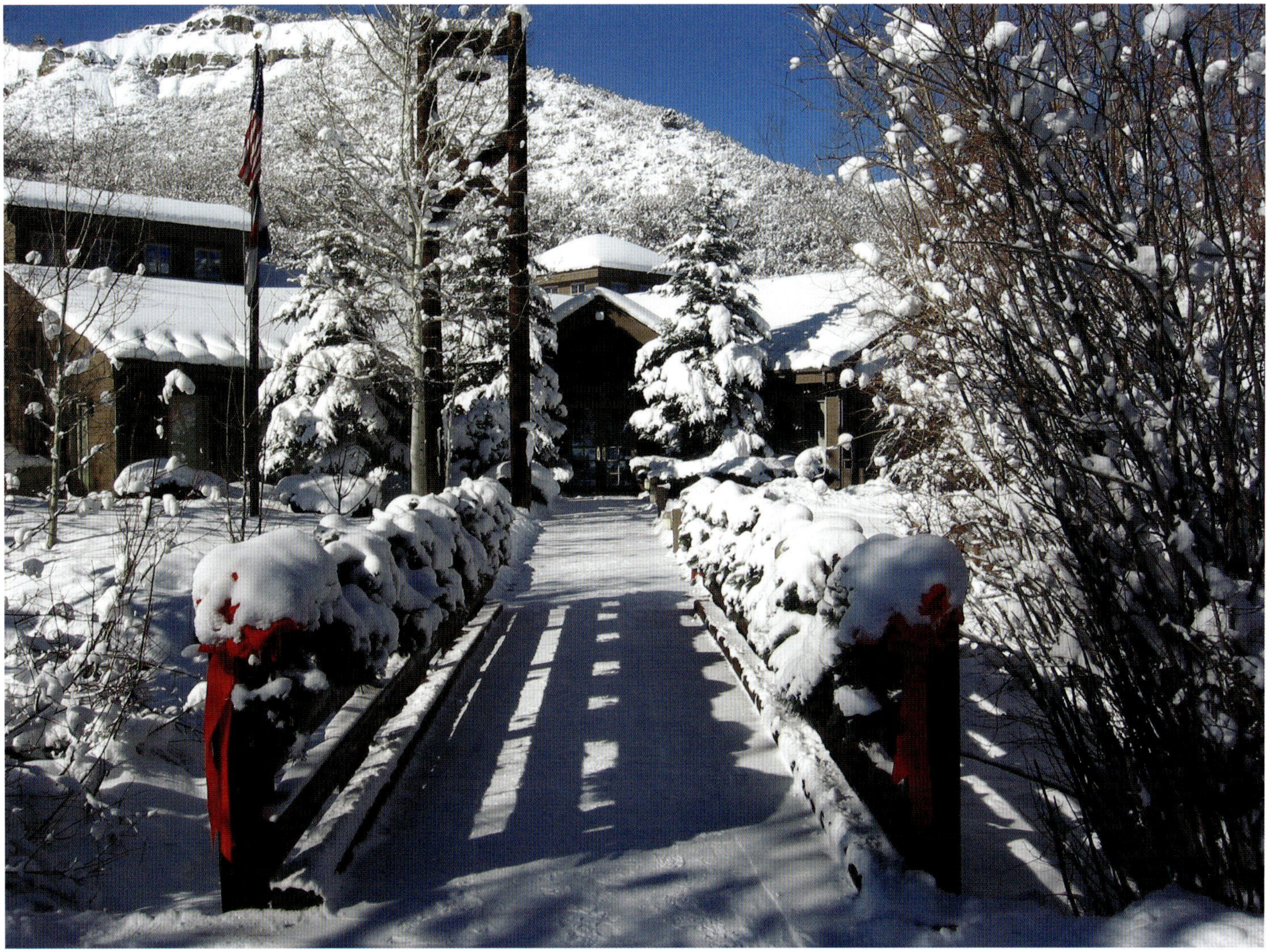

Bridge to Snowmass Chapel, Snowmass

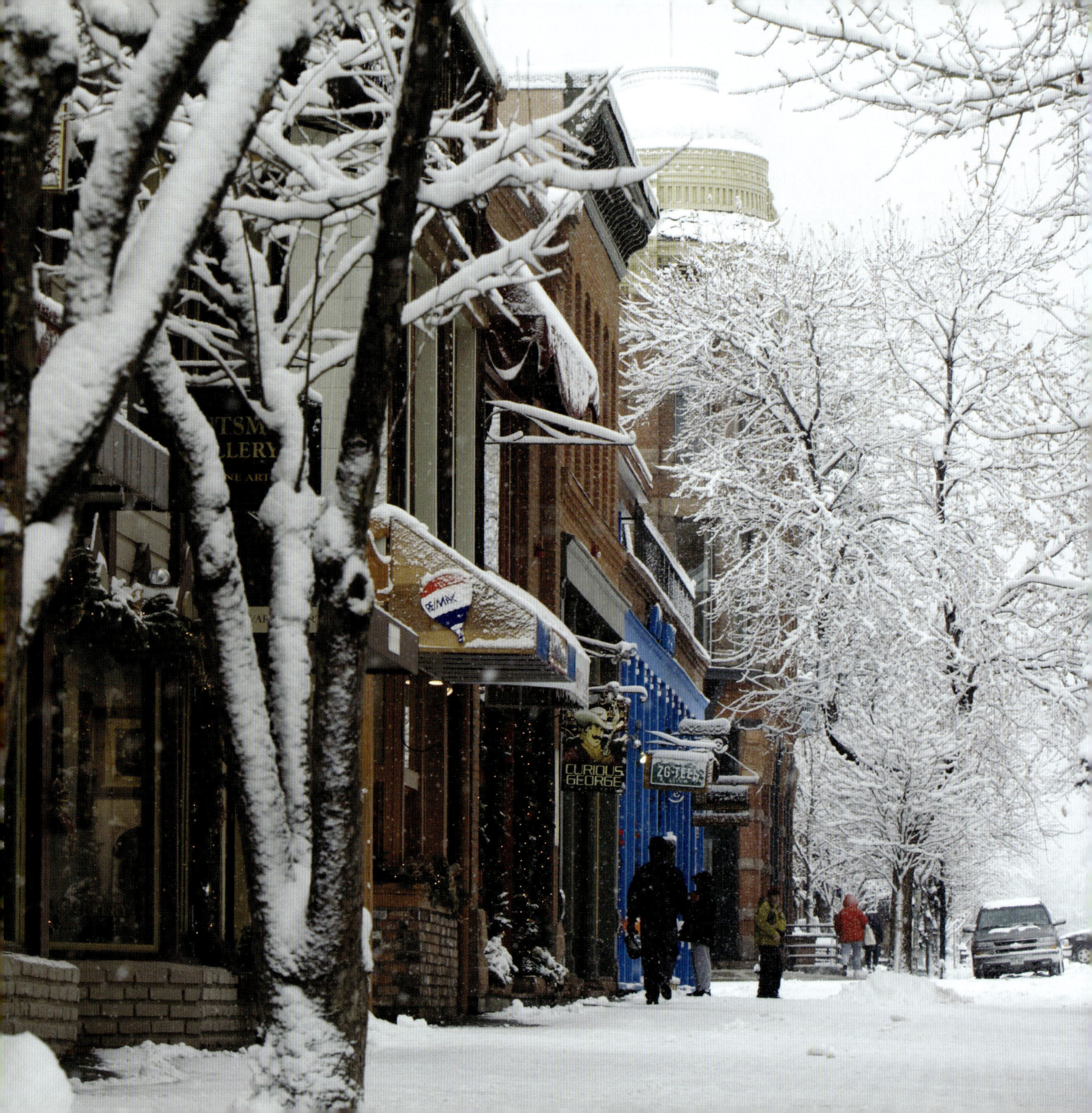
CURIOUS
GEORGE

No matter what kind of winter adventure you're after, Aspen is the flawless locale for experiencing it. Aspen and Snowmass boast Colorado's best ziplines as well as great sledding and Nordic skiing. You'll also find skating at the Silver Circle Rink and dogsled rides in Snowmass Village.

Of course, you just can't go to Aspen or Snowmass without strapping on a pair of downhill skis—these towns boast some of the best ski resorts in North America. And with 90 percent of the hotels within walking distance of the lifts, the runs are all easy-access. Come back from a day on the slopes to live music at the Snowmass Village Mall. Local and regional bands from around the state play each afternoon for the ideal après-ski treat.

For a memorable family celebration and some holiday cheer, visit Santa at the Silvertree Hotel. There, you'll find the annual Holiday Open House with candy canes and a 17-foot Christmas tree. In the days leading up to Christmas, head back to the Silvertree for storytelling and fireside chats with Santa.

Explore Aspen's hip art scene at the Anderson Ranch Arts Center Holiday Exhibi-

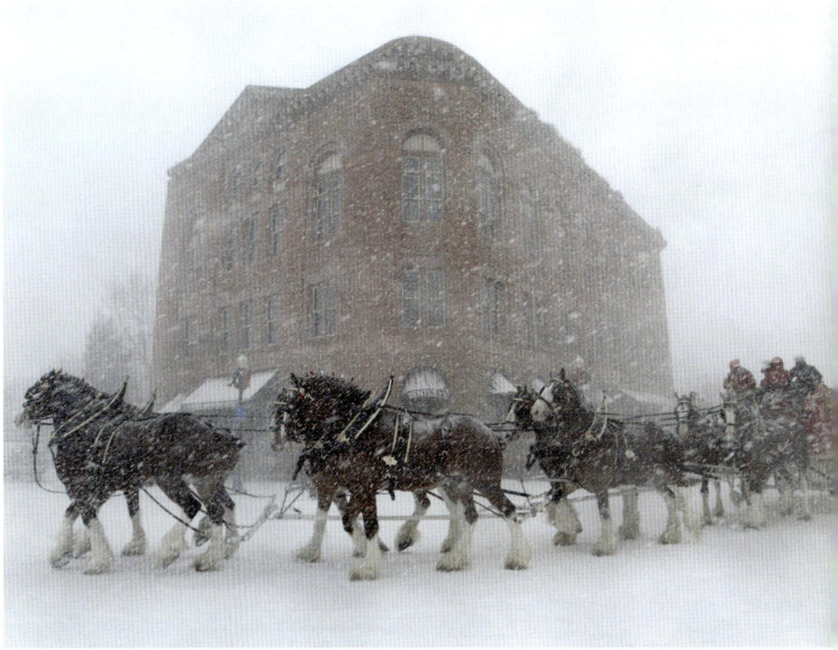

Above: Clydesdales in front of the Wheeler Opera House, Aspen
Left: Snow-covered Hyman Avenue, Aspen

tion for artists in residence as well as staff artists. All artist galleries are open nightly for holiday festivities and walk-in viewings. For an impressive array of contemporary art, the Aspen Art Museum is superb.

Bask in elegance at some of the world's finest hotels—the Hotel Jerome, a Rock Resort; the St. Regis Resort, rated one of the top 25 resorts in North America by the Zagat Survey; and The Little Nell, which bears a prestigious Relais & Chateaux designation. Any time of day is a good time to celebrity watch from one of Aspen's finest bistros while enjoying a delectable home-away-from-home Christmas feast.

For a true Aspen Christmas, hike down Main Street to the historic Sardy House tree lighting. More than 5,000 people crowd around the nation's largest living Christmas tree for a show of lights that gets more spectacular every year. Christmas Eve services with candle lighting and vocal choirs at Snowmass Chapel are heartfelt and cherished. And the Aspen Santa Fe Ballet's production of *The Nutcracker* is always a classic. Be sure to catch the Wheeler Opera House's annual rendition of *It's a Wonderful Life* as well, perfect for a night out on the town.

Aspen also offers an incomparable New Year's Eve experience. Surrounded by mountain panoramas, the historic little town hosts celebrations that range from elegant galas to rockin' street parties. Dancers light up the floor at the Hotel Jerome's annual bash while the glitterati dance on tables at Montagna in The Little Nell. Fabulous food, beautiful people, free-flowing champagne, and world-class people watching with celebrity sightings—what more could you ask for?

Right: Solitary Nordic skiing, Aspen

Next page: A dogsledding date, Aspen

Following page: A couple strolls down snowy streets, Aspen

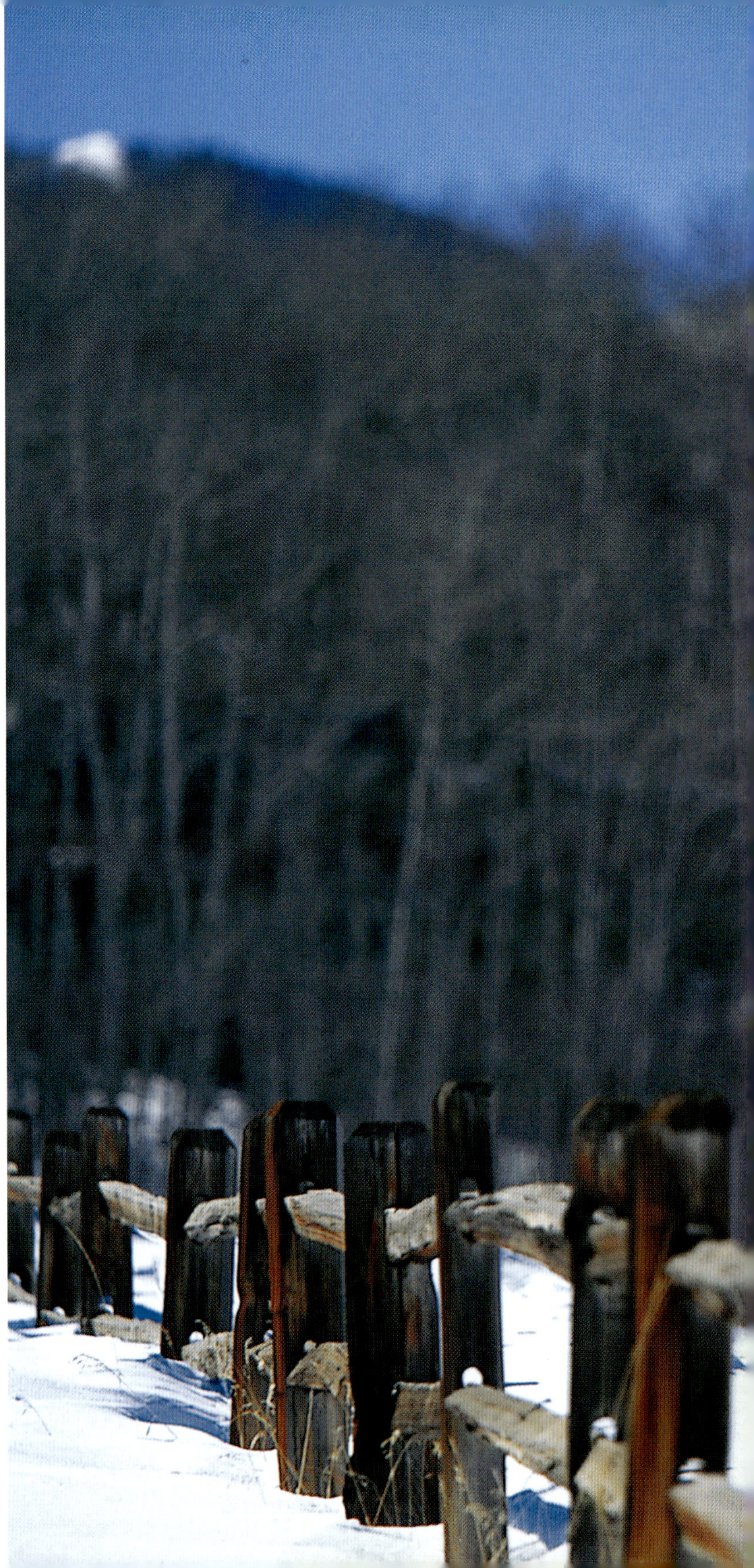

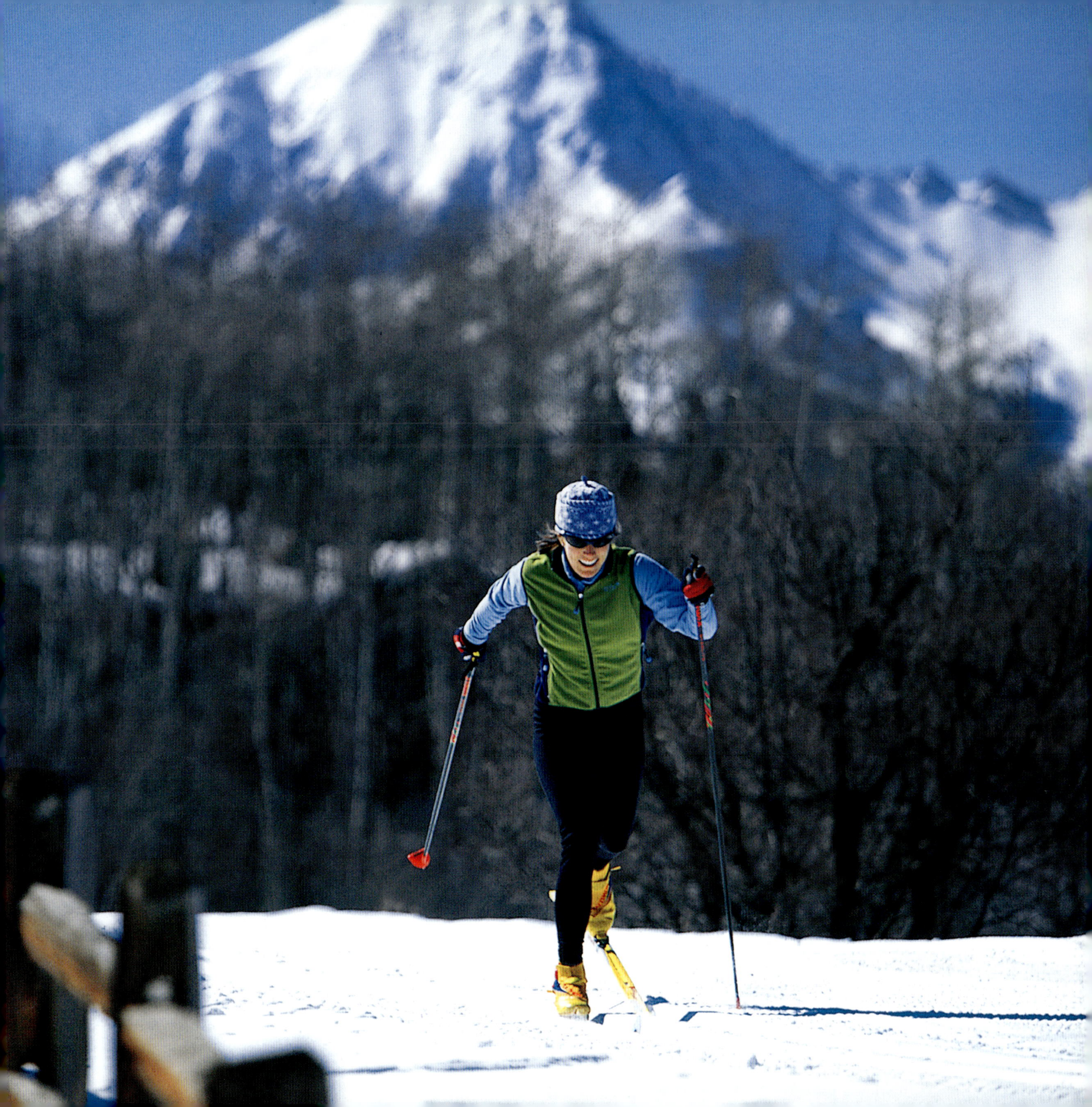

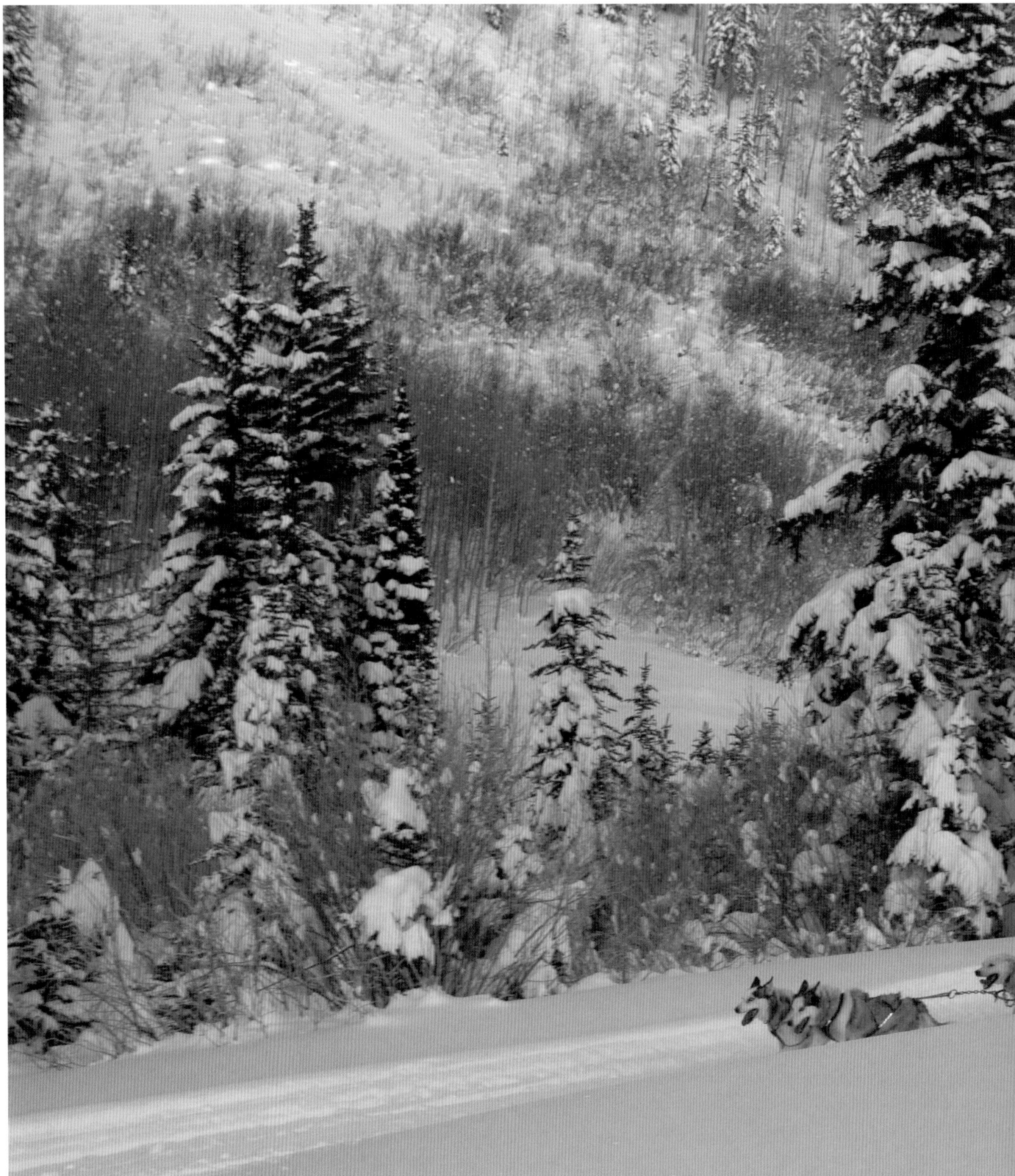

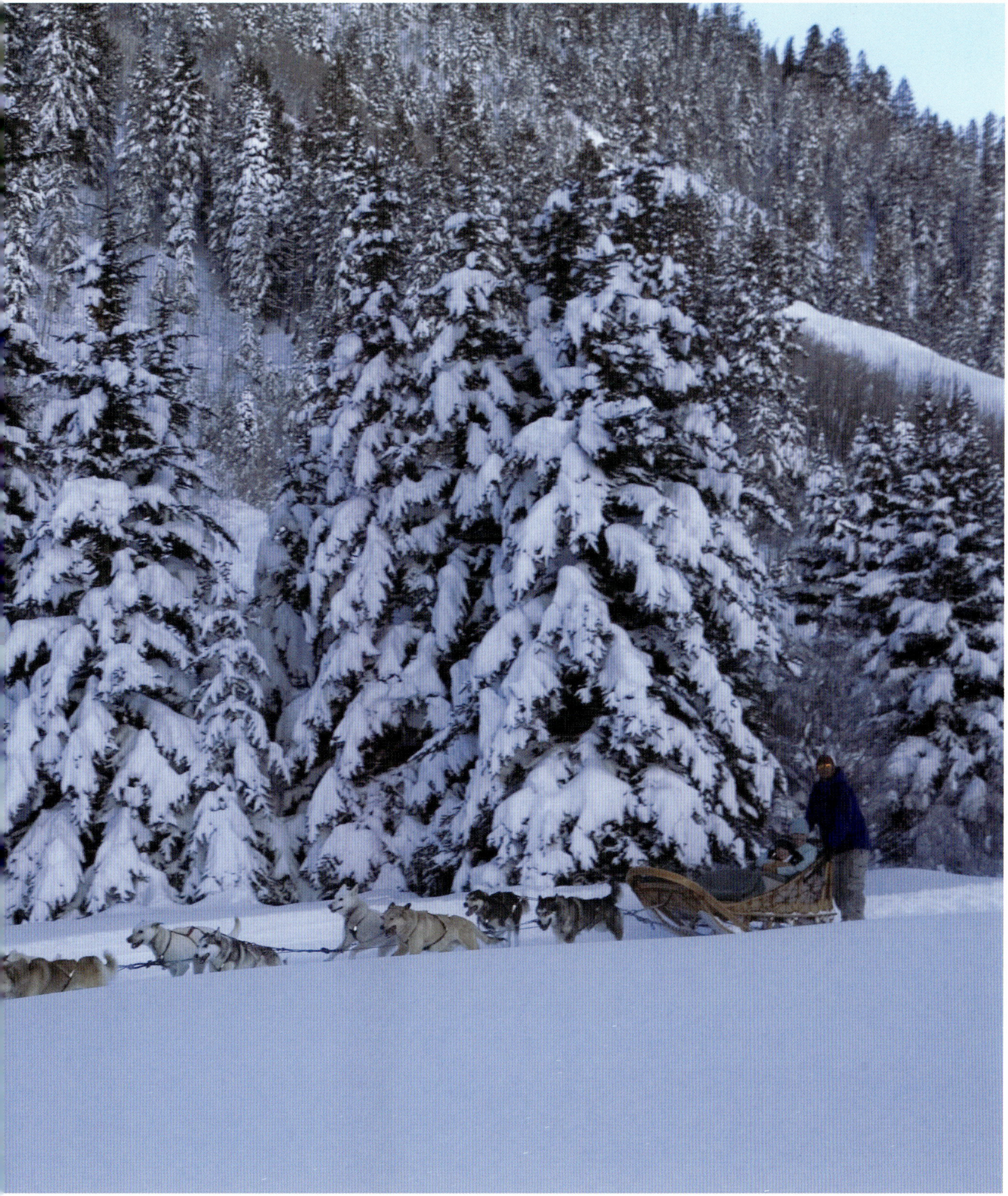

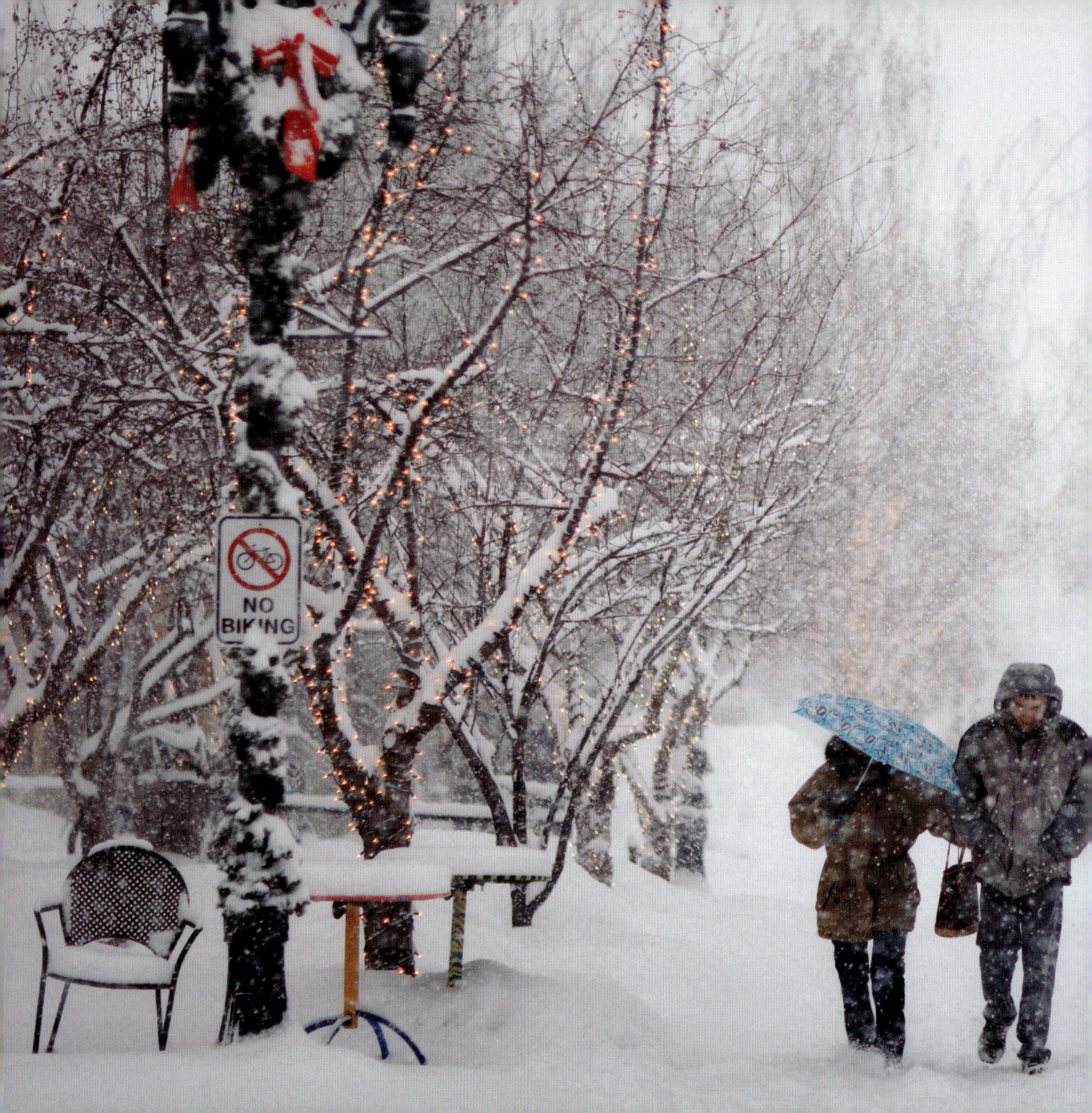
NO
BIKING

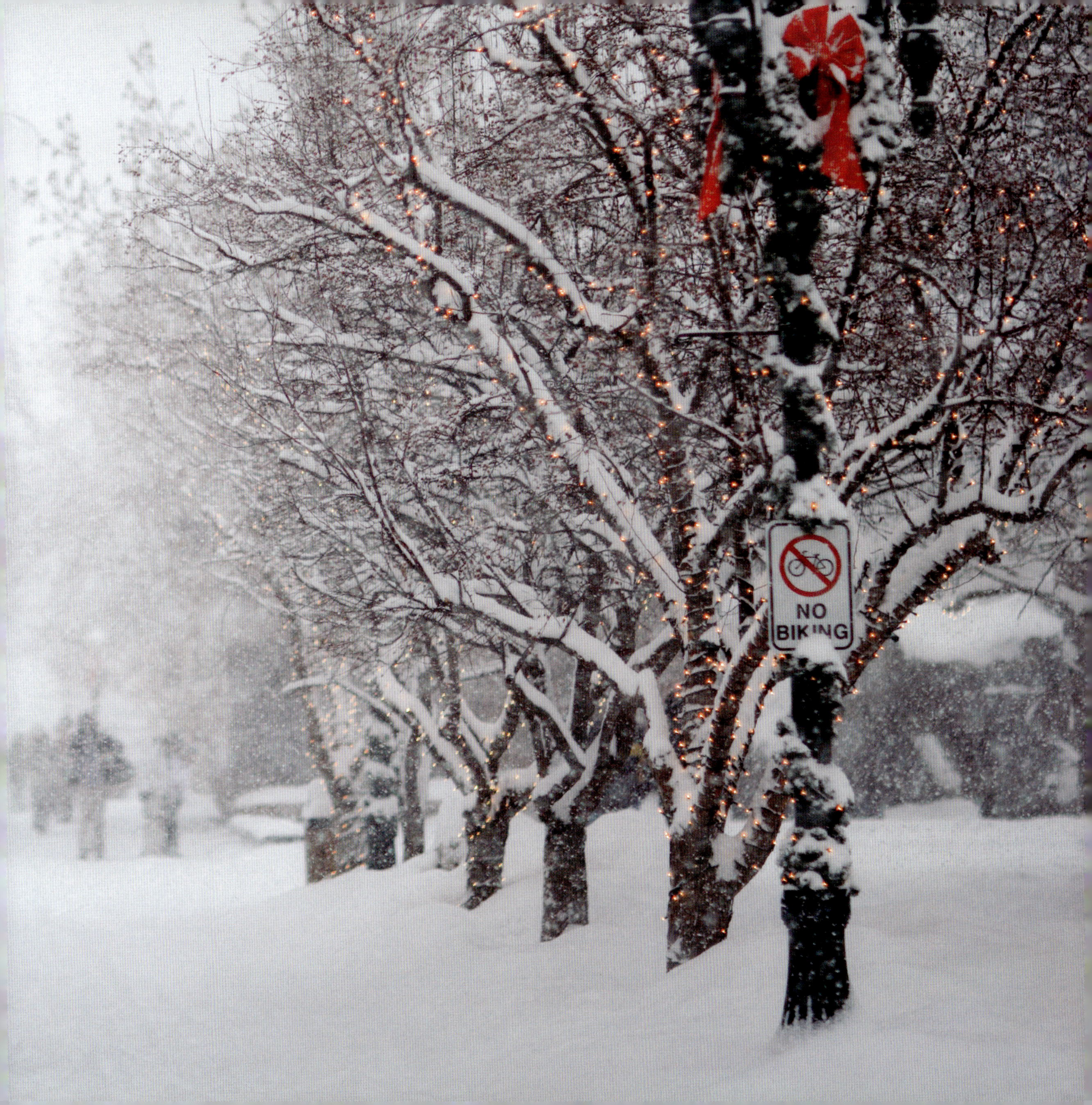
NO
BIKING

Boulder

& FORT COLLINS

Heap on the wood!

The wind is chill;

but let it whistle as it will.

We'll keep our

Christmas merry still.

—SIR WALTER SCOTT

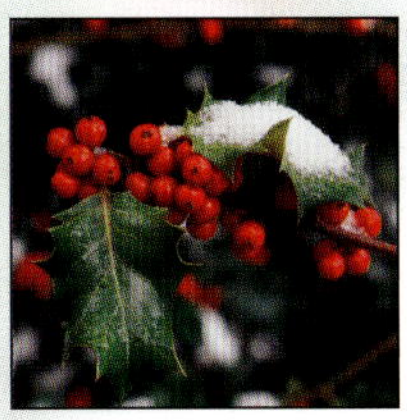

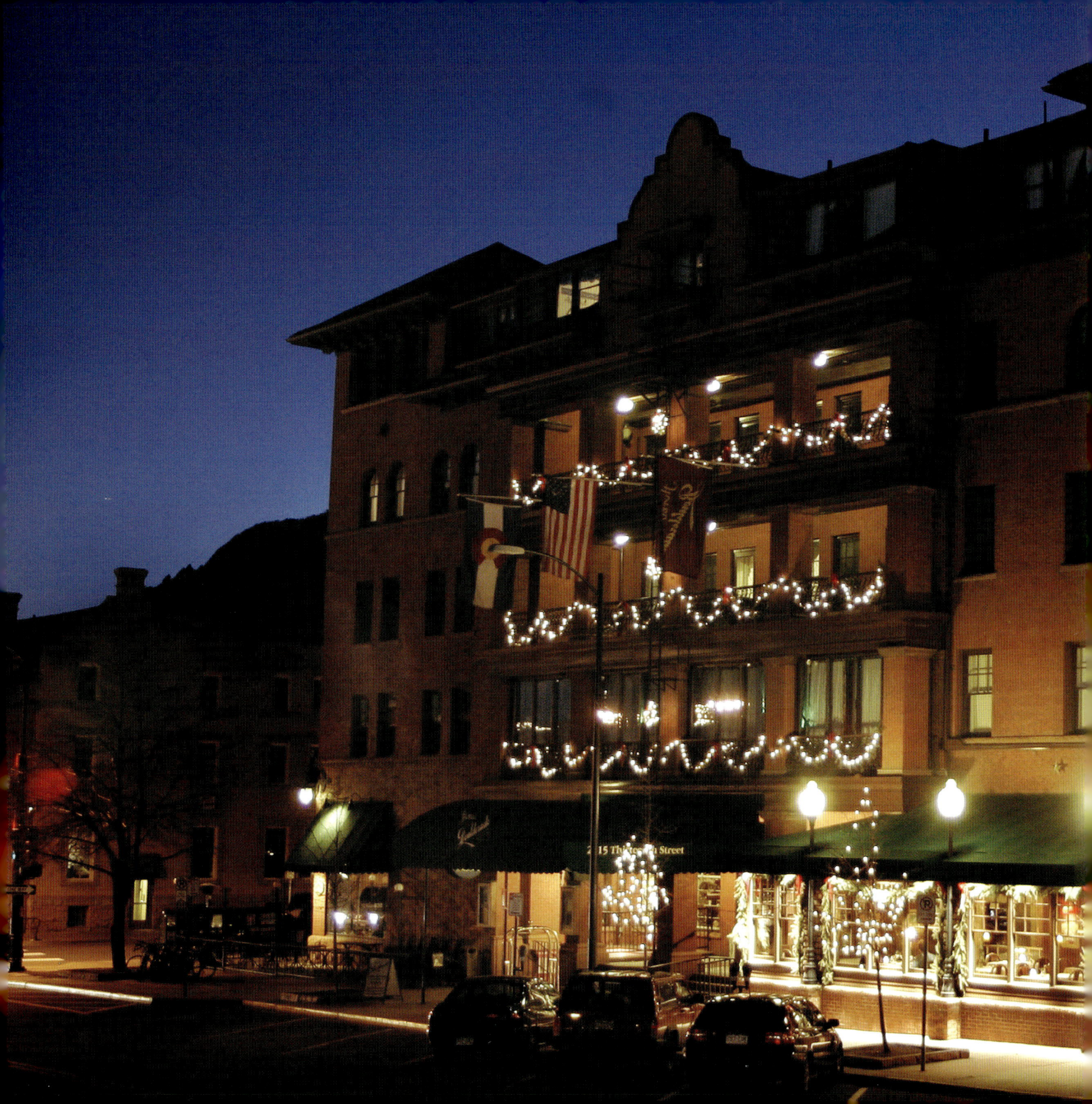

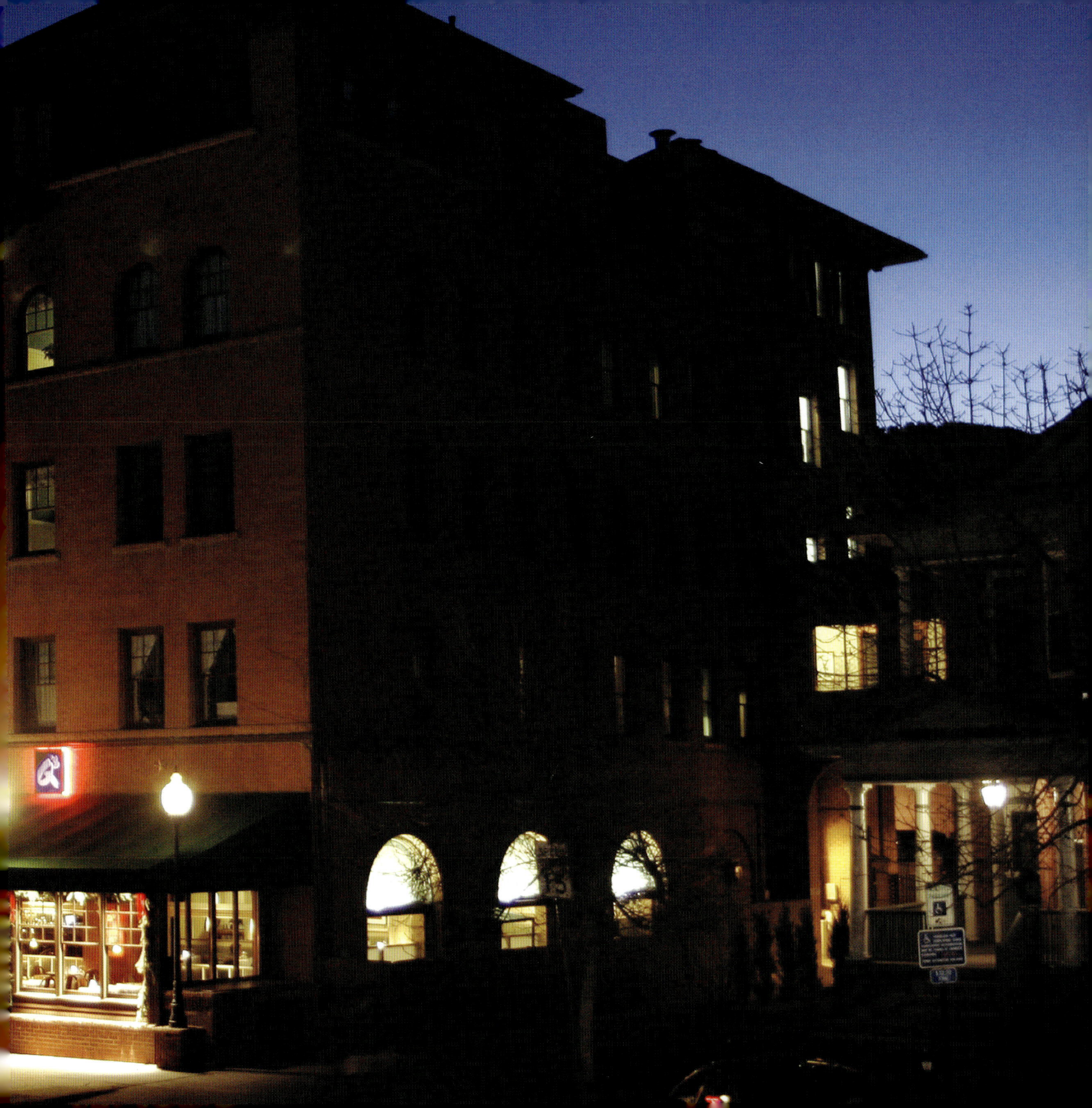

BOULDER, LOCATED JUST 40 MILES northeast of Denver, is nestled on a balance beam between the breathtaking Rocky Mountains and the Mile High City. For a magical Christmas, it's the picturesque combination of earth-friendly lights and natural scenery.

Everything culminates on Boulder's Pearl Street Mall. For Christmas shopping, live music, and holiday performances, it's the place to be. After the shopping day is done, the town Christmas tree illuminates the town square on Pearl Street. The Lights of December Parade brightens the streets with bands, dancers, floats, and a truly Boulder touch: eco-conscious elves and the traditional "St. Nick's on the Bricks" Santa visit. Stroll a few blocks down to 29th Street for horse-drawn carriage rides through the snowy streets of this famous college town.

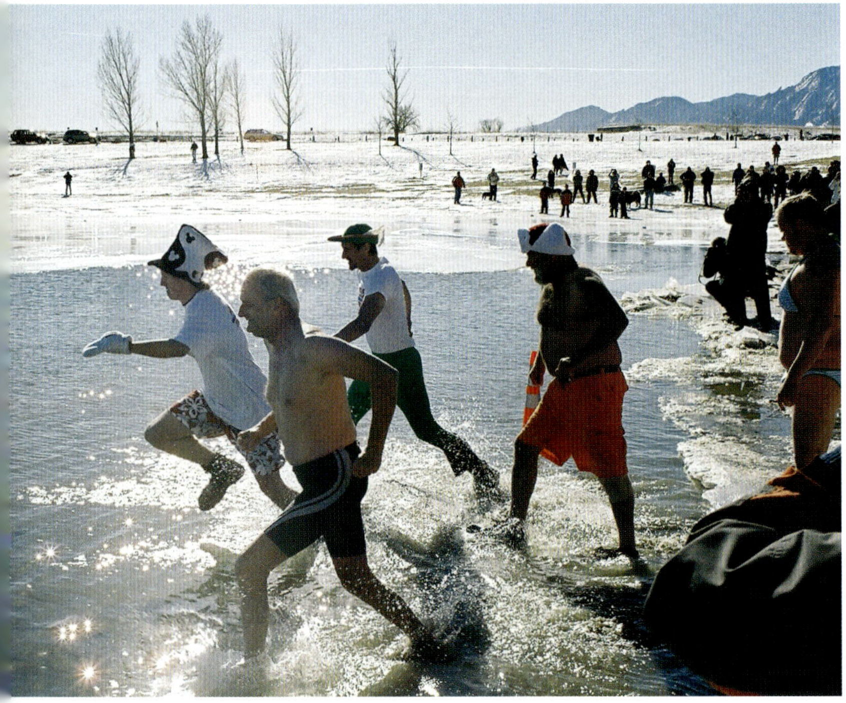

Above: The Polar Bear Plunge, a fundraiser for the Alzheimer's Association of Colorado, Boulder
Right: A peaceful rural scene in east Boulder
Previous page: The Hotel Boulderado, Boulder

Take a snowy tour of the charming University of Colorado campus and attend the Holiday Festival of Trees, an early-December holiday brunch and themed Christmas tree raffle held at the Folsom Field. Another ever-evolving Boulder tradition is the University of Colorado Festival of Christmas music program, first organized by the late Dean Warner Imig in 1942 and since revived and rewritten to awe-inspiring success.

All throughout December take the guided Historic Homes for the Holidays tour through one of Boulder's premier neighborhoods and enjoy spectacular displays of lights and architecture. A different neighborhood is featured each year, so no two tours will ever be alike.

Experience the casual elegance that is Boulder at the luxurious St. Julien Hotel and

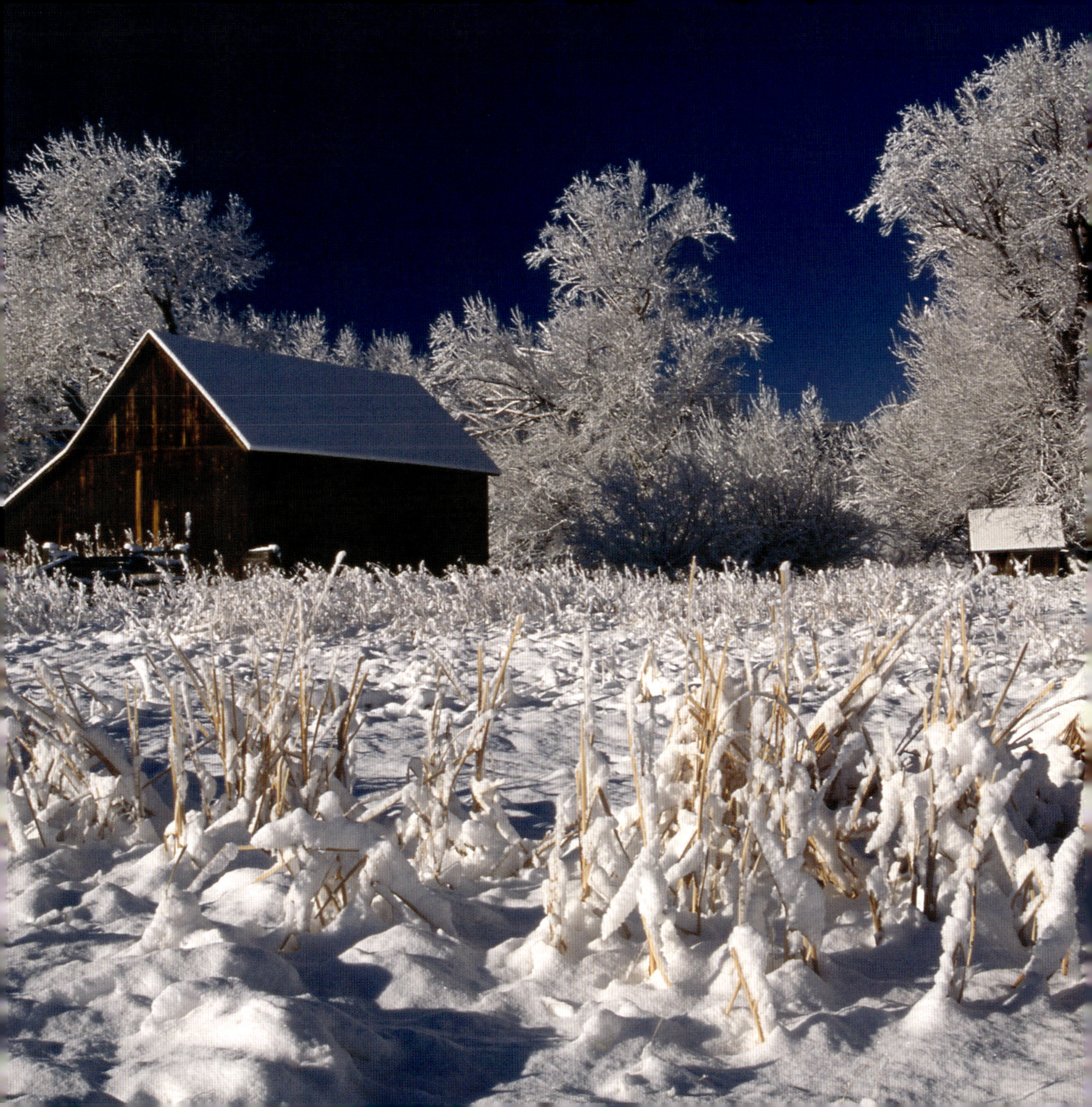

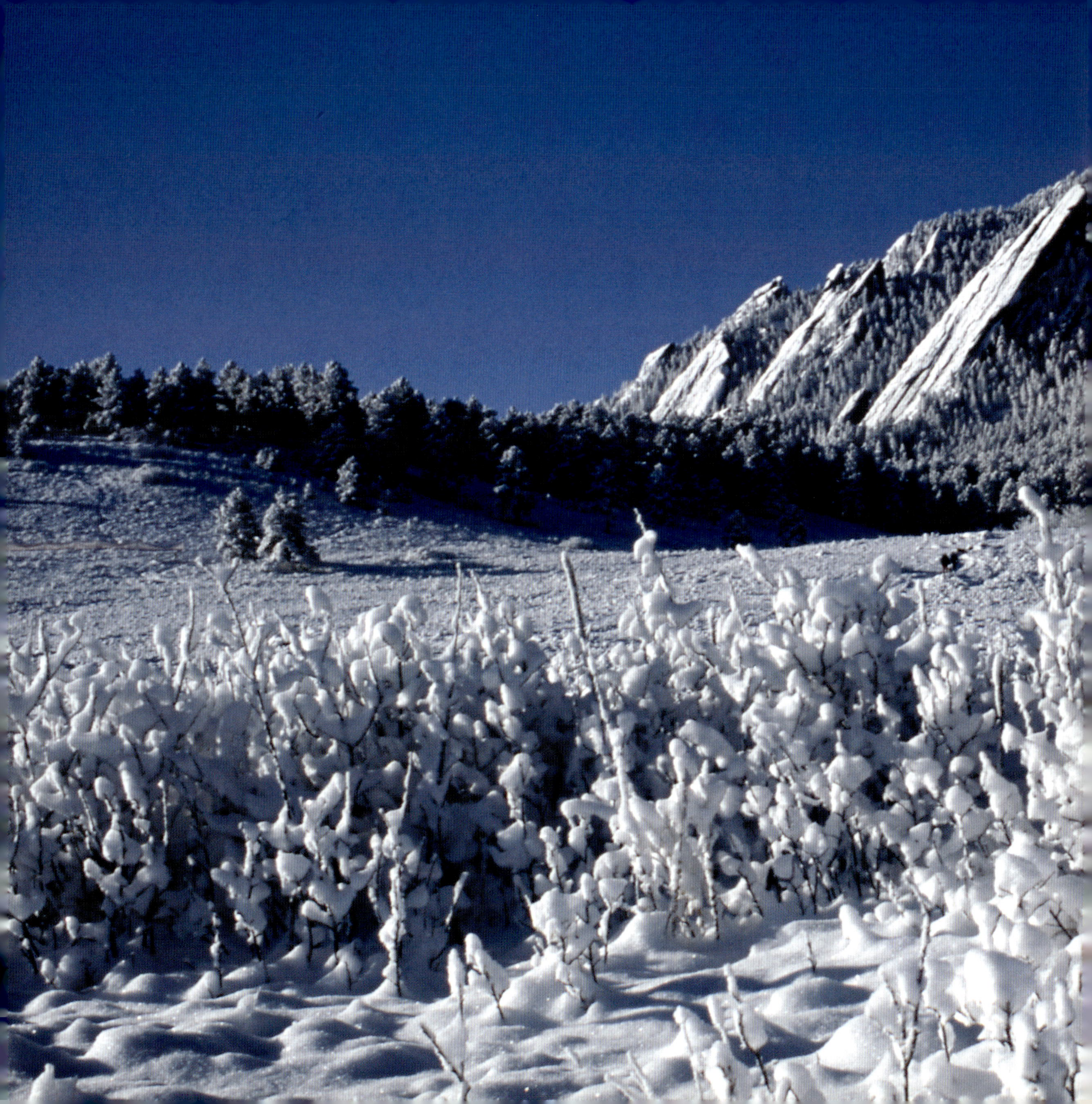

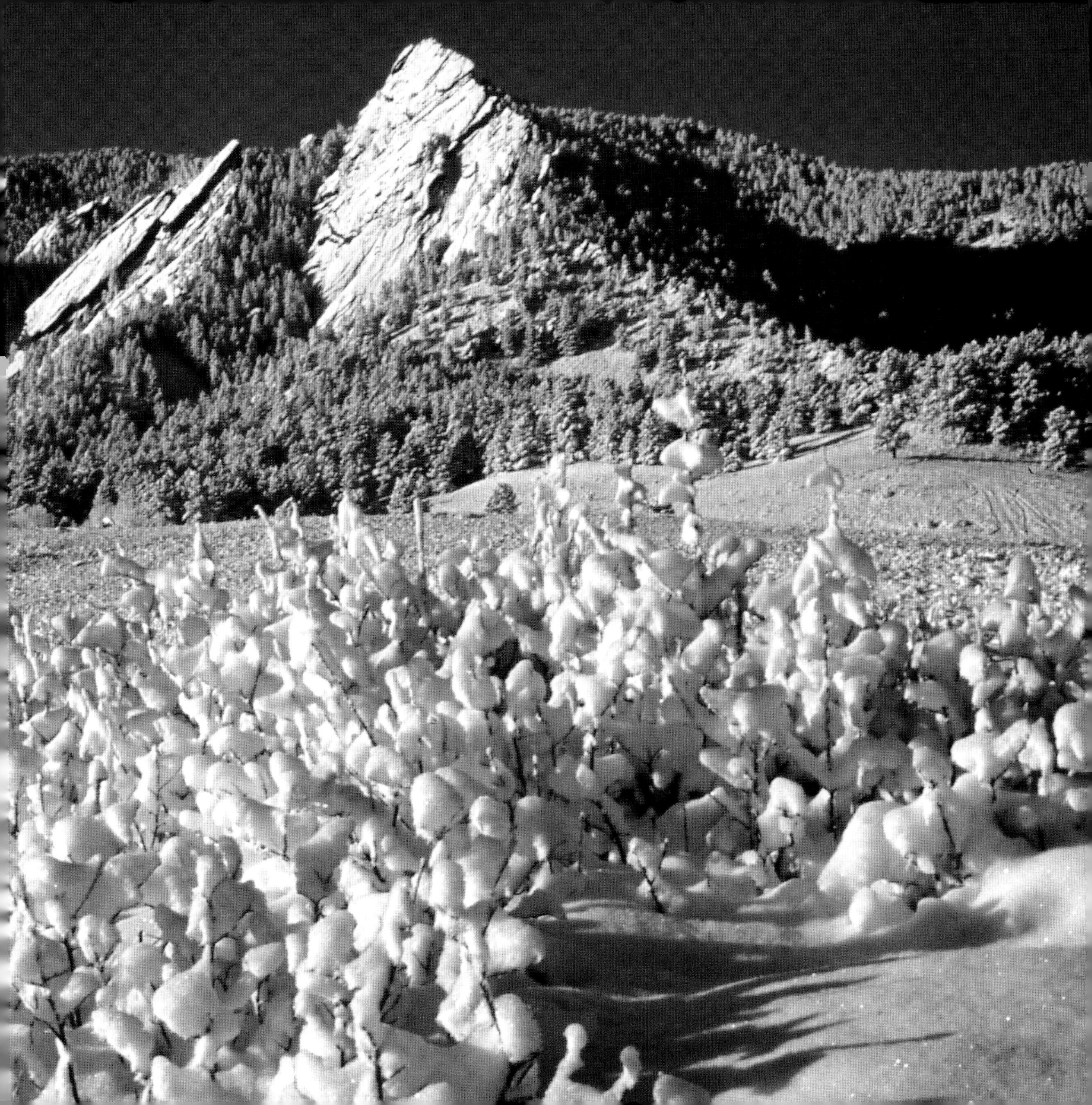

Spa, just steps from the Pearl Street Mall. The top-notch creature comforts and service are matched by the hotel's inspiring mountain views. Or, try the Hotel Boulderado, a Boulder landmark founded in 1909 that combines Victorian splendor with modern luxuries and conveniences.

The Hotel Boulderado spreads holiday cheer every December with an annual Christmas Day brunch. In the early days of December, dress up for their annual Teddy Bear Tea—then return a few weeks later for The Nutcracker Tea. To get your tea for the holiday season, take a tour of the always-in–season Celestial Seasonings™ factory. Their Peppermint™ or Sleepytime™ tea will keep you curled up by the fire all winter long.

For some fresh mountain air, bundle up and take in the Winter Boulder Farmers' Market at the Boulder County Fairgrounds. There, seasonal treats, handmade and unique art and jewelry, and entertainment are plentiful. Next, hit the town for the Rocky Mountain Revels annual Christmas play, sure to be a hot-ticket event.

If you're in town for Christmas Day, make reservations at the one-of-a-kind Italian eatery Trattoria on Pearl, always open Christmas Eve and Christmas Day. Then twist and twirl at the outdoor Ice Rink at One Boulder Plaza, which hosts themed skating parties in the weeks leading up to Christmas.

Following the Christmas festivities, join the bravest of the brave in the Polar Bear Plunge, an icy swim in Boulder Reservoir held every year on Jan. 1—a truly original way to splash into the New Year! Even if you don't take the leap, cheer on those who do.

Before you leave, be sure to take in the picturesque panoramas of the town from afar.

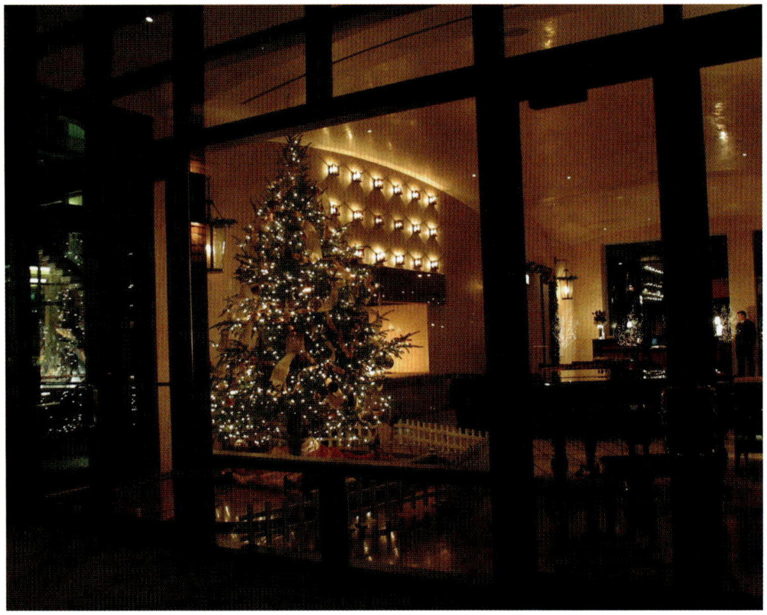

Above: Christmas tree at the St. Julien Hotel & Spa, Boulder
Right: A Victorian home flecked with snow, Boulder
Previous page: The Flatirons of Green Mountain, Boulder

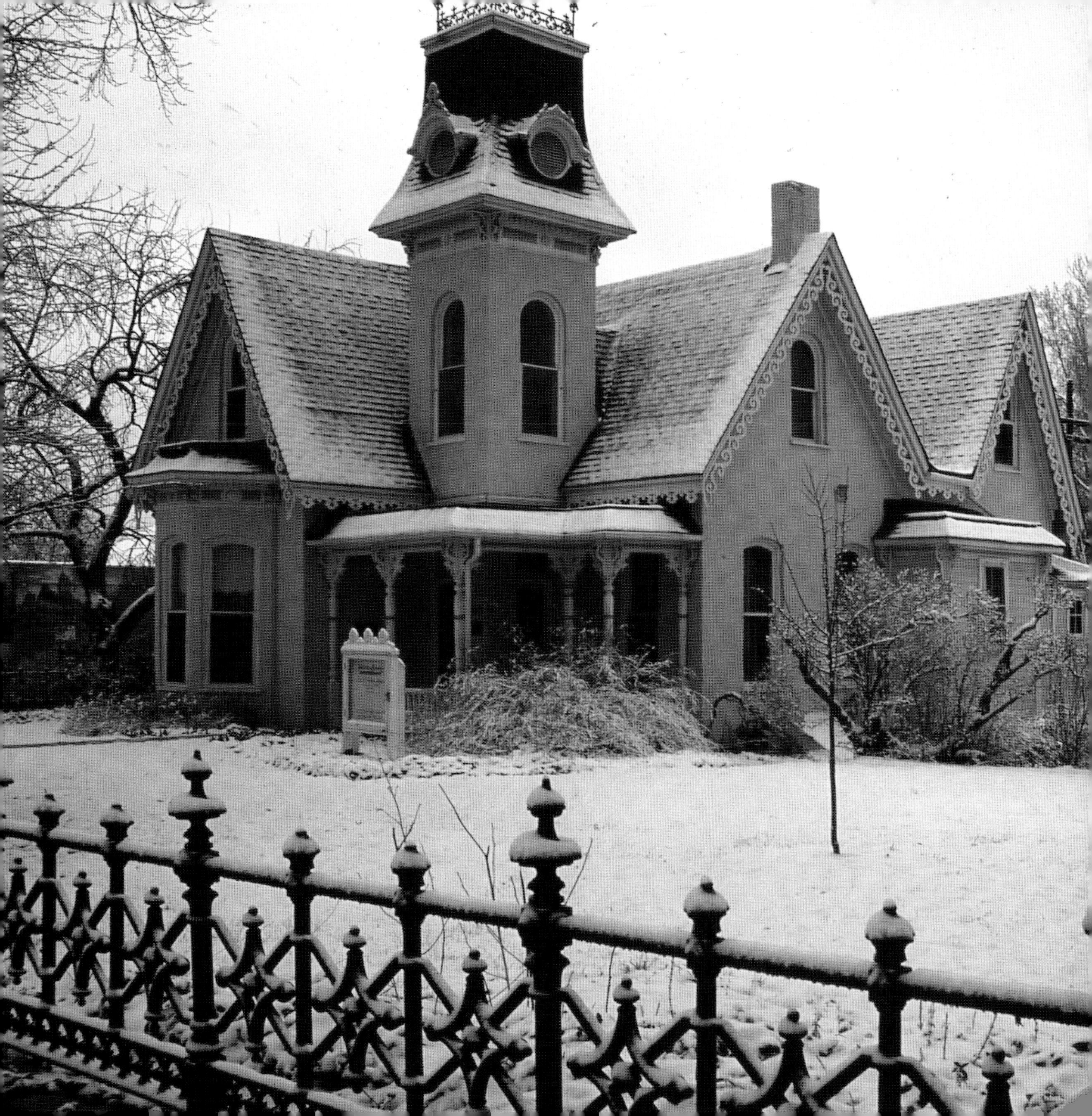

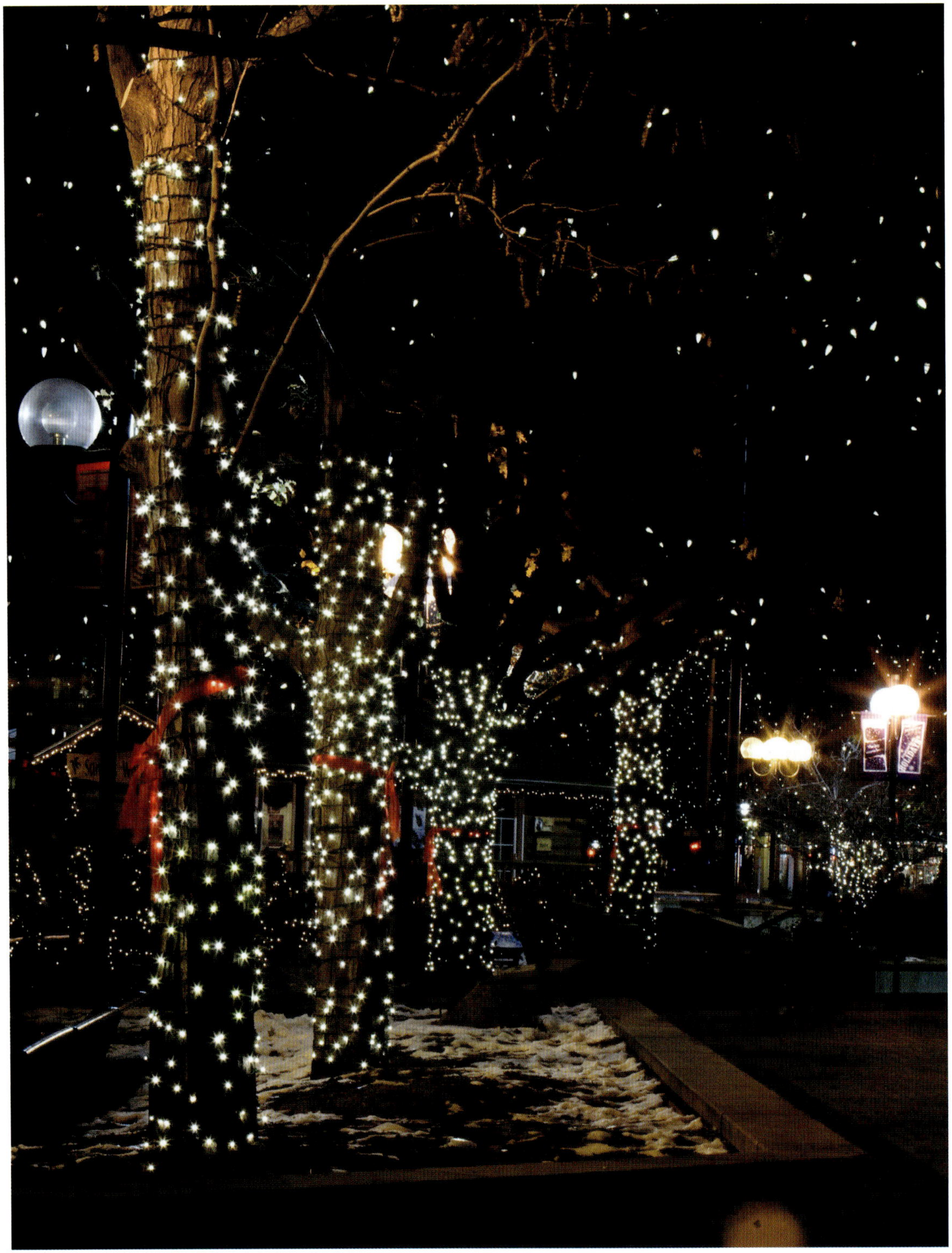

FORT COLLINS

Sixty-five miles north of Denver is a city ideal in every sense of the word. Recently named the No. 1 best place to live by *Money Magazine,* Fort Collins is the kind of place dreams are made of—it's charming, safe, and set against a beautiful Rocky Mountain backdrop. So, it's no surprise that Christmas in Fort Collins is delightful, to say the least.

Begin your festive journey with a trip to *The Nutcracker* ballet. The Lincoln Center's annual presentation of this enchanting classic is sure to lift your spirits, and the talented dancers performing it are sure to pirouette their way into your heart. Follow the dancing to the ice and attend the Winter Wishes Ice Show at EPIC ice arena. More than 250 skaters perform choreographed routines to holiday classics. Snuggle under a blanket in the bleachers or treat the family to a gourmet dinner at a rink-side table. No matter where you sit, the costumes, jumps, solo performances, and holiday spirit are sure to wow you.

In Old Town Fort Collins, enjoy Carolfest, an annual singing celebration and party for the whole family. The caroling begins at the Opera Galleria and everyone is invited to participate, so follow the procession through the Northern Hotel lobby to Santa's Workshop and then to the Fort Collins Museum. Stay there and enjoy the company of loved ones, the songs of choirs, and the taste of hot cocoa and homemade cookies as you light the community Holiday Tree.

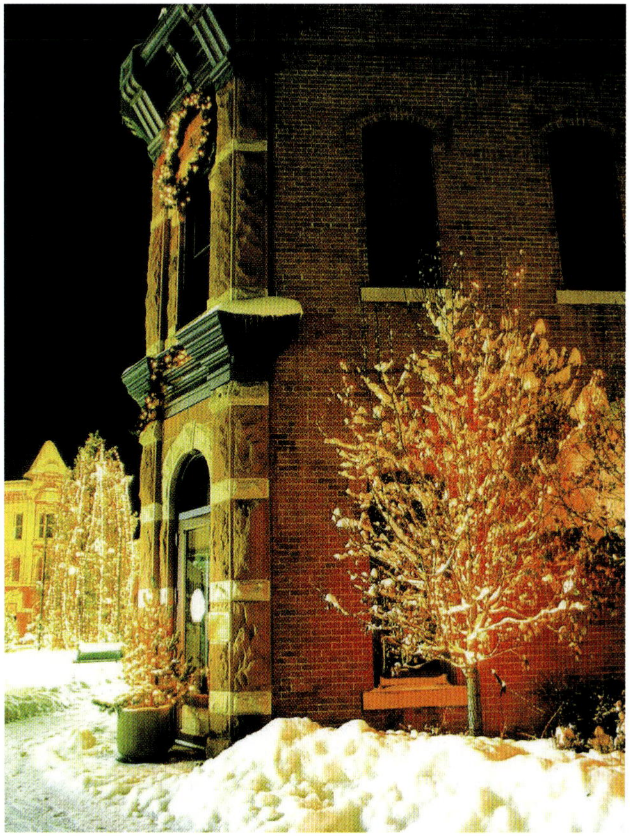

Above: Historic building alight at Christmas, Fort Collins
Left: Old Town sparkles with seasonal decorations, Fort Collins

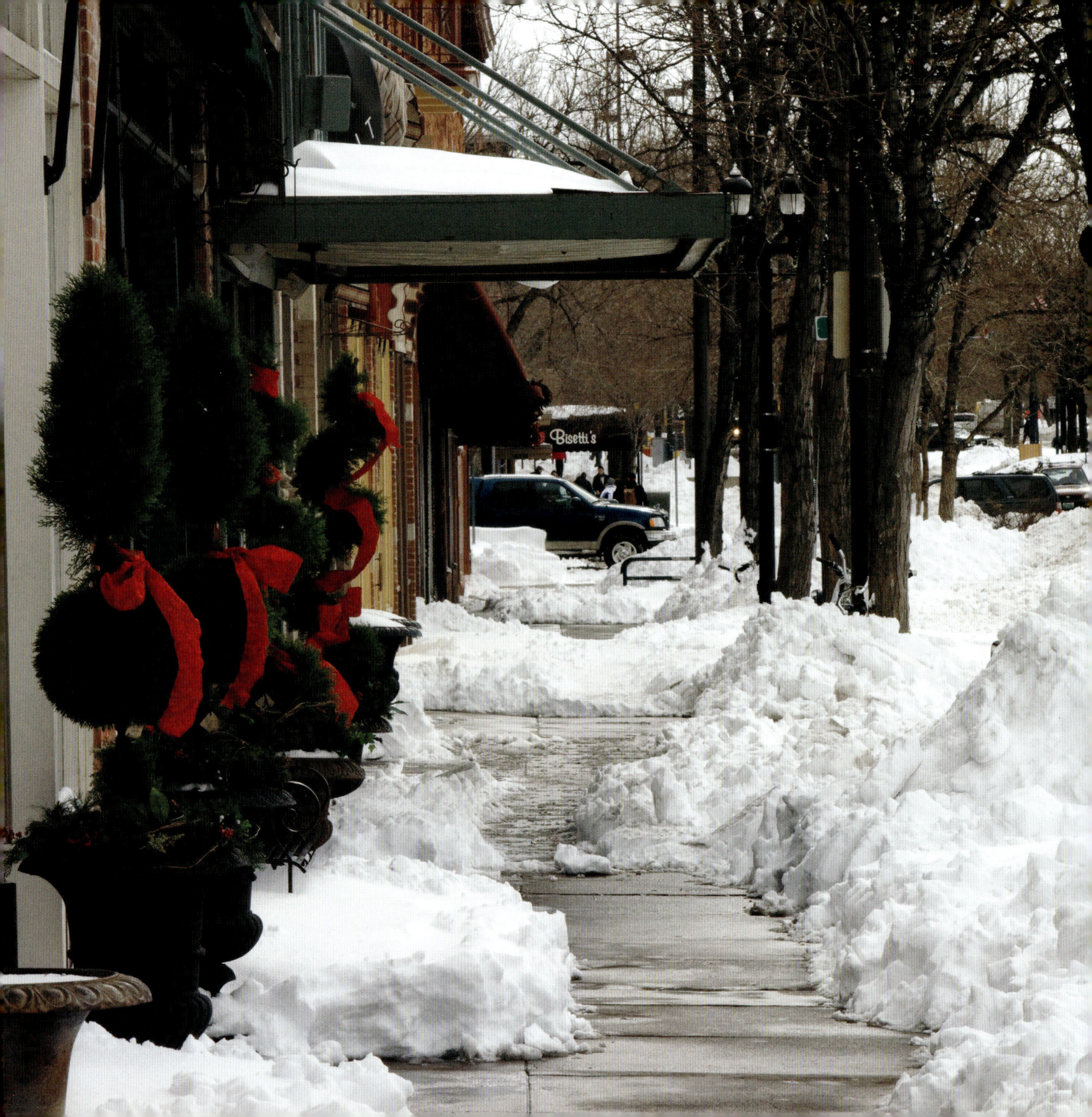
Bisetti's

While in town, catch a holiday flick at the Lyric Cinema Cafe. You're in for a treat at this theater, which offers beer and wine as well as delectable hors d'oeuvres. Enjoy independent and foreign films year-round at this fabulous venue. Head to Harmony Library for a cultured afternoon for the kids—throughout the month of December, they host Santa's Coming readings where enthusiastic library staff get the little ones "read up" and ready for St. Nick's visit with stories, picture books, puppets, and songs.

For a quick romantic getaway and breathtaking views of lights, walk around the Spring Creek Garden Lights exhibit. In these community botanic gardens, thousands of lights twinkle and wink in the peaceful winter nights. Then take a trek downtown and explore the city by horse and carriage.

Winter is a lovely time to stride through town and tour local galleries during the First Friday Gallery Walk, which takes place year-round on the first Friday of every month. Pick up gifts and works of art for your home while enjoying the local scenery of Fort Collins. Fort Collins is also one of the fittest cities in Colorado, so get into the spirit of fitness by participating in or watching the Christmas 4K and Kids Santa Chase races at the foot of the Rockies.

After Christmas has come and gone, ring in the New Year with First Night Fort Collins, a celebration throughout downtown. With performances, storytelling, crafts, street performers, international dancing, magicians, and, of course, a countdown, downtown is the perfect place to spend the last night of the year.

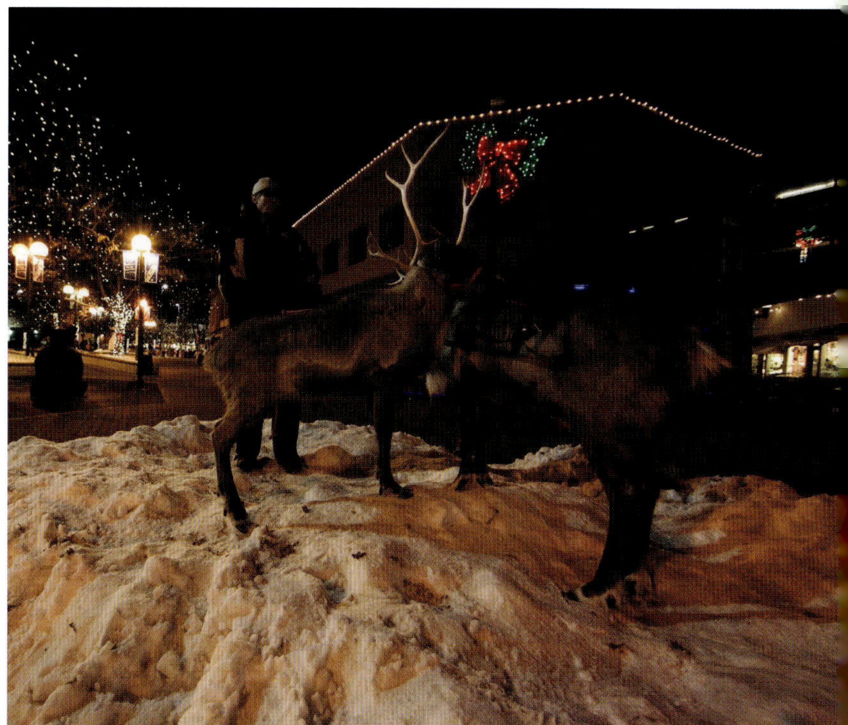

Above: Santa's reindeer take a break, Fort Collins
Left: College Avenue piled with snow, Fort Collins

Breckenridge

& FRISCO

*Our hearts grow tender
with childhood memories
of love and kindred, and
we are better throughout the
year for having, in spirit,
become a child again at
Christmastime.*

—LAURA INGALLS WILDER

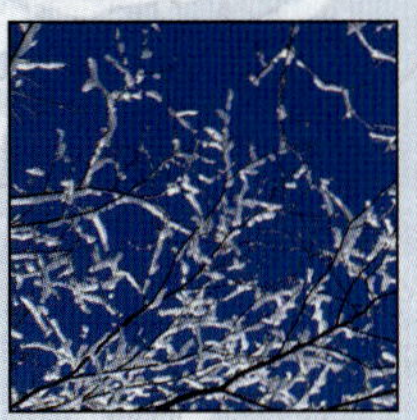

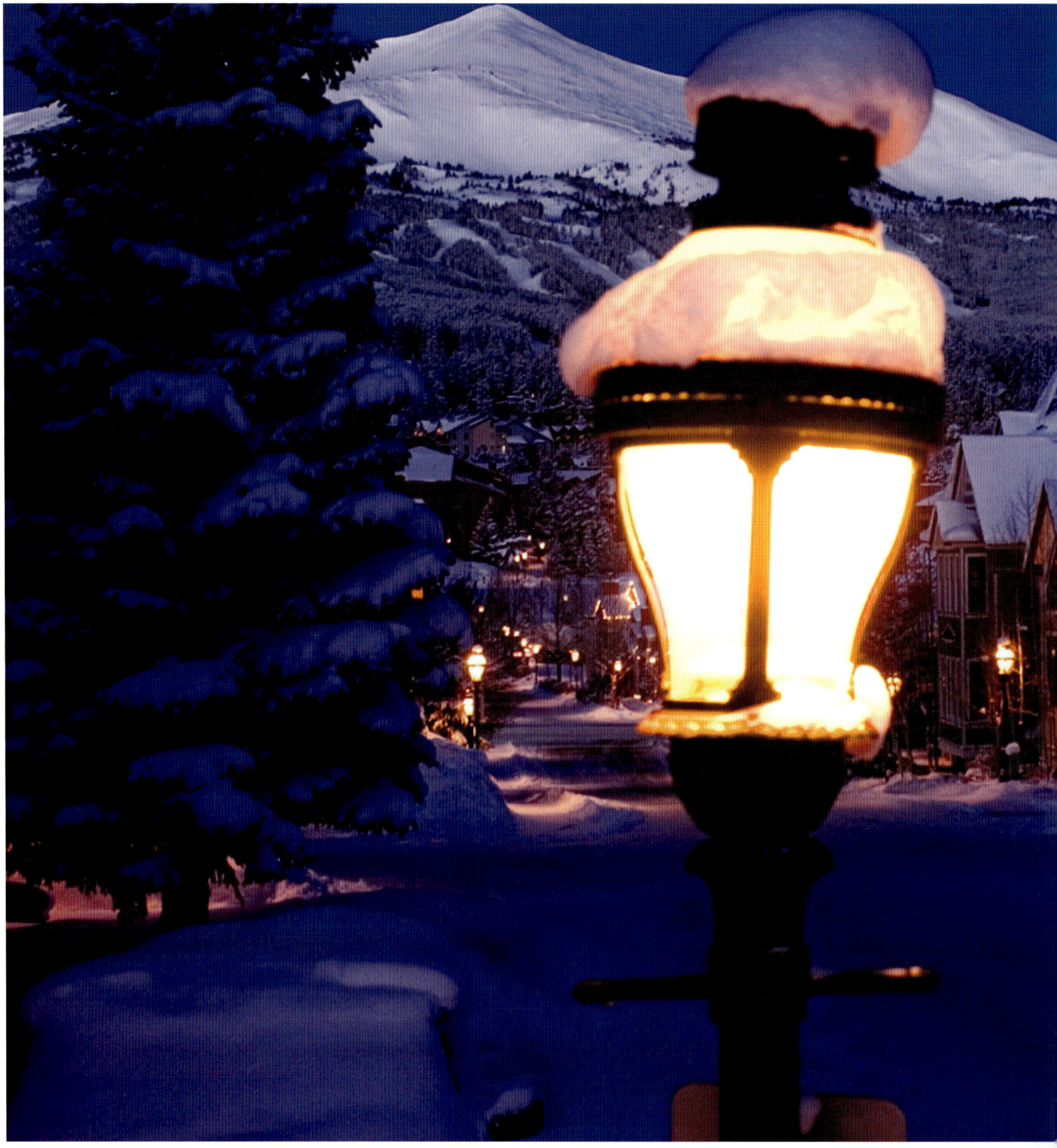

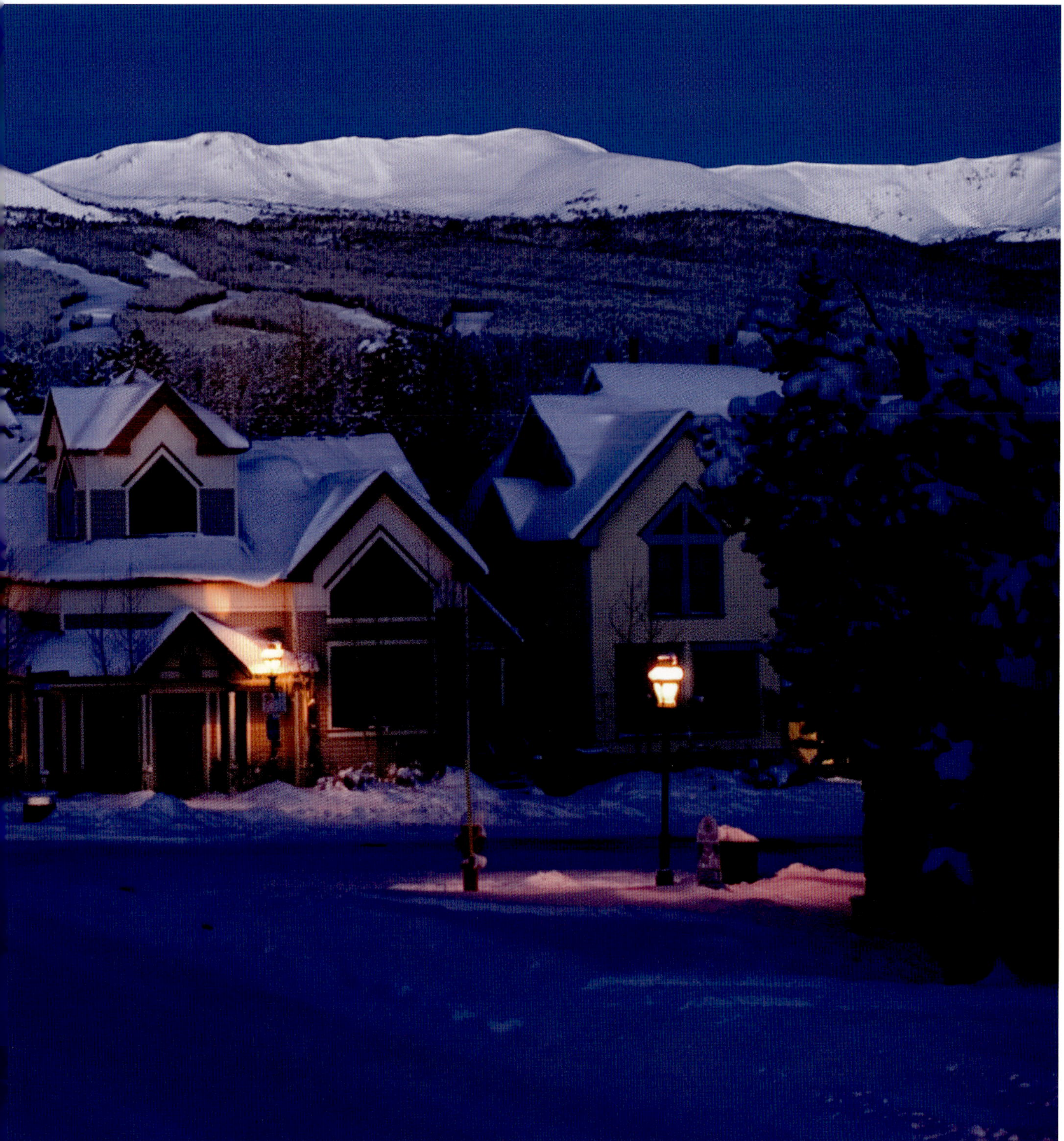

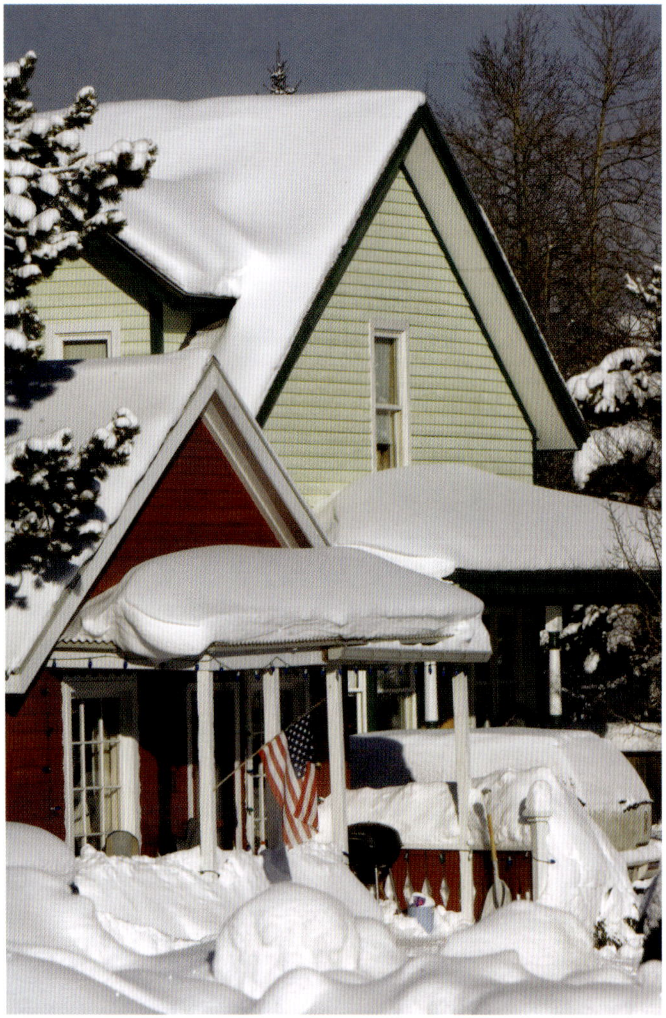

Above: A foot of snow accumulates on houses in town, Breckenridge
Right: Sleigh rides bring Christmas spirit to Breckenridge

Previous page: Gaze up at the ski trails from Breckenridge

NINETY MILES WEST OF DENVER, a glistening town awaits exploration. Breckenridge, Colorado, population 2,400, is one of Colorado's oldest continuously populated towns. At Christmas, the town is full of tradition.

A holiday visit to Breckenridge begins at the historic 1896 Victorian Briggle House. With period entertainment, music, and costumes, the holiday season is never far away at this elegantly restored home. Follow the Briggle House with the Lighting of Breckenridge, an annual all-day festival that begins in the early hours with storytelling and a holiday craft workshop at the Firehouse Museum, and ends with a procession of carolers and a stroll down Main Street beginning at Daniel's Cabin. The stroll concludes in Blue River Plaza with a tree lighting, fireworks, and, of course, Santa Claus.

Home of the Victorian Winter Wonderland, Breckenridge boasts some of Colorado's most exceptional holiday activities. In addition to going skiing, snowboarding, and shopping, take a tour of one of Breckenridge's famous Victorian-era houses. The Barney Ford House Museum and Edwin Carter Museum

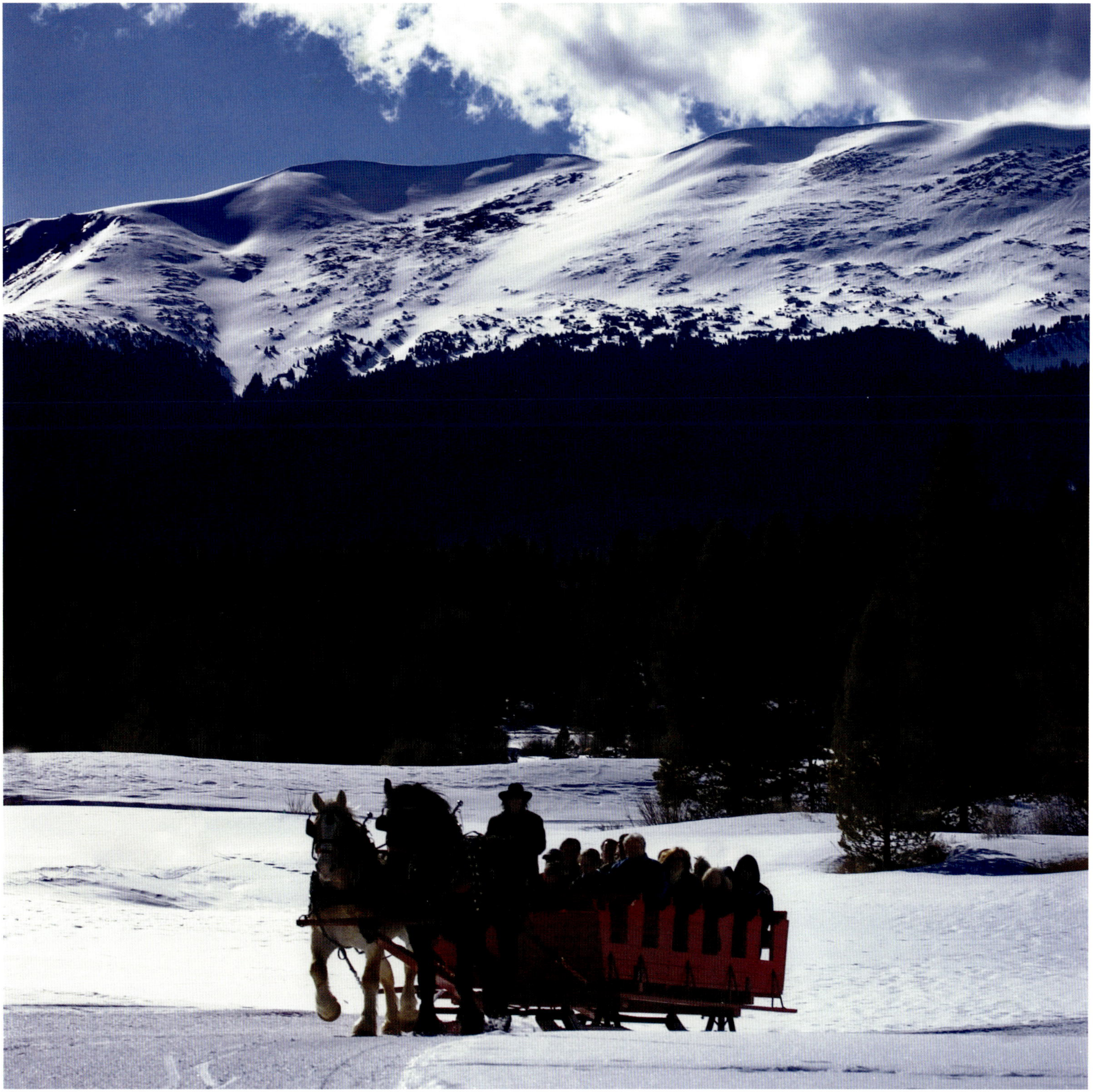

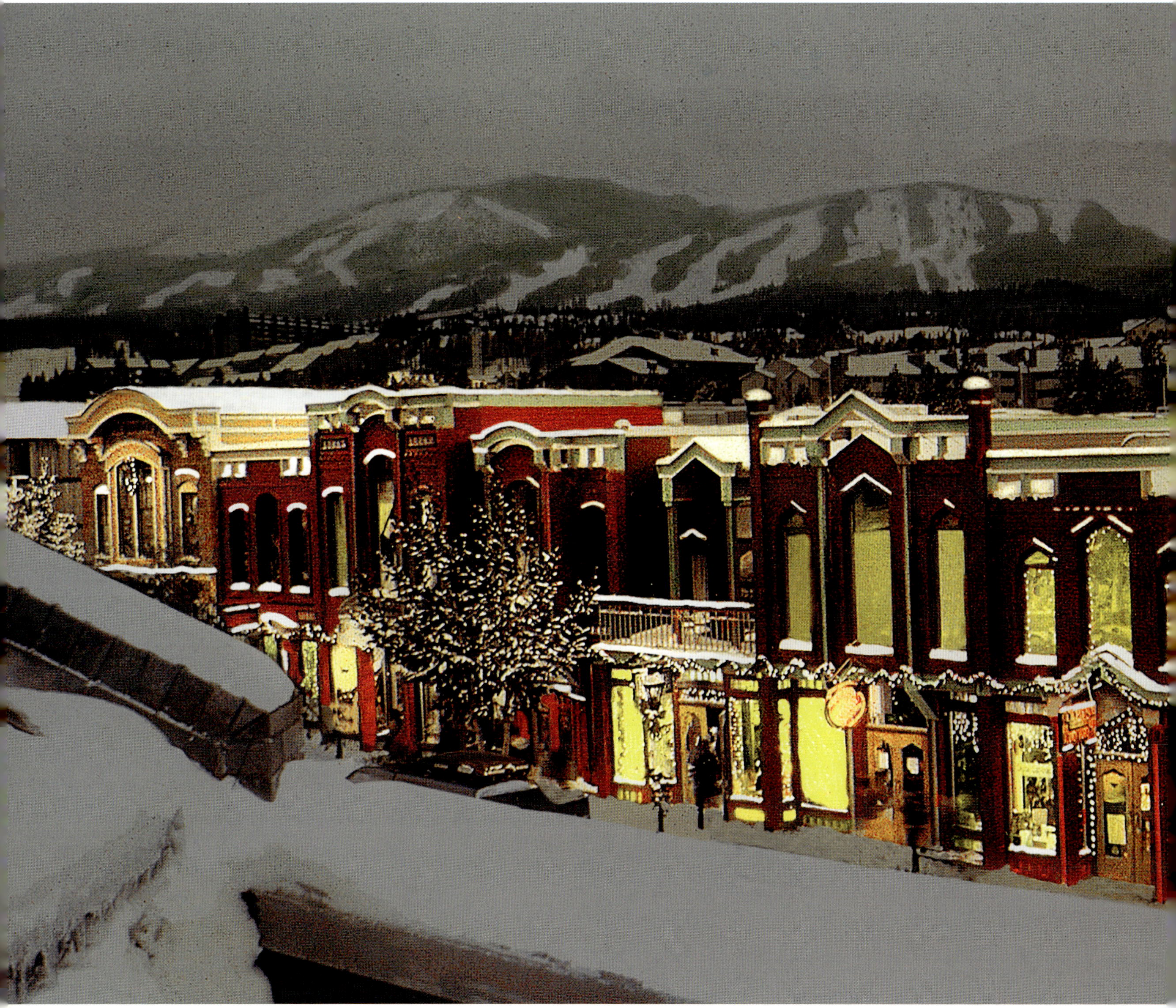

Main Street exudes mining-town charm, Breckenridge

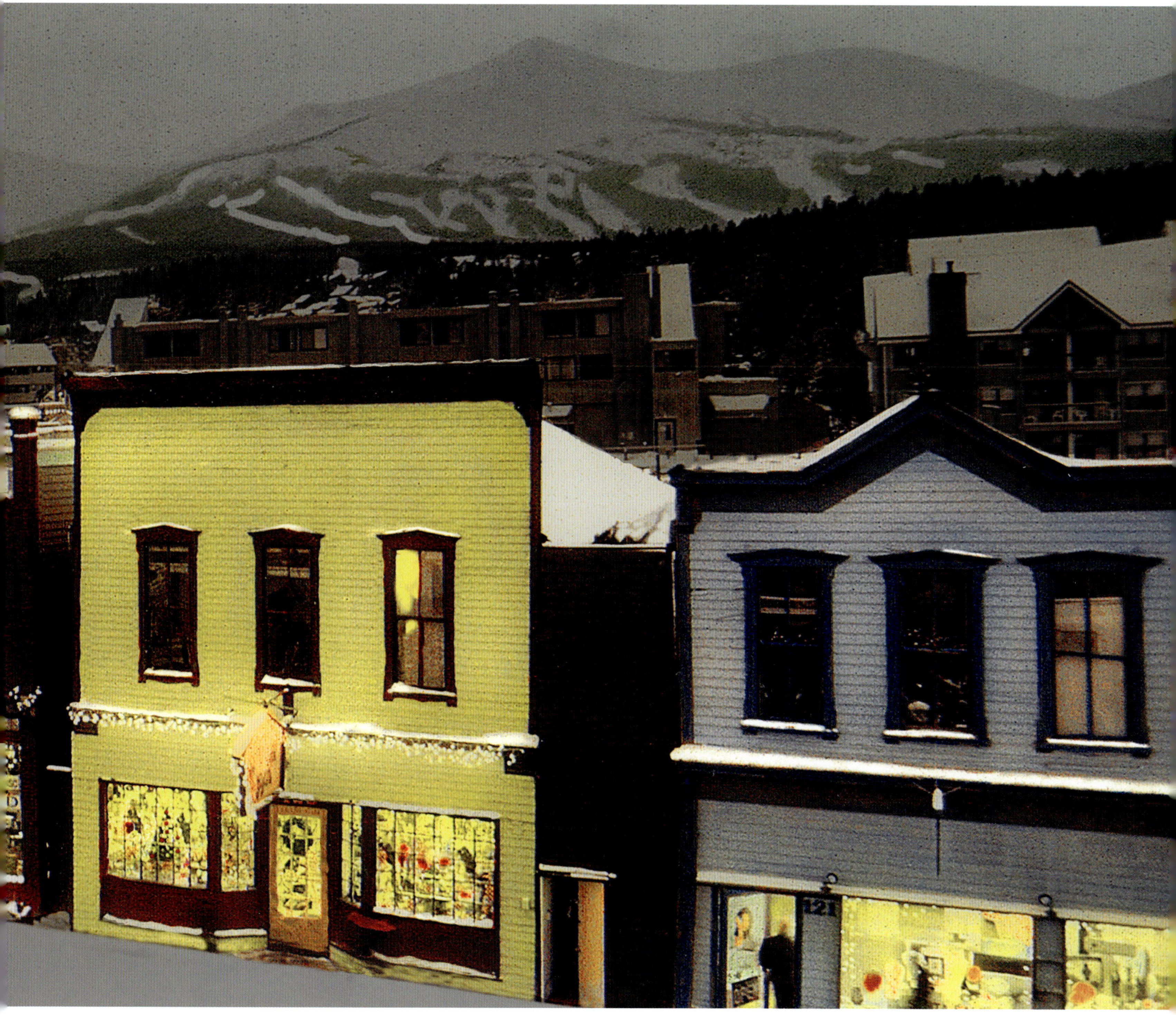
121

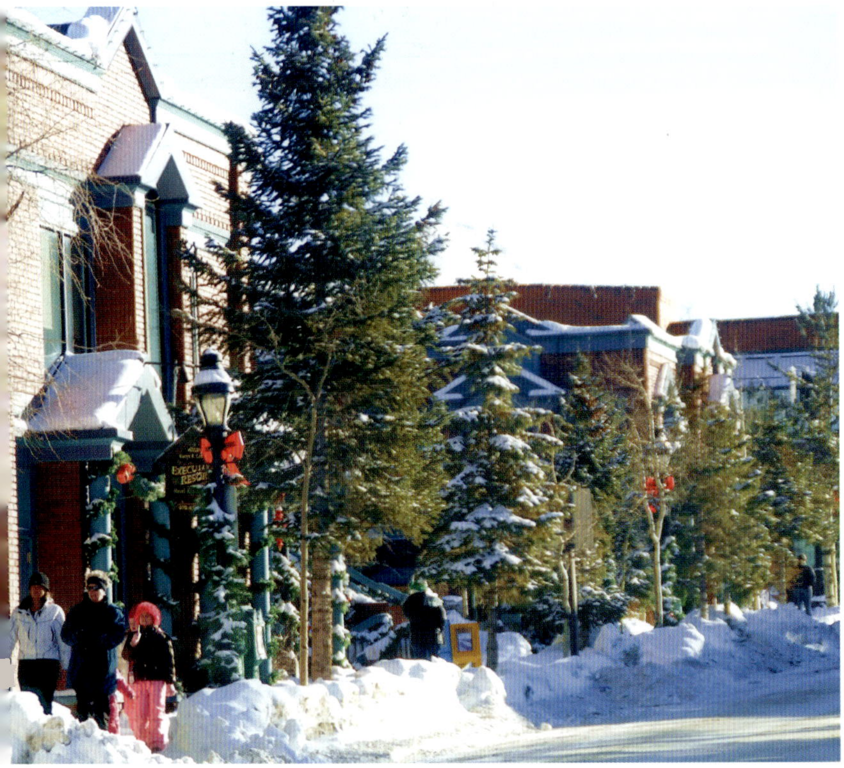

Above: Town Square Mall ready for the holidays, Breckenridge
Right: Nordic skiers enjoy scenery, Breckenridge

both attract visitors from around the state with their dazzling Victorian decor and festive holiday atmospheres. See Santa at the Lincoln West Mall on Main Street, also part of the Wonderland.

For fine dining complemented by breathtaking views, try The Top of the World restaurant. The Cellar features tasting menus and an award-winning wine list while The Hearthstone Restaurant treats you to wild game, fresh seafood, and hand-cut steaks in a 120-year-old Victorian home.

For cocktails and ales formulated to bring holiday cheer, be sure to pay a visit to the Breckenridge Brewery. Famous for their Avalanche Ale™ and seasonal Christmas Ale™, the legendary brewery opened in 1990. The microbrewery is also a highlight of the Breckenridge nightlife, with some of the best food and views of the mountain in town.

Glide gracefully through winter at the new Stephen C. West Ice Arena with adjoining indoor and outdoor rinks. Strap on your own skates, or attend the rink's annual Christmas ice show, featuring some of Colorado's best ice skaters.

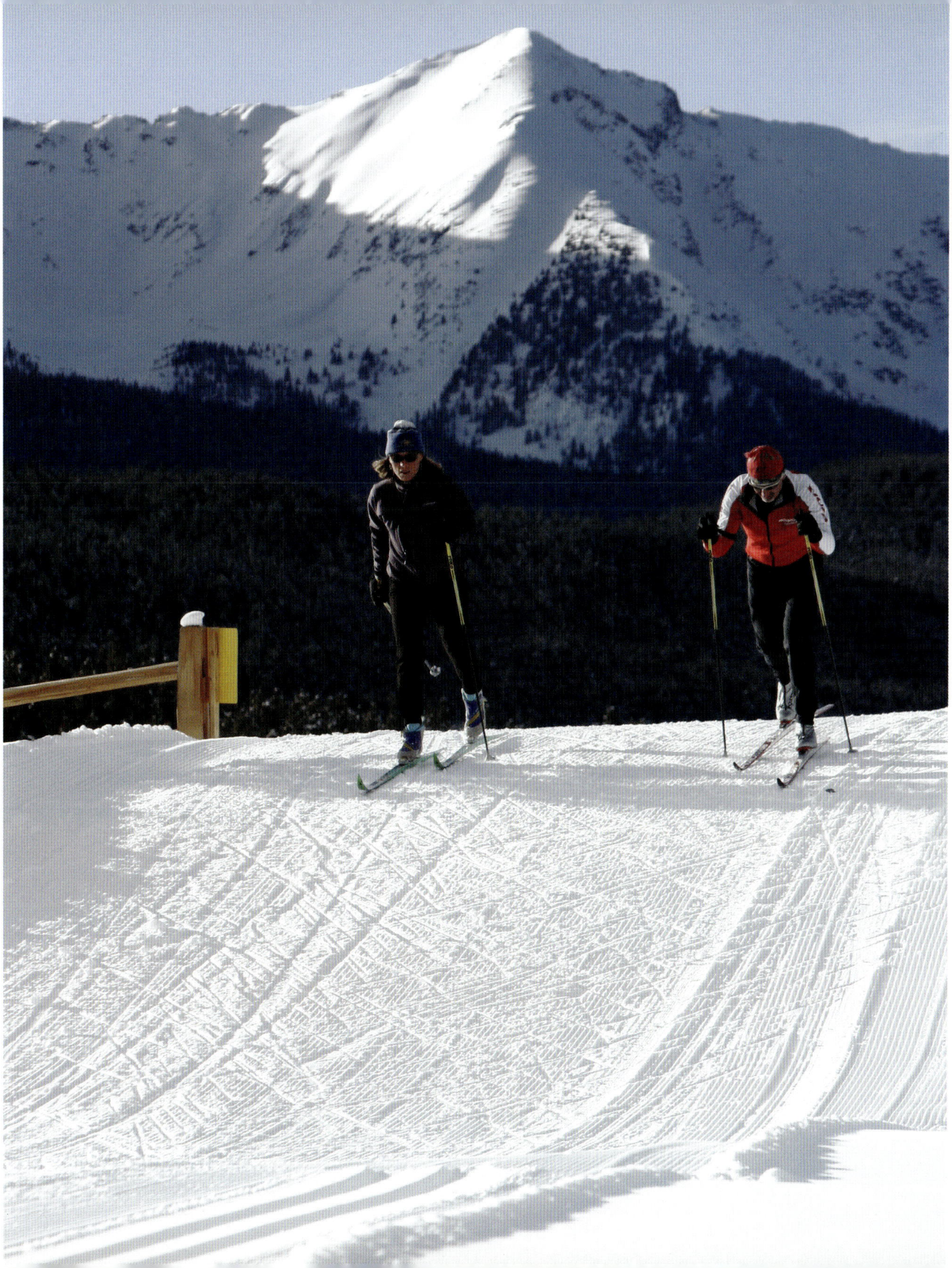

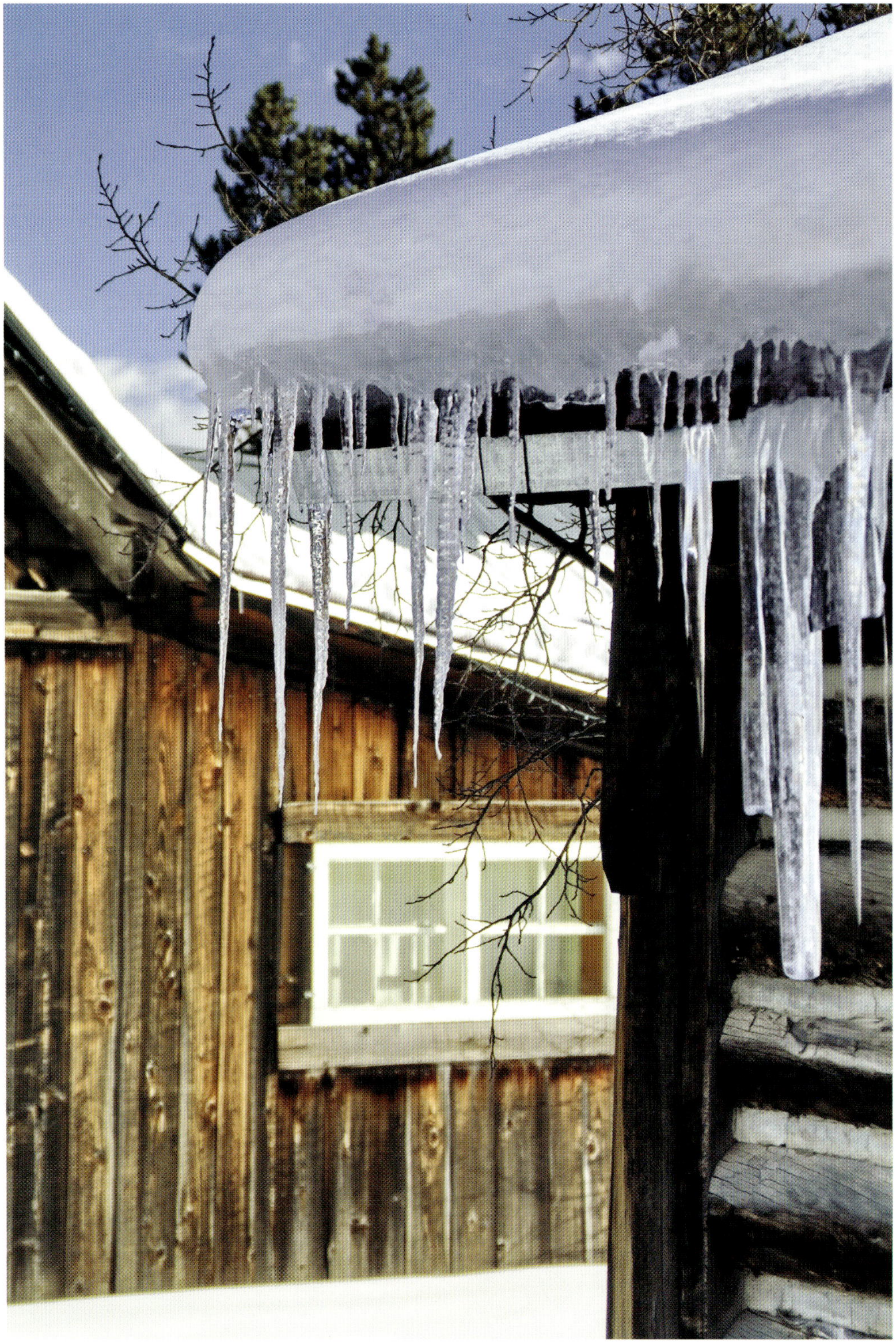

Breckenridge and nearby Frisco mix mountain and urban charm, offering world-class shopping—including a Christmas Bazaar at Old Town Hall—as well as adventure sports like snowmobiling, dogsled touring, cross-country skiing, and snowshoeing. For those seeking something in between, special Christmas sleigh rides through downtown fit the bill.

Families cherish their holiday time in Breckenridge at the Mountain Top Children's Museum, which features interactive experiments and Christmas cheer crafts. Kids can also take photos and train rides with Santa at the Main Street Train Station while their parents enjoy historical walking tours of downtown Breckenridge. In late January, don't miss the museum's international snow sculpture championships, in which artists transform 20-ton, 12-foot blocks of snow into artistic masterpieces.

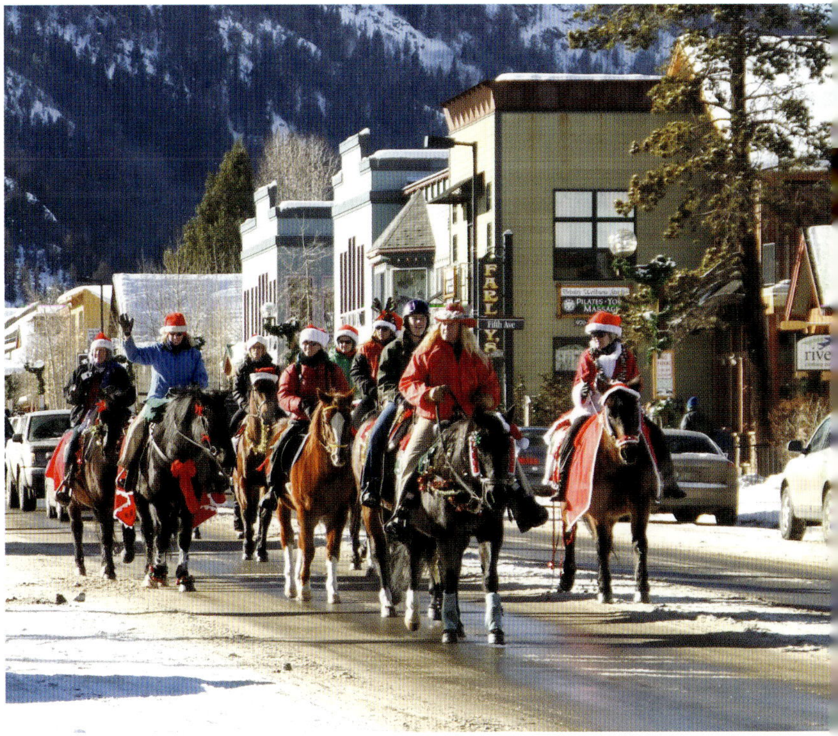

Above: Horses parade through downtown, Frisco
Left: Sun warms icicles hanging from a log cabin

Colorado Springs

& PUEBLO

Silent night, holy night

All is calm, all is bright

Round yon Virgin

Mother and Child

Holy Infant so tender

and mild…

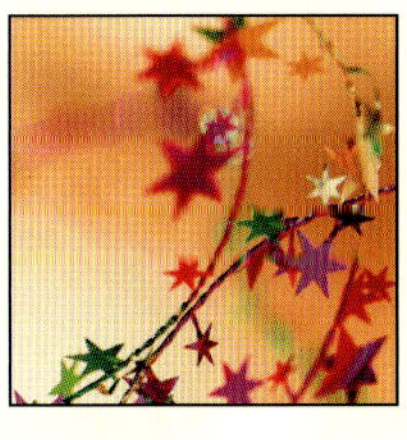

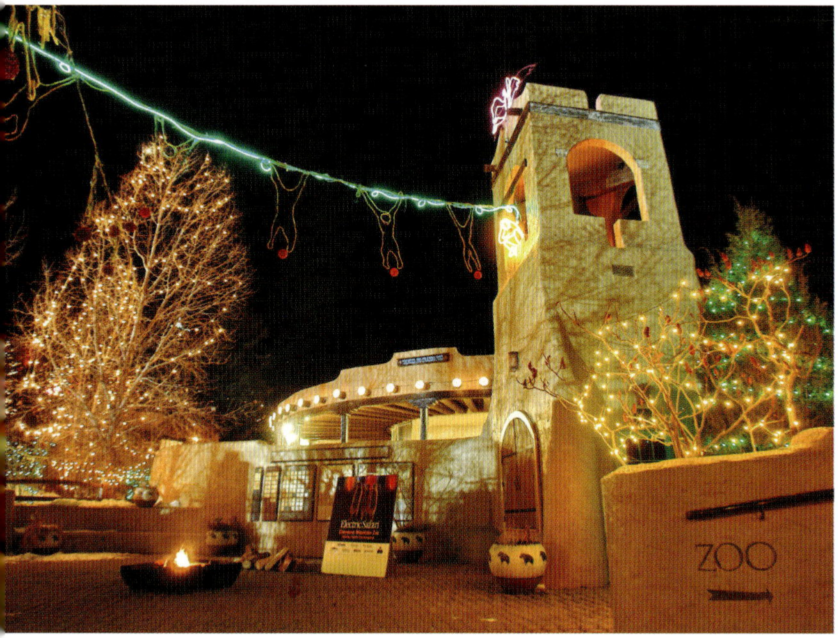

Above: The Electric Safari consumes Cheyenne Mountain Zoo, Colorado Springs
Right: The Broadmoor Hotel shines during the holidays, Colorado Springs

Next page: Looking out over the city, Colorado Springs

MAKE A ROYAL ENTRANCE into the holiday season at the Glen Eyrie Castle Christmas Madrigal Banquet in Colorado Springs, 75 miles south of Denver. This festive five-course meal features period singing, dancing, and an introduction to the Lady and Lord of the castle. An enchanting fantasy world come to life, this Renaissance-themed dinner is the perfect way to usher in Christmas.

For a taste of Christmas any time of year, The North Pole in Colorado Springs is ideal. Comprised of an entire enchanting village of elves and Christmas-themed rides with holiday lights galore, this amusement park, opened in 1956, is truly magical. The idyllic home of Mr. and Mrs. Claus completes this tiny wonderland and allows holiday fairy tales to come to life.

Just around the river bend from The North Pole are the Seven Falls, an all encompassing taste of natural Colorado beauty. Each of the seven waterfalls is individually decorated for the holiday season, making it more than worth braving the cold to see them. Red, green, yellow, and blue lights flash and illuminate the already gorgeous surroundings, spreading joyous holiday cheer to all viewers.

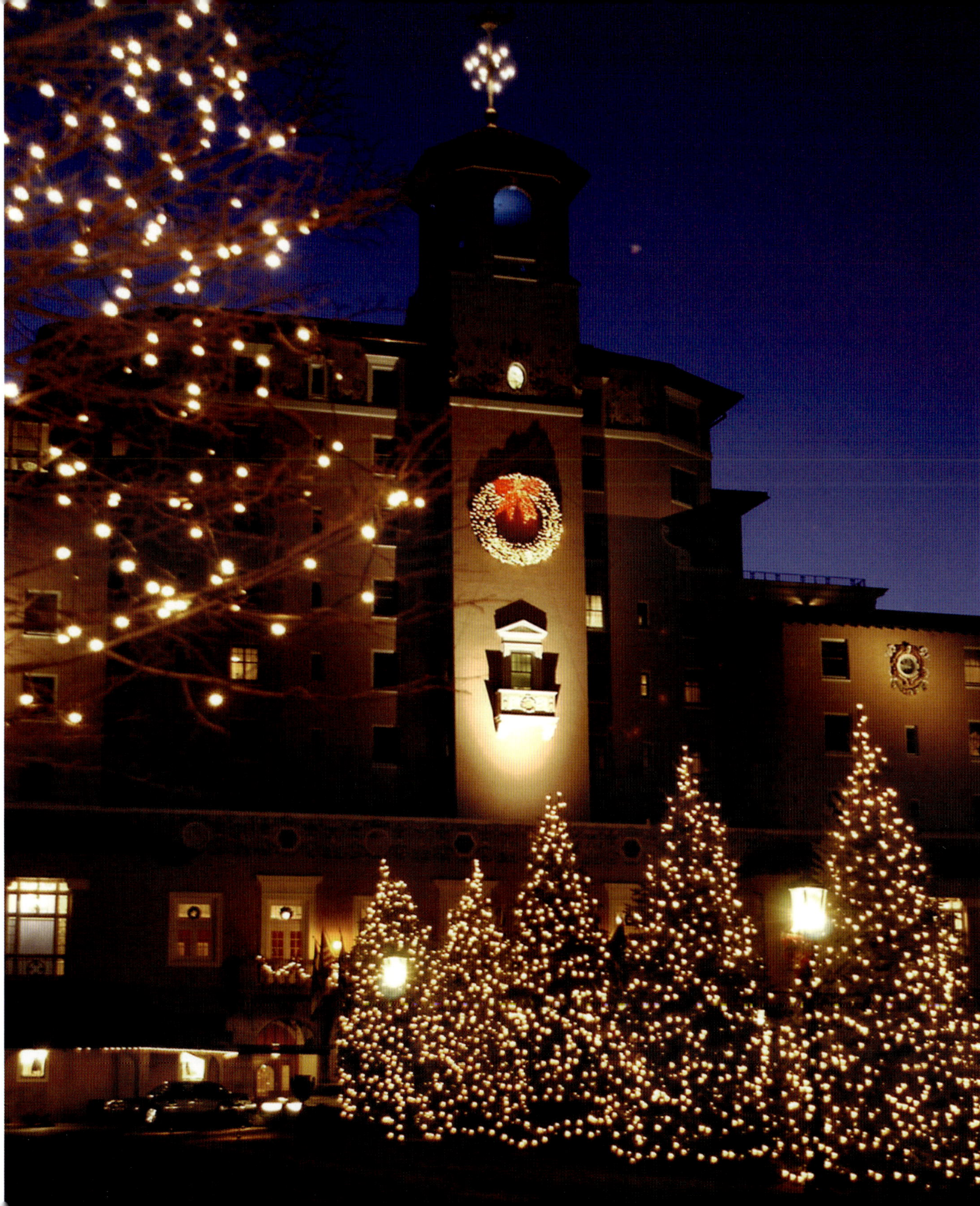

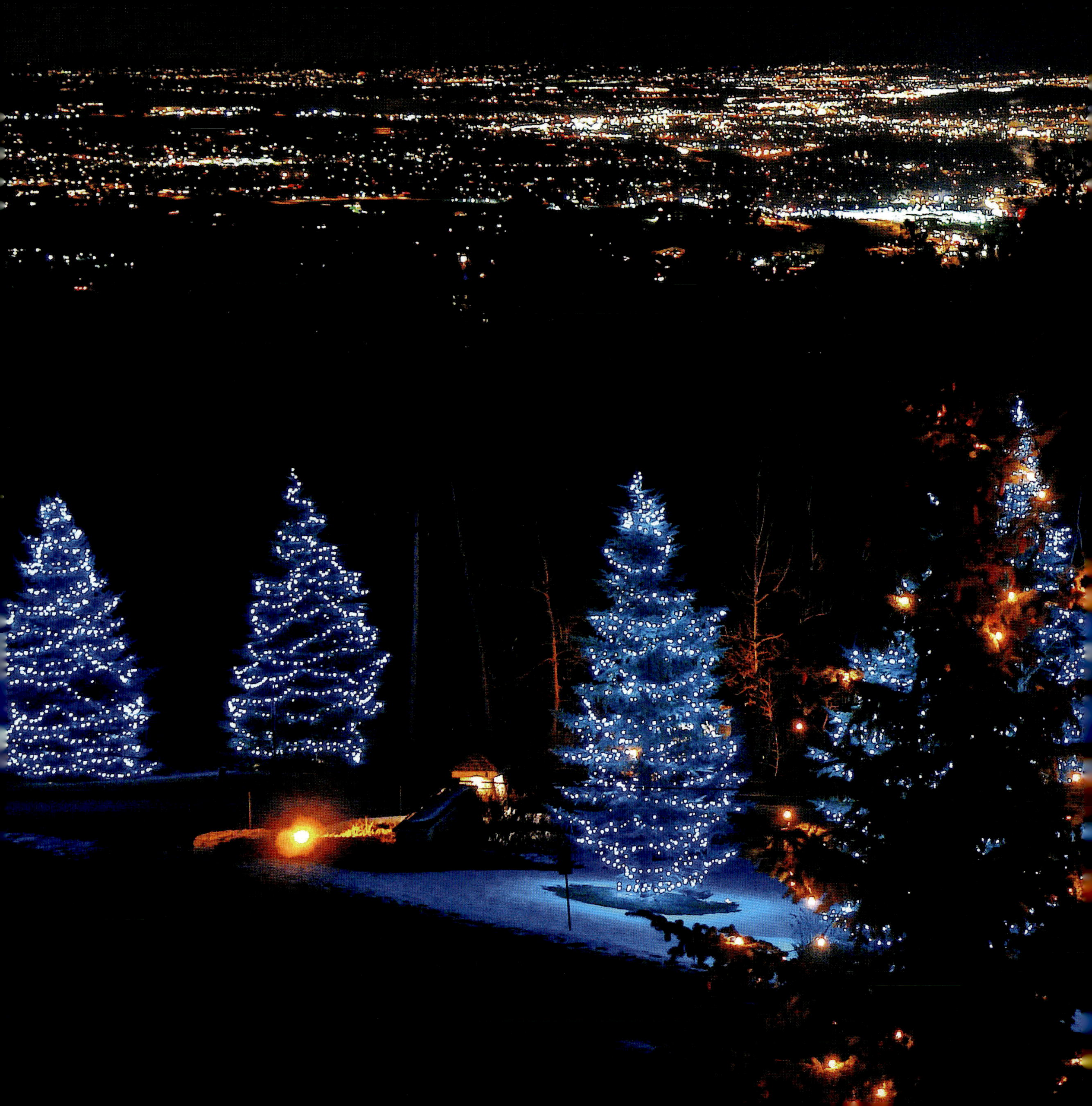

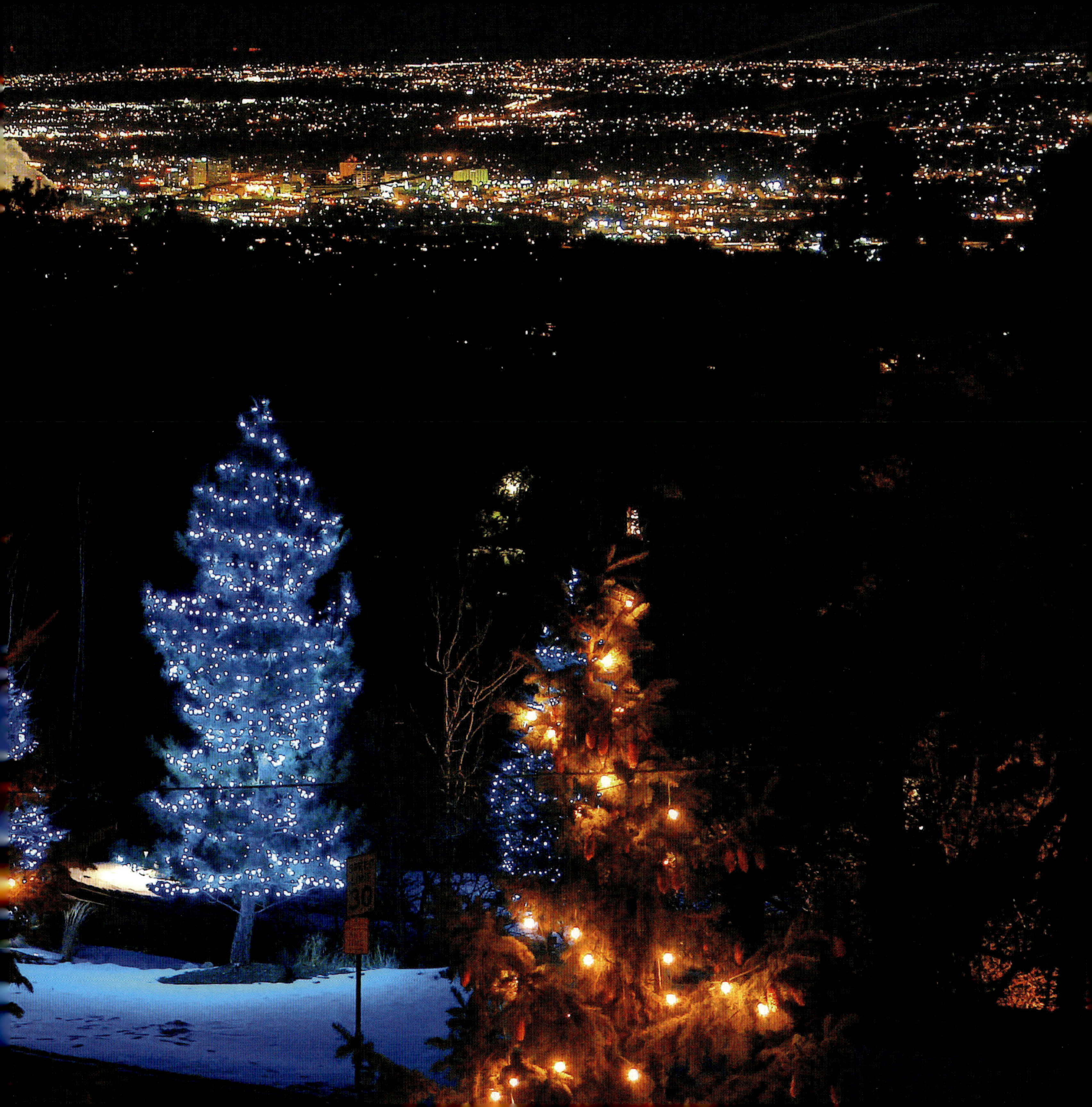
30

Christmas performances abound at the Pikes Peak Center, which starts the holiday season in early December with presentations of an eclectic mix of holiday favorites. Don't miss the Colorado Springs Chorale choir's yearly performance of The Best Way to Celebrate Christmas, a combination of classic and original carols all directed by the Chorale's renowned directors. Following that stunning vocal performance, the Pikes Peak Center hosts the Colorado Springs Philharmonic, playing even more holiday classics.

Head out for a mountainside adventure along the Cheyenne Mountain Zoo Electric Safari, an annual celebratory holiday light display. With more than a million lights, it's the largest light display in Western Colorado. Enjoy the light display as well as great panoramic views of the second-largest city in Colorado at this mountainside zoo.

Downtown Colorado Springs dazzles with its annual Festival of Lights Parade, full of delightful horse-drawn carriages, classic cars, floats, and live music. The parade boasts the

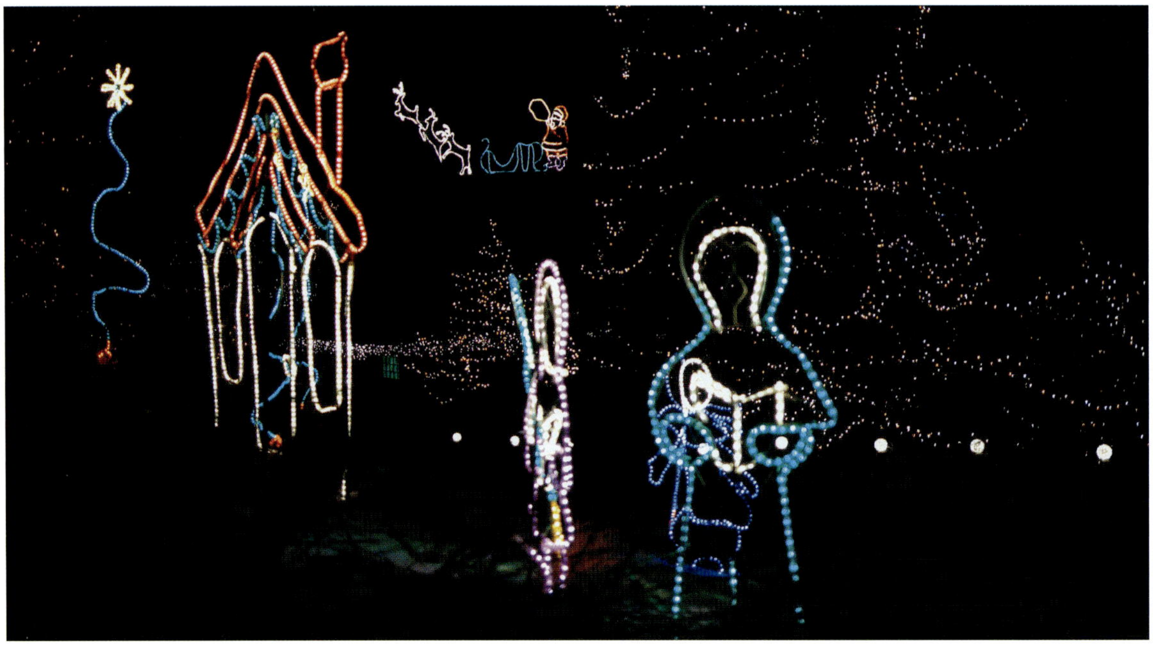

Electric Safari at Cheyenne Mountain Zoo, Colorado Springs

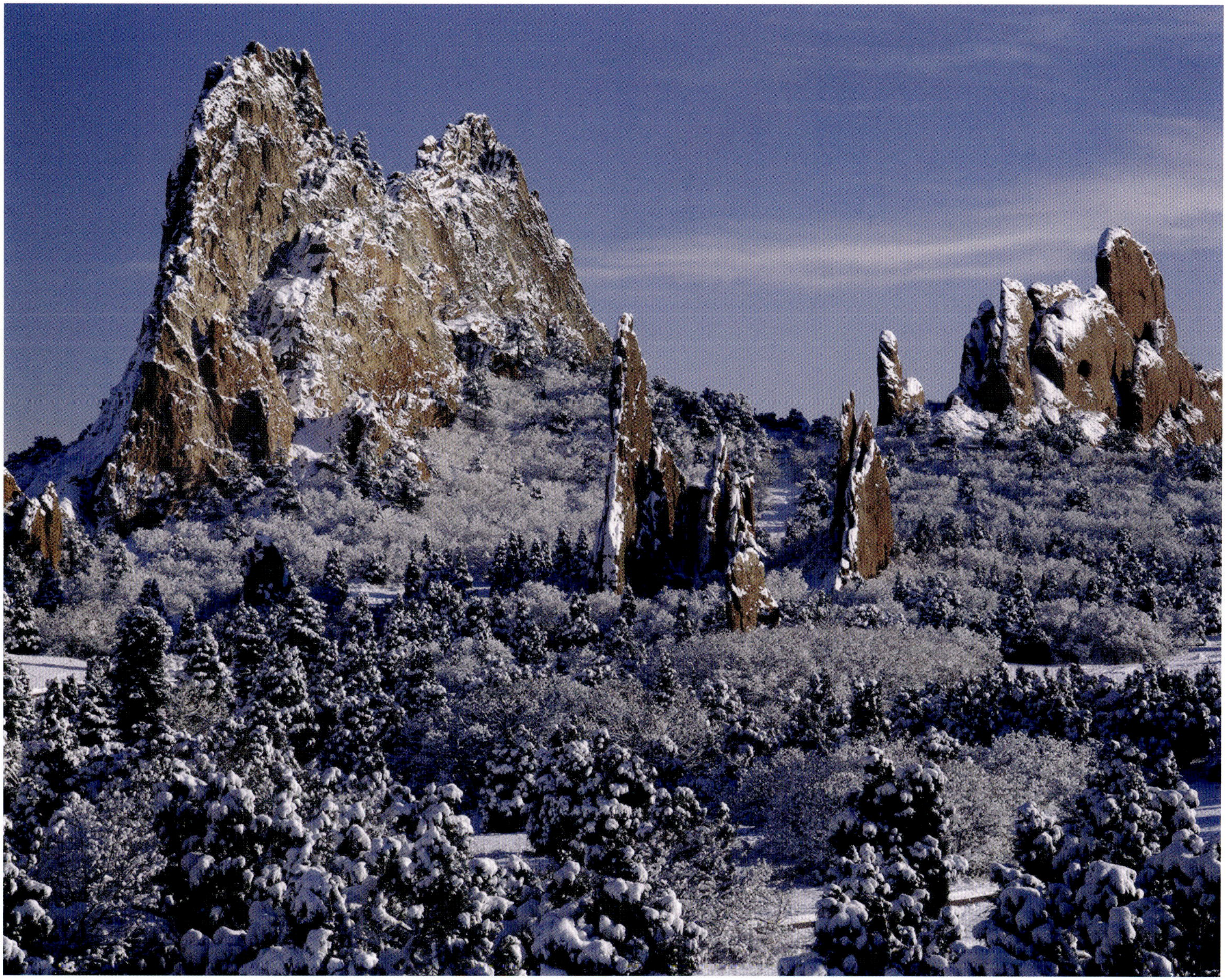

Garden of the Gods Park dusted with snow, Colorado Springs

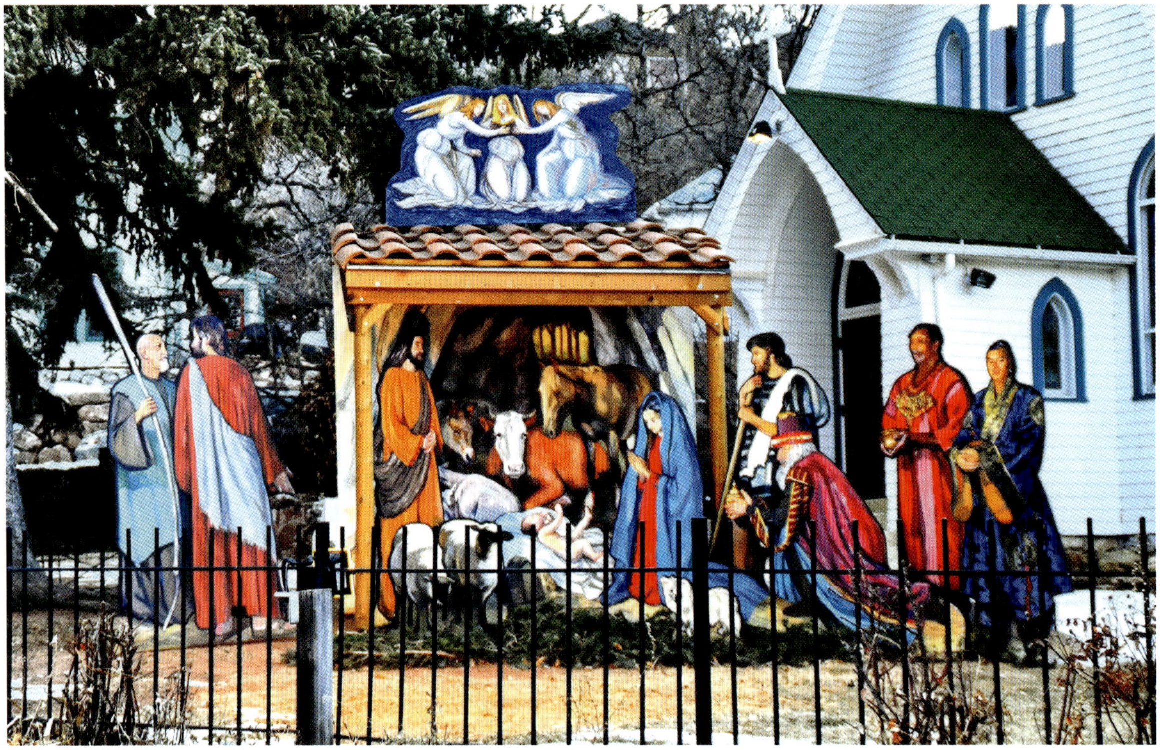

A nativity scene graces a church yard, Colorado Springs

second largest attendance of any holiday parade in the state and is a thrilling experience for holiday-lovers of all ages.

Don't forget your ice skates. Colorado Springs is home to the World Arena, where the Broadmoor Skating Club—which has spawned eight Olympic medal winners to date, including Peggy Fleming—trains. Stop by for a lesson, an event, or just for fun.

Colorado Springs wouldn't be The Springs without the Broadmoor Hotel. The lovely hotel, famous for entertaining celebrities and celebutantes alike, comes alive during the holiday season. With a fairy-tale light display and the most courteous service you'll ever receive, the hotel is nothing short of extravagant. Stay the night and grace one of the hotel's semiannual Christmas plays or theaters with your presence. The Colorado Christmas Dinner Theater hosts nightly performances from Thanksgiving until Christmas. Finish the year off right with their New Year's Eve Gala, featuring a live orchestra, a stunningly decorated ballroom, and dining in true Colorado style.

PUEBLO

In a town best known for hosting the Colorado State Fair, Christmas is a big affair. To get into the spirit, attend the annual Christmas Posada. School choir members begin this singing procession at the Pueblo Convention Center, chanting biblical quotations as they parade through town. The ceremony culminates in a breathtaking live nativity scene, sure to bring faith and spirit to the holiday. As you enjoy the crowds and liveliness of downtown, take in the classic adobe architecture of Pueblo.

Next, visit the Pueblo Zoo for fun with animals, nature, and lights. In the Electricritters Light Display, holiday lights and shimmering animal sculptures illuminate the night. It's a holiday light extravaganza with more than 250,000 tiny colorful lights. The zoo's holiday music festival and Candy Cane Café are also big draws. Pick up some great stocking stuffers in the gift shop and sip hot cocoa as you take a safari through the mountains. The whole family will enjoy this glowing night on the town surrounded by animals of fur and lights alike.

For a taste of history, spend a day at the Rosemont Museum, a 113-year-old Victorian house offering a festive Christmas atmosphere with period décor along with staff and docents decked out in authentic Victorian attire. To keep the enchanting spirit going, catch a performance of *The Nutcracker* downtown and watch the Christmas fairy tale come to life on stage.

Get to know the natural geography of Pueblo, located along the swishing Arkansas River, with a Historic Arkansas Riverwalk Tour. Take an informational boat tour and learn about the amazing life within the river as you sip on cocoa and chew cookies with Santa Claus. Later, watch as the Pueblo Express transitions to a Polar Express at the Pueblo Railway Association by the Union Depot. Take a ride with a loved one in the two antique cabooses and then have a snack and explore Santa's workshop, housed in a little red caboose.

The Holiday Lighting Extravaganza, right after Thanksgiving, lights up Pueblo's Riverwalk and features hot chocolate and live music. NORAD tracks Santa's arrival and fireworks burst over Lake Elizabeth in a grand finale to the evening.

Just 20 miles away from Pueblo is the tiny town of Beulah. Beulah plays host to the Yule Log Festival, a customary community Christmas activity. This town tradition was first established in 1952 when a couple from Beulah attended a yule log festival in Palmer Lake; they enjoyed the ceremony so much that they brought a splinter of the Palmer Lake log back to Beulah to begin their own tradition. Now, every year, community members from the entire town search for a hidden log in Mountain Park in a colorful and celebratory ceremony. The finder is carried back to a community fire ring on the log, which is then used to spark a bonfire. Friends and family gather around the warm blaze to enjoy cookies and warm cider.

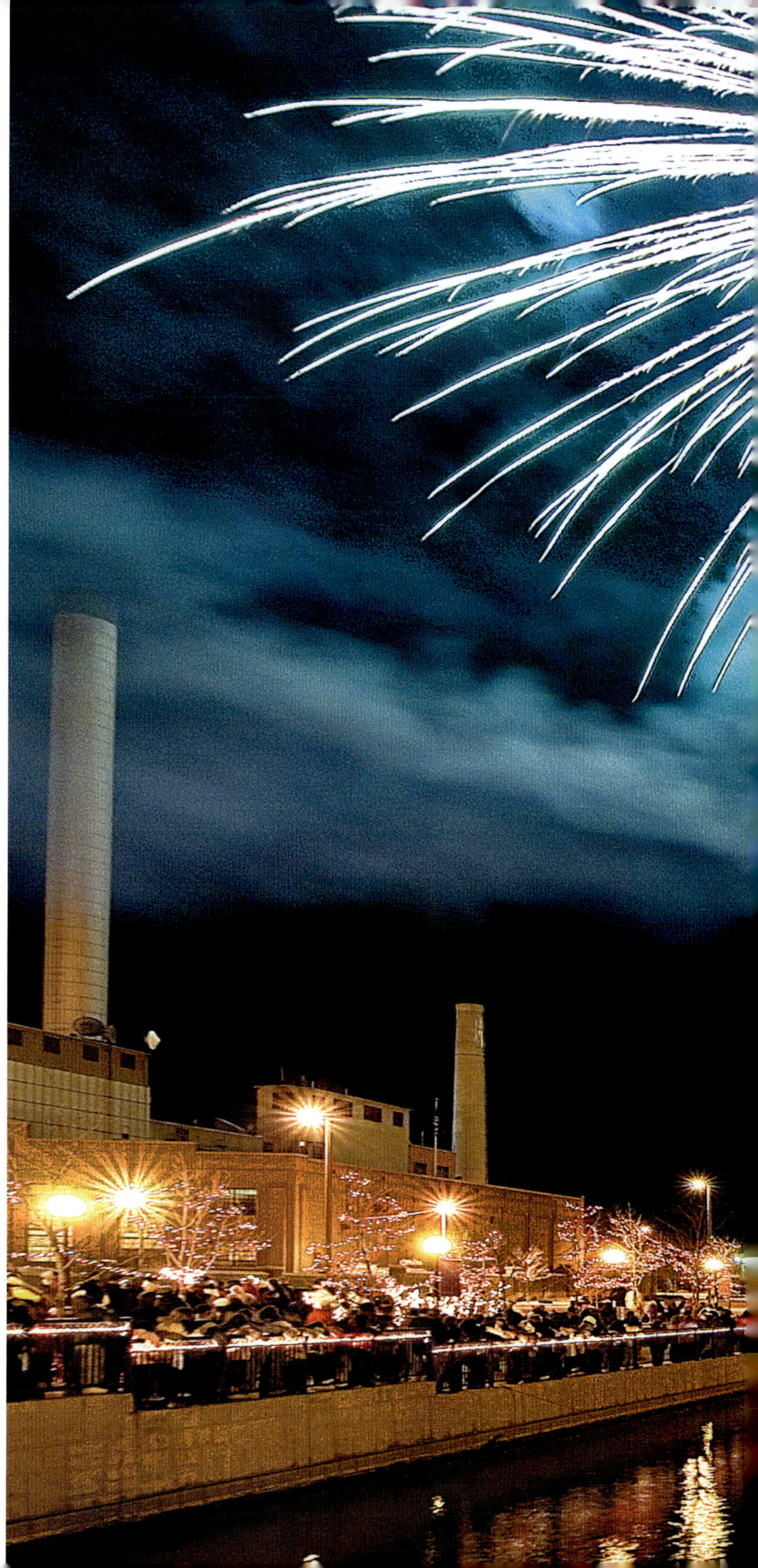

A fireworks show over Lake Elizabeth during the Riverwalk's annual Lighting Extravaganza, Pueblo

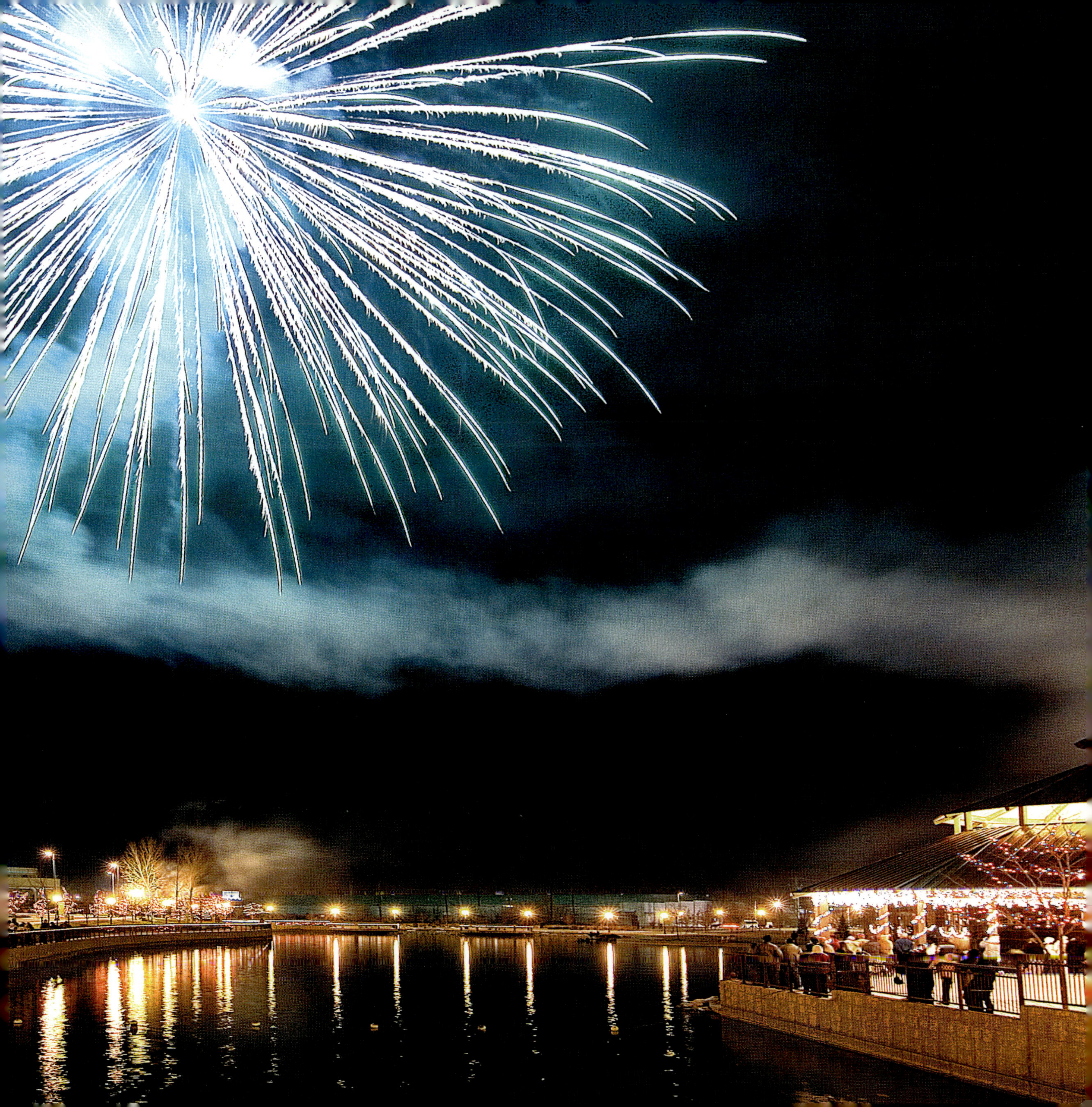

Crested Butte

& GUNNISON

Come,

bring with a noise,

My merry, merry boys,

The Christmas Log

to the firing...

—ROBERT HERRICK

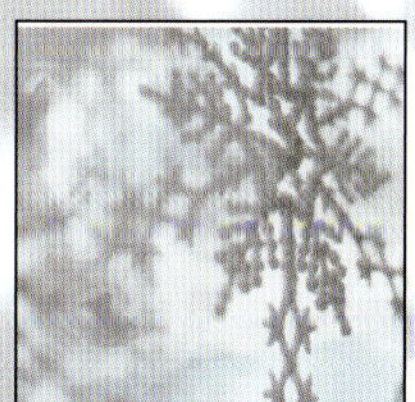

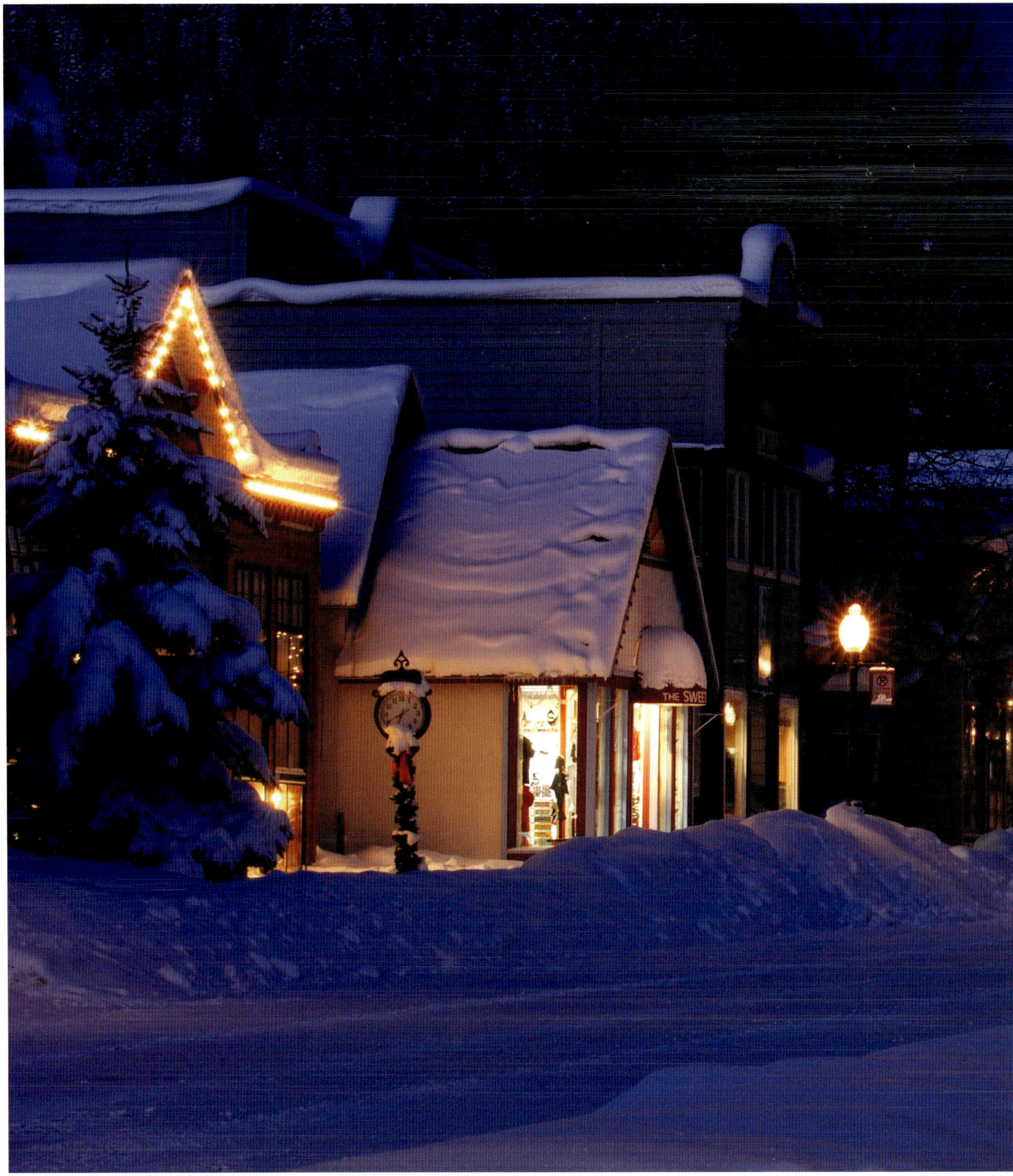

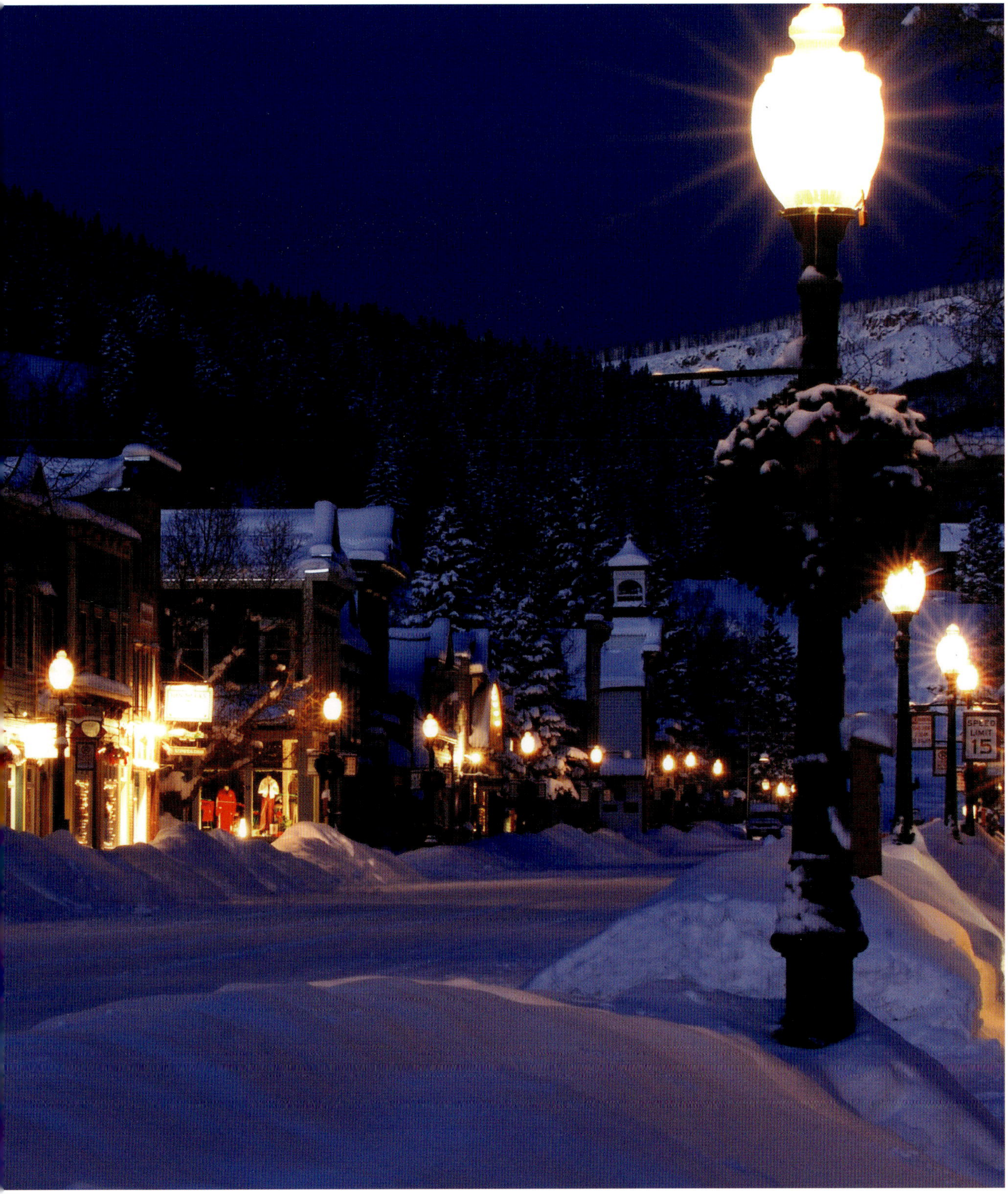
SPEED
LIMIT
15

EFFERVESCENT BEAUTY surrounds Crested Butte in western Colorado. Covered in a soft, white blanket of snow, the valley bears only the marks of those who yearn to tackle its flowing terrain. Here, and in nearby Gunnison, you can celebrate the holidays in true Colorado fashion—in the midst of pristine snow, glowing lights, and the festivities of a lively mountain town.

Near the end of November, the streets of Gunnison come alive with the sounds of Good Samaritans buzzing about the annual Sugar Plum Festival. This arts-and-crafts show, which takes place in The Field Western Heritage Center in Gunnison, stirs up quite the excitement. With handmade wreaths, tree skirts, and table runners, this 75-booth artisan festival offers the perfect entrance into the holiday season and draws a crowd anxious to get a jump-start on their holiday gift shopping.

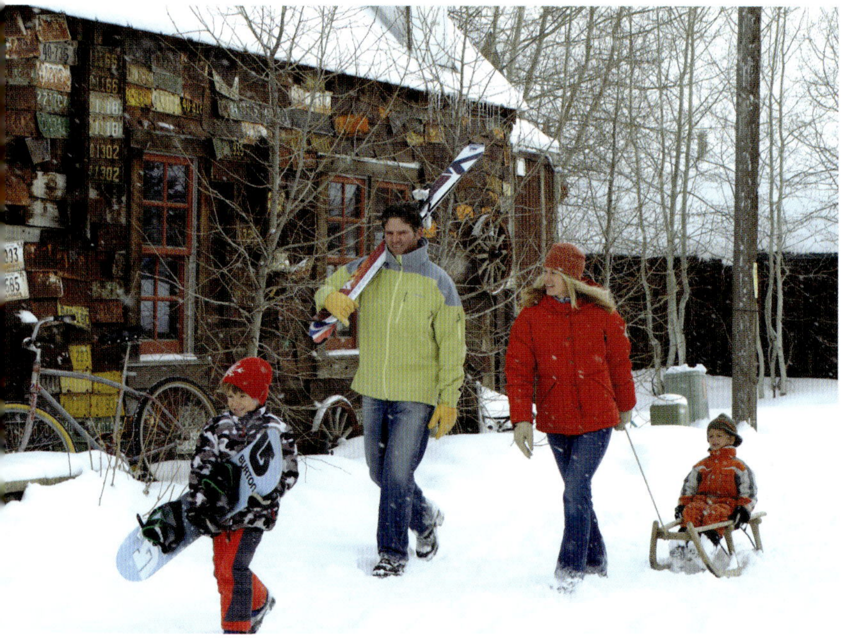

Above: A family heads out for skiing, snowboarding, and sledding, Crested Butte
Right: Christmas lights glow through the fence detail and light up the porch, Crested Butte

Previous page: Elk Avenue, the town's main street and a National Historic District, Crested Butte

A few weeks later the Butte's yuletide events kick off with the Nordic Center Citizens Race Series, offering ski, skate, and skiathlon events for all ages and abilities. This town's competitive spirit is definitely kicked into high gear during the holiday season.

Gunnison's Night of Lights spreads joy as trees all down Elk Avenue are lit up. The ceremony, featuring musical accompaniment by Western State College's lively orchestra, is a favorite of natives and visitors alike. Local businesses compete for awards for best lights, best food vendor, and best stationary light sculpture. There's live entertainment all over the town, culminating with a visit from Santa himself, who lights the town Christmas tree.

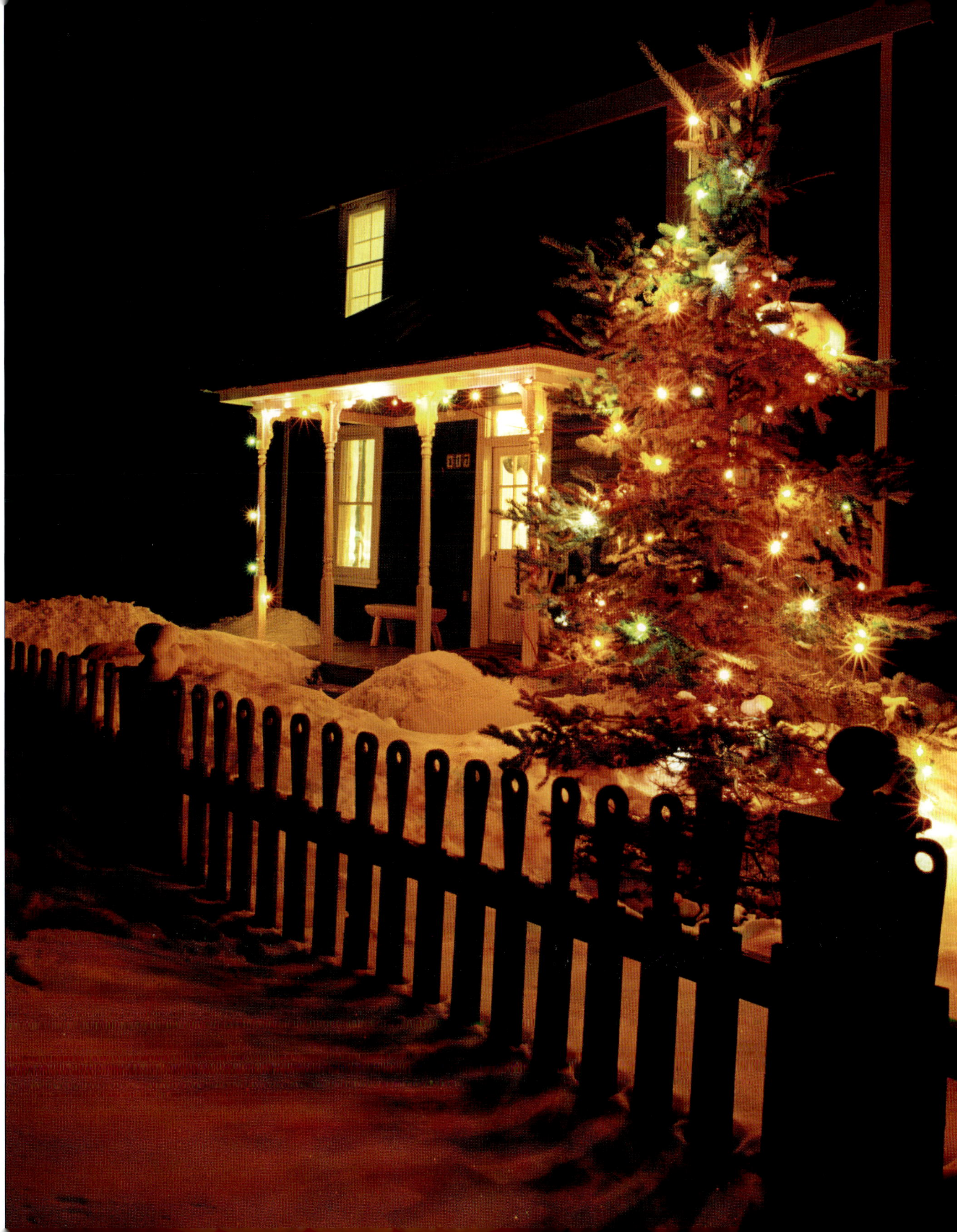

Trek back to Crested Butte and take a romantic fantasy carriage ride. Travel back more than a century during the 20-minute historical tour of the town, basking under the warmth of a blanket and the guidance of a charming horseman.

Housing some of Colorado's most isolated and untamed terrain as well as plenty of beginner and intermediate hills, the ski area at Crested Butte invites anyone coming to town for the holiday festivities to hit the slopes. Free "learn to skate ski" lessons along with ski specials throughout the month of December make the offer almost irresistible. The astounding natural beauty of the town's surroundings only add to the lure.

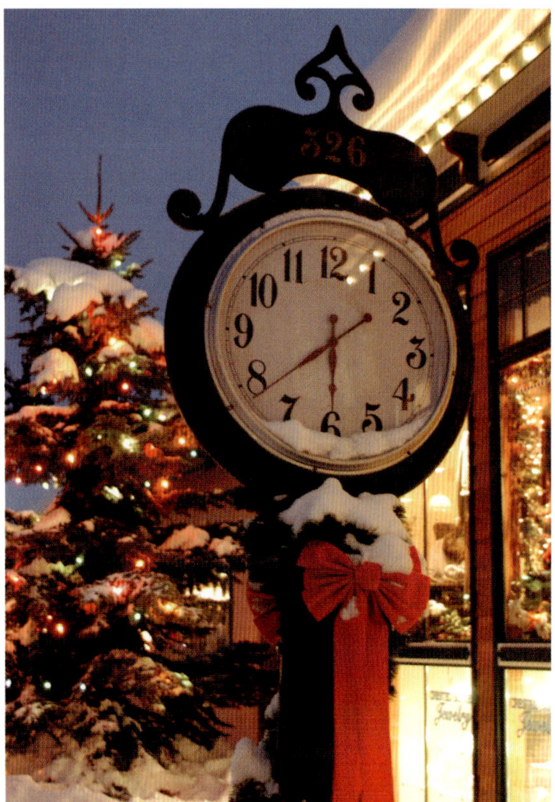

Panoramic views of the town and mountains are a sunny sight from the chairlift—but they're even more picturesque by night. Moonlight snowshoe tours of the town offer a rare view of the mountainside glory. A nighttime tour for both skiers and snowshoers takes place on the last full moon before Christmas.

Yet another lighting festivity is the Christmas Eve Torchlight Parade, a final glowing evening welcoming St. Nick to town. Matched only in energy by the New Year's Eve celebration and fireworks, this parade draws nearly the entire town out to cheer.

As soon as the holidays are over and done, thoughts of snow sink back into the minds of the powder-craving natives as the Profurious Park and Pipe Series of ski and snowboard competitions cruises through the valley. These events draw crowds that watch in amazement as children, teens, and adults get aggressive on the jumps and rails. Another holiday season may be over, but the cheer of a community is never far from the heart in these spirited mountain towns.

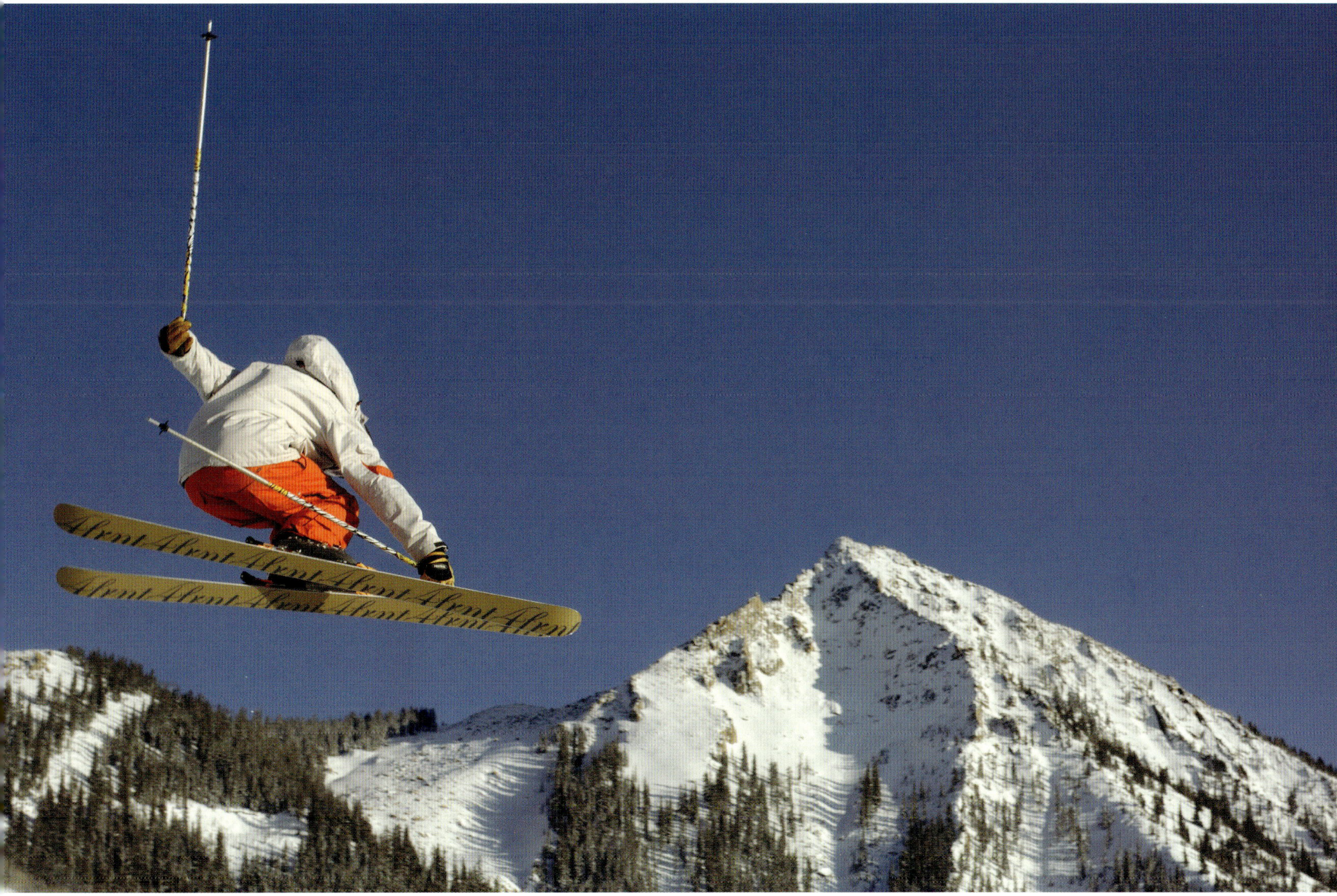

Left: The town clock in the town's National Historic District, Crested Butte

Above: A skier catches some air at Crested Butte Mountain Resort

Next page: Santa offers sleigh rides on historic Elk Avenue

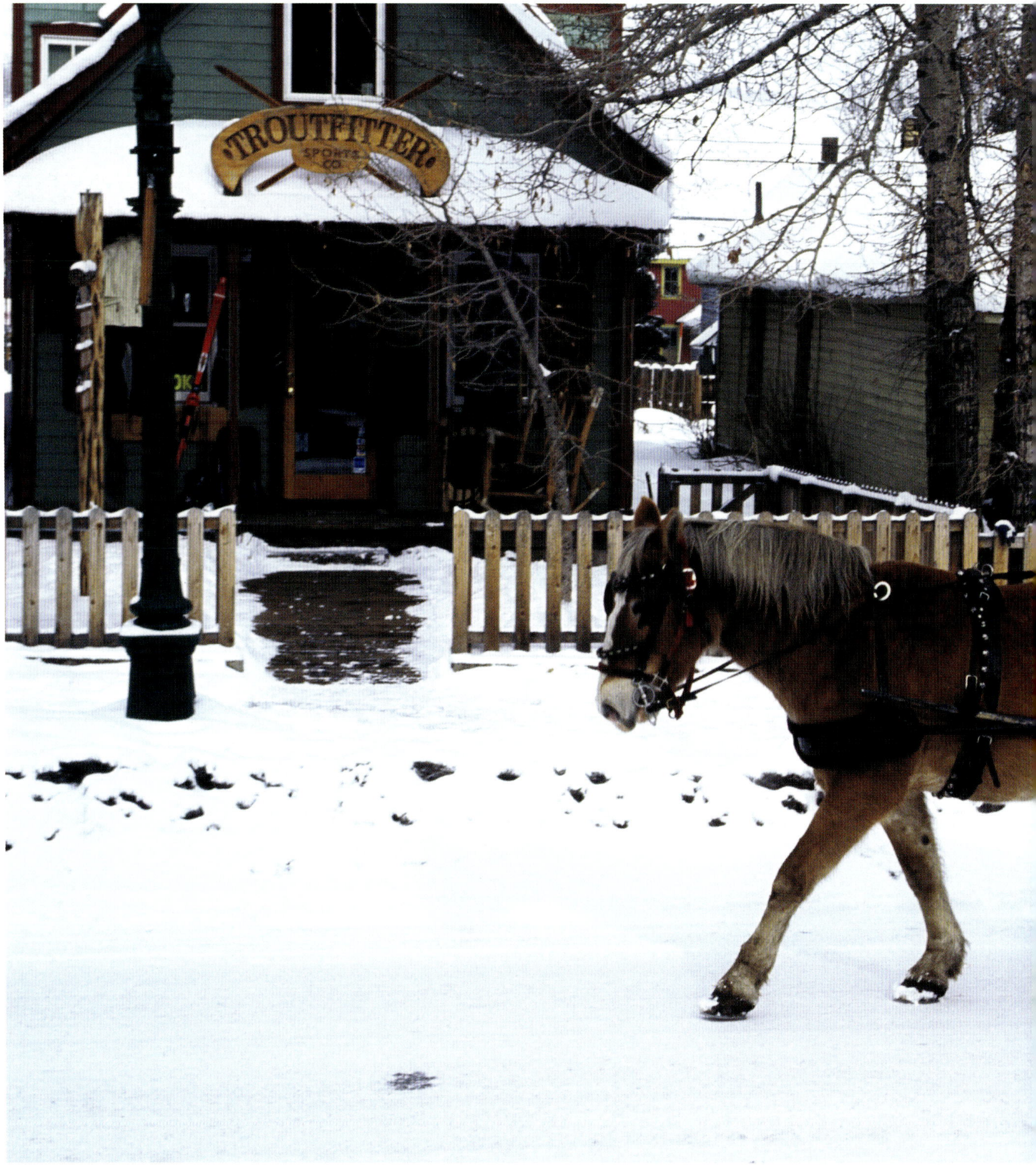
TROUTFITTER
SPORTS CO

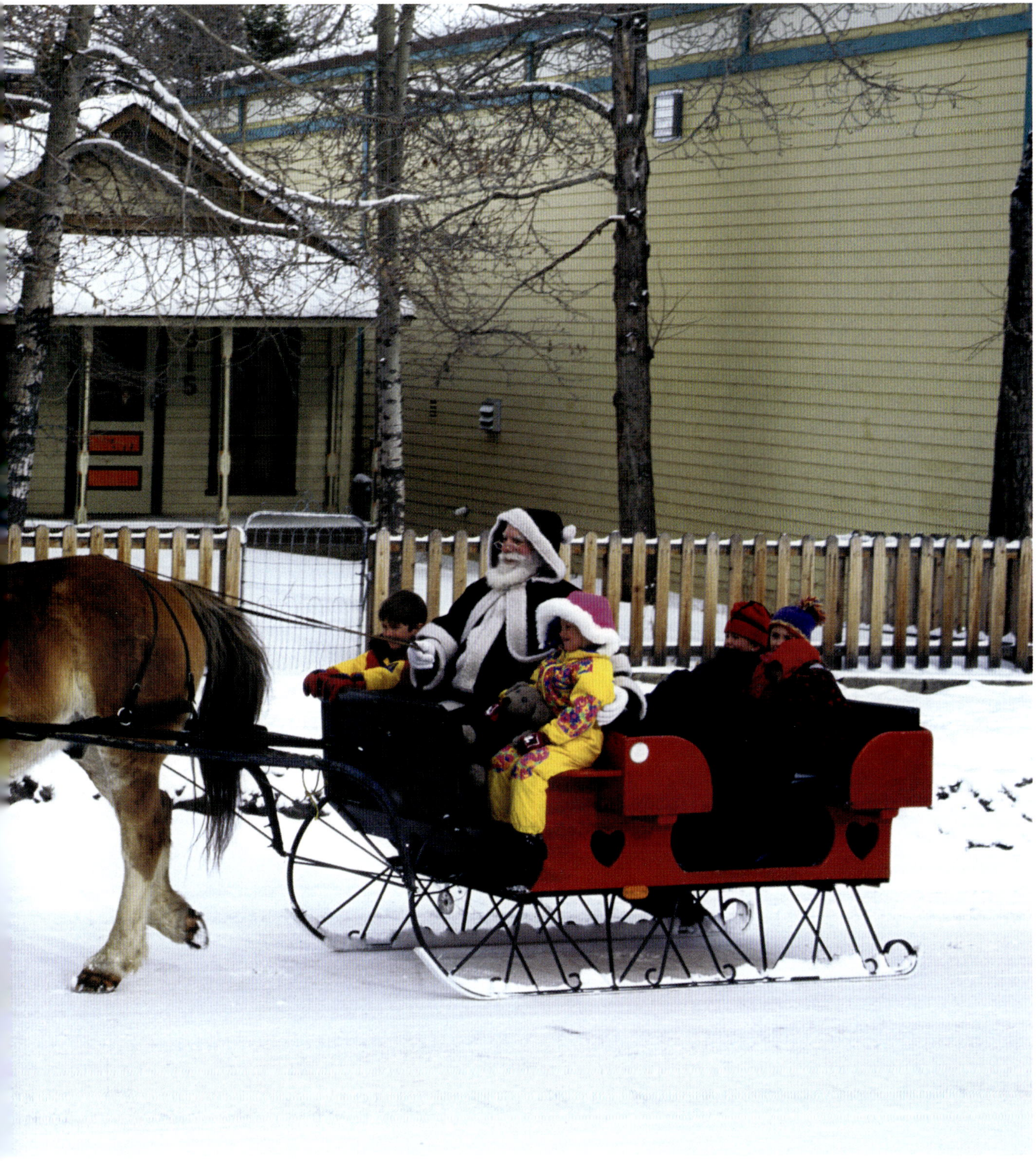

Denver

It is Christmas

in the heart that puts

Christmas in the air.

—W.T. ELLIS

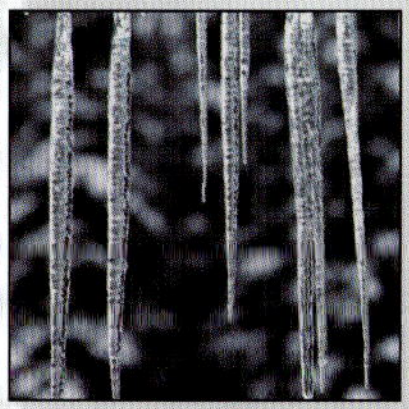

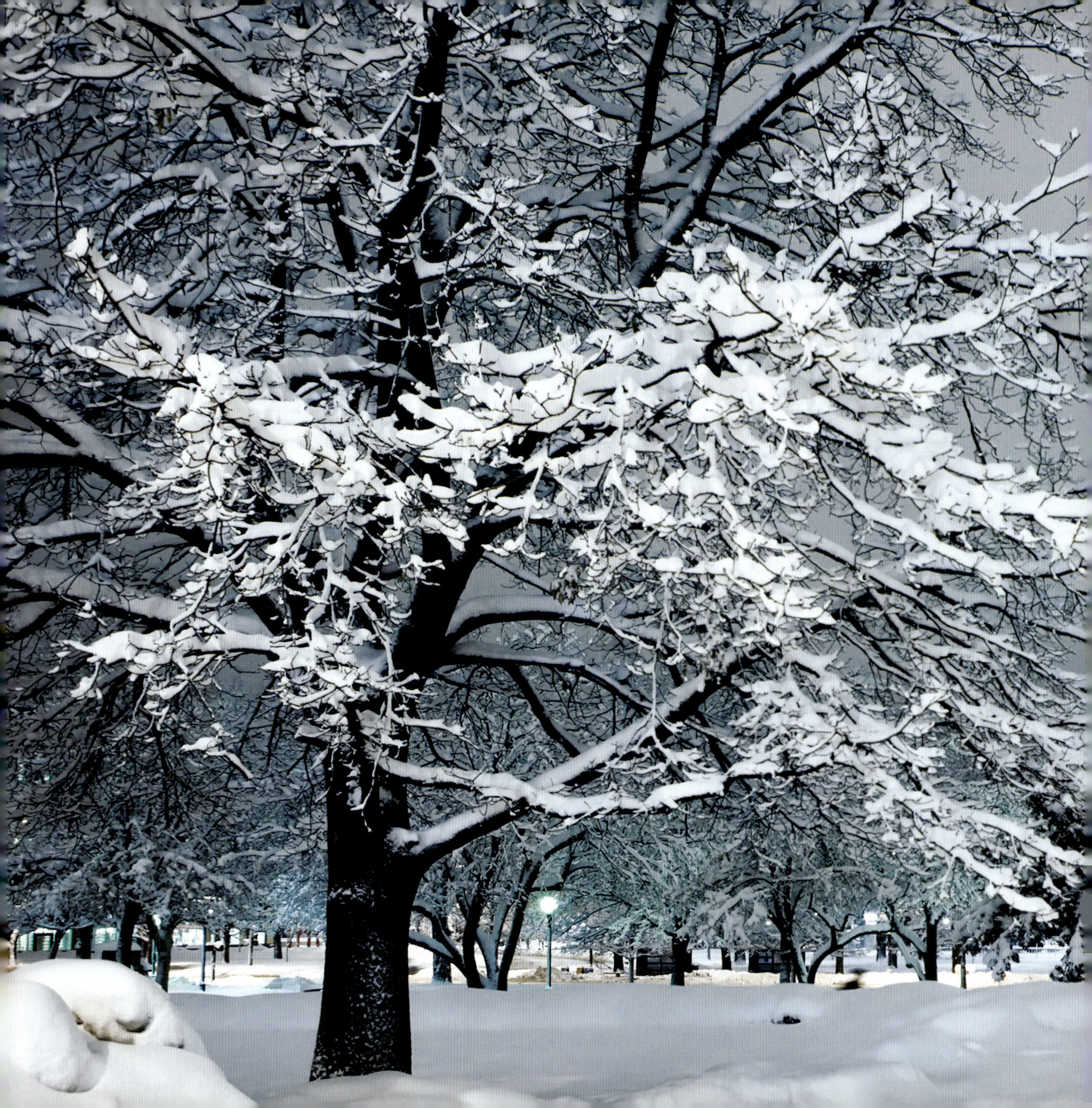

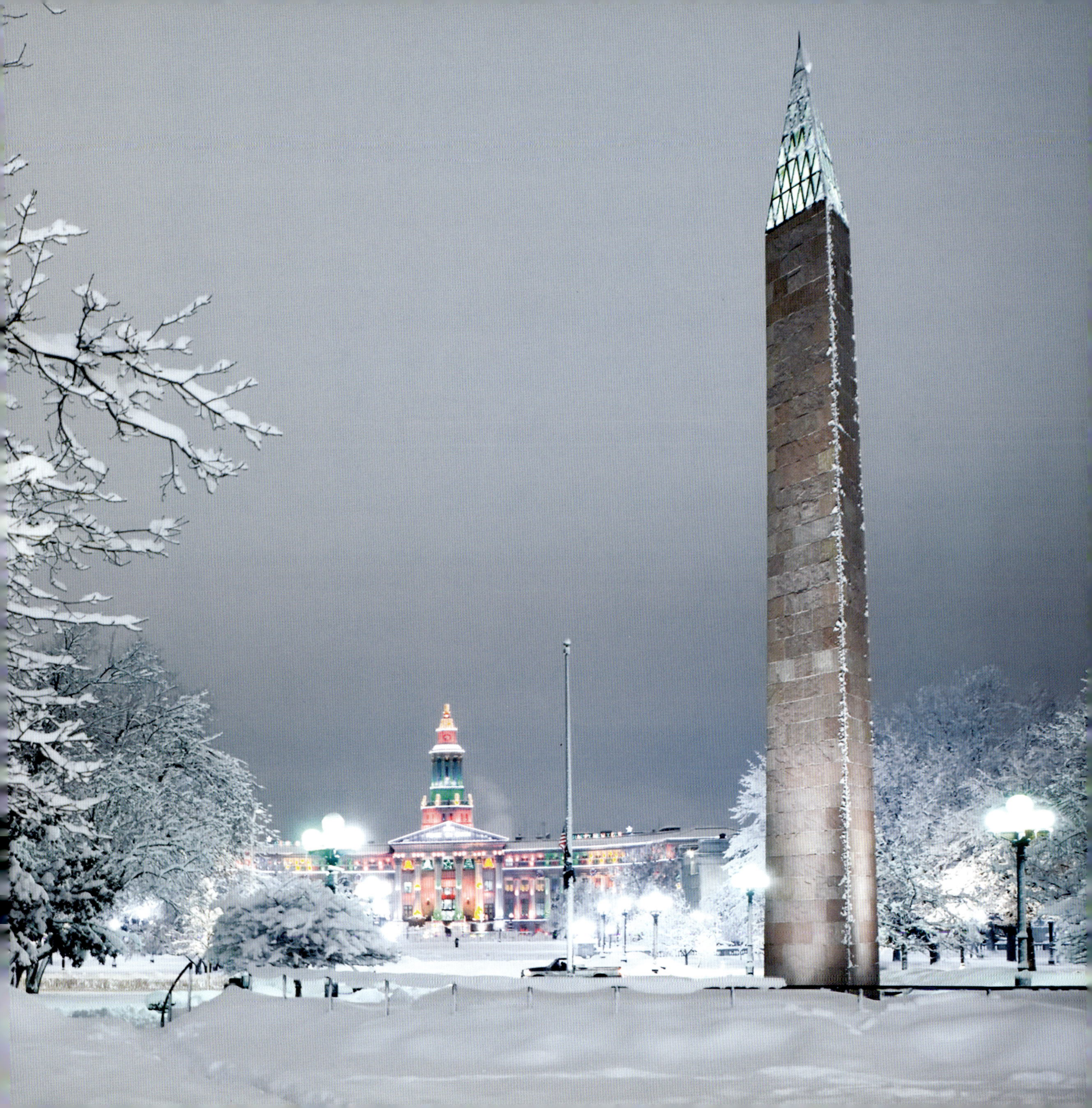

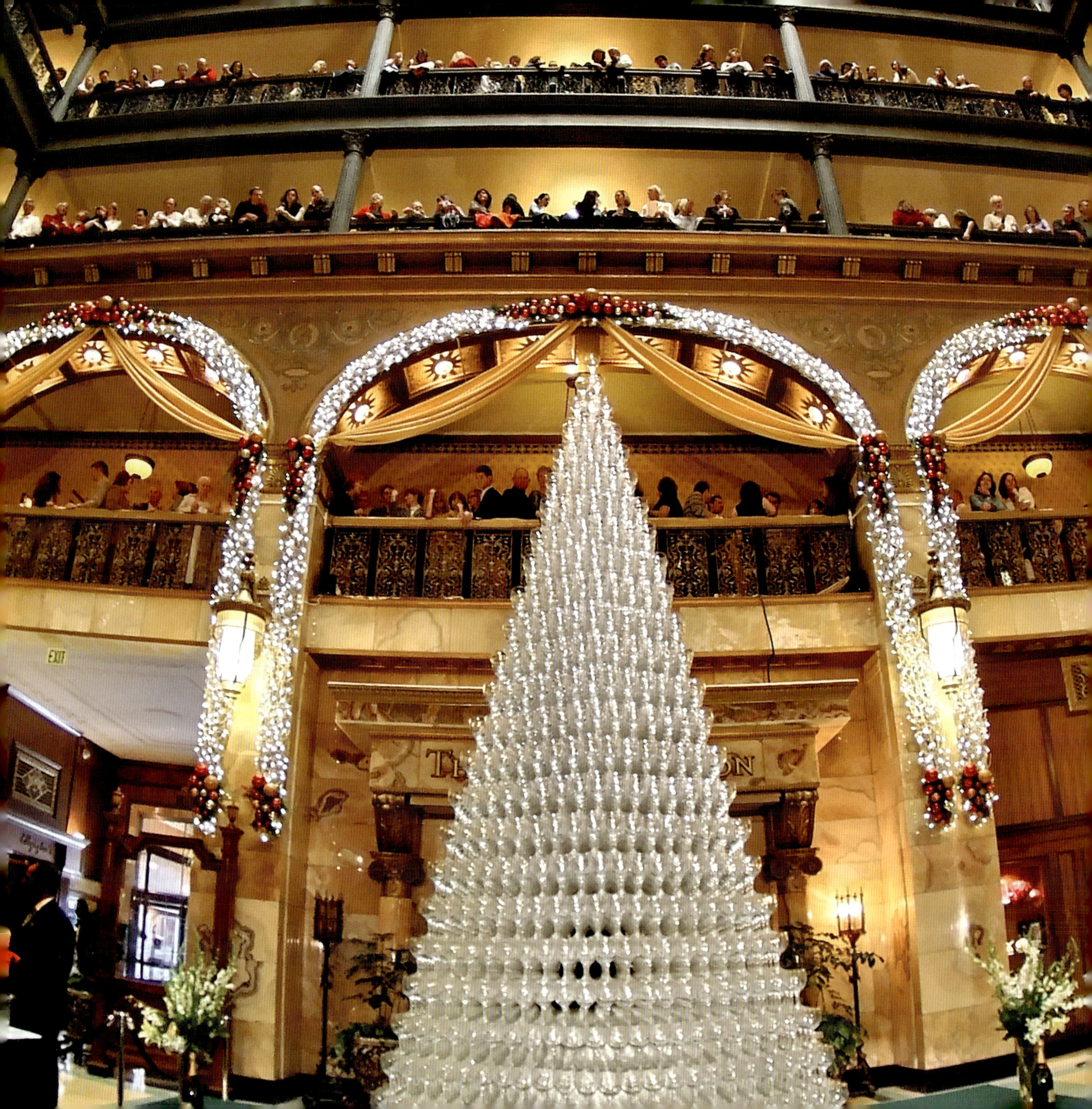
EXIT

LIVE LIKE ROYALS IN THE QUEEN CITY, celebrating Christmas with cascades of champagne, loads of lights, and scores of cultural events. The holiday season in Denver kicks off at no less than the historic Brown Palace Hotel. The annual Champagne Cascade in mid-November features a master swordsman, an antique Napoleonic saber, and a 6,000-glass pyramid. With one precise blow, the swordsman severs the neck of a bottle of champagne, allowing the bubbly to sparkle its way down the two-story glass tower. Once the champagne is flowing, the hotel flips the switch, delighting visitors with thousands of twinkling lights adorning the landmark hotel's elegant atrium, archways, and chandelier.

For a small-town Christmas experience, take the Light Rail to the Downtown Littleton Station for the Candlelight Walk and Tree Lighting the day after Thanksgiving. Stroll down historic Main Street with lit candles, stopping in shops and sipping hot cider as you wait for Santa to arrive on his sleigh and illuminate the tree-lined streets. Lights abound in the Denver metro area during the holidays, so if you miss this tree lighting, head to Denver Botanic Gardens Blossoms of Light at 10th Avenue and York Street. Featuring more than a million colorful lights, this display is rivaled only by the Zoo Lights display at Denver Zoo in City Park.

Denver wouldn't be Denver without the fully lit City & County Building, its colorful display glowing from the day after Thanksgiving through New Year's and then again for the National Western Stock Show. Stroll by on your way to a viewing spot for the annual

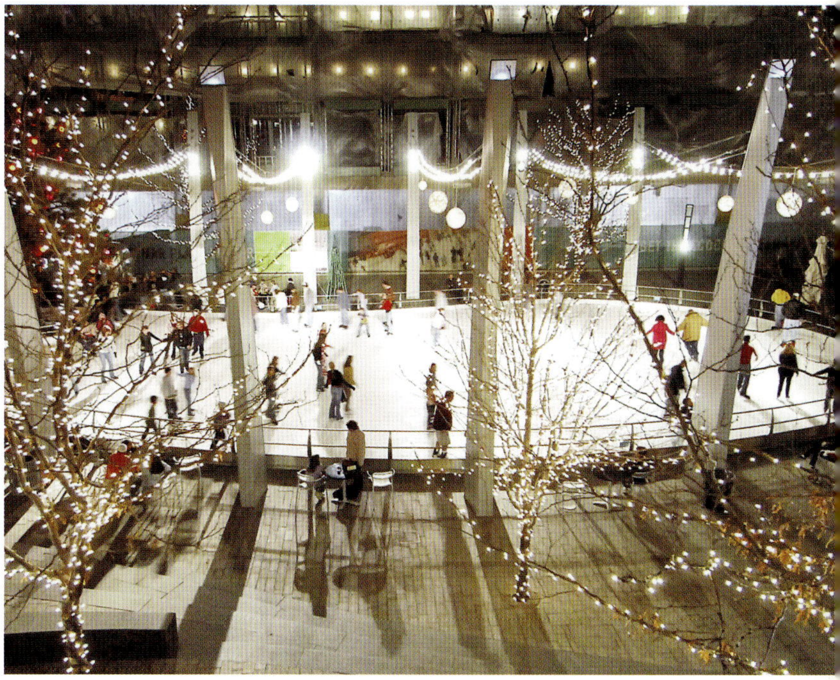

Above: Outdoor skating rink, Belmar, Lakewood
Left: The annual champagne cascade tower, The Brown Palace Hotel, Denver

Previous page: Vietnam War Memorial, Civic Center Park and City & County Building, Denver

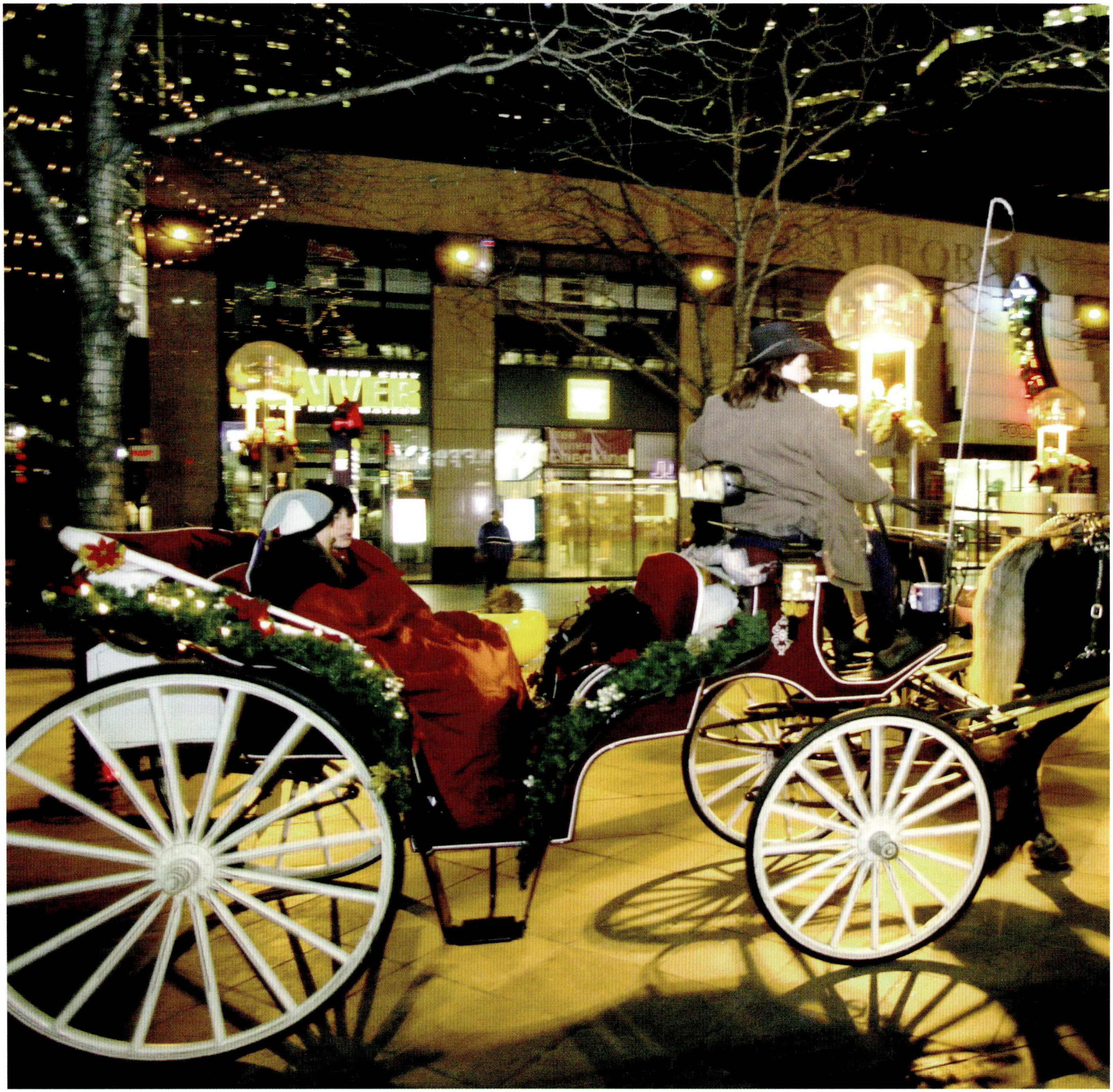

Horse-and-carriage rides on 16th Street Mall, Denver

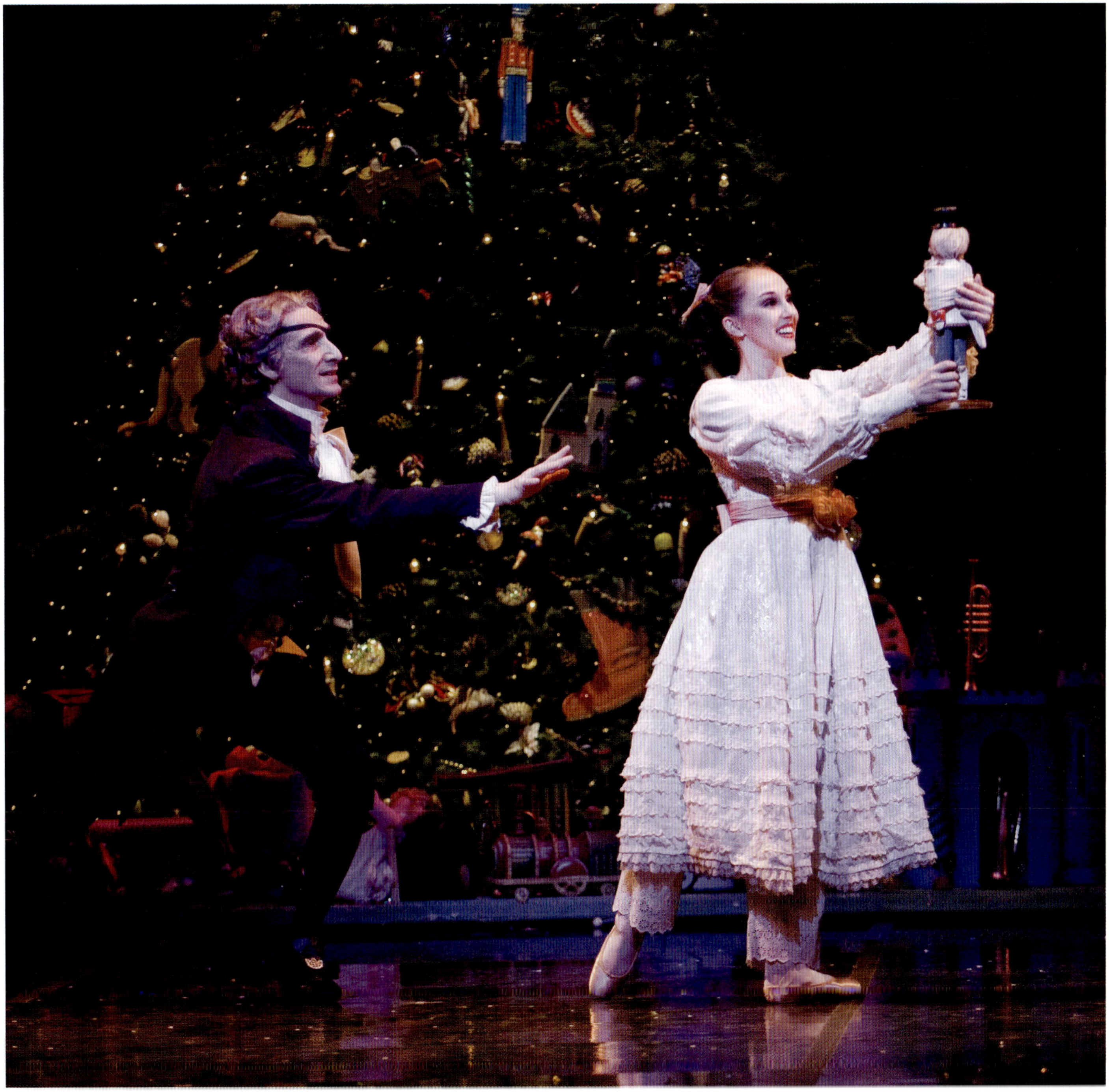

Colorado Ballet's Gregory Gonzales and Dana Benton in *The Nutcracker,* Denver

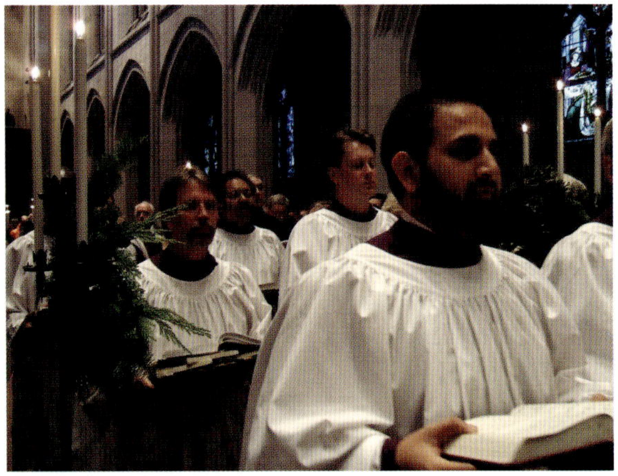

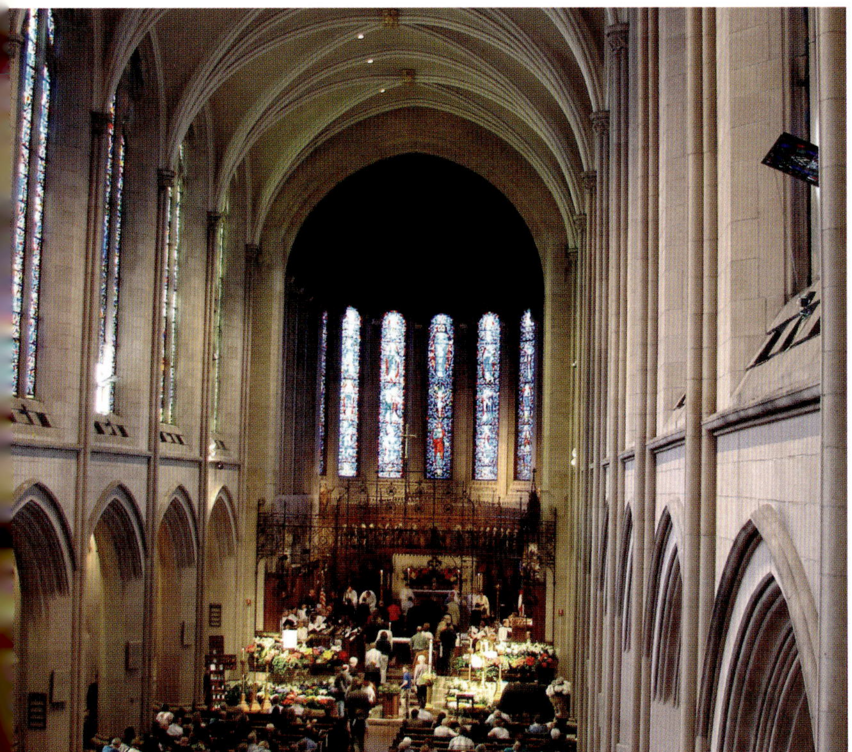

Top: The choir at Saint John's Cathedral, Denver
Above: Saint John's Cathedral decorated for Christmas, Denver
Right: Christmas trees and poinsettias adorn an altar at Holy Ghost Catholic Church, Denver

Parade of Lights, a festive parade featuring bands, giant balloons, and billions of twinkling lights. If it's Santa you need to see, Larimer Square offers the best photo opportunities amid the charming shops and restaurants on Denver's oldest city block. The metro area offers plenty of opportunities for outdoor recreation at Christmas as well, including outdoor ice rinks at Belmar Center shopping district in Lakewood and Southlands Shopping Center in Aurora.

The Denver Center for Performing Arts gets you in the Christmas spirit with annual performances of *The Nutcracker* by the Colorado Ballet and *Too Hot to Handel,* a glorious take on Handel's *Messiah*, performed by the Colorado Symphony Orchestra. After the show, spend the night across the street at the Hotel Teatro, regularly rated tops by Travel + Leisure, Condé Nast, and Zagat. The Newman Center for the Performing Arts at the University of Denver usually augments the season with shows from the Cleo Parker Robinson dance troupe and Young Voices of Colorado.

Saint John's Episcopal Cathedral's Festal Eucharist celebrations are beautiful and the choir and organ performances at the Cathedral

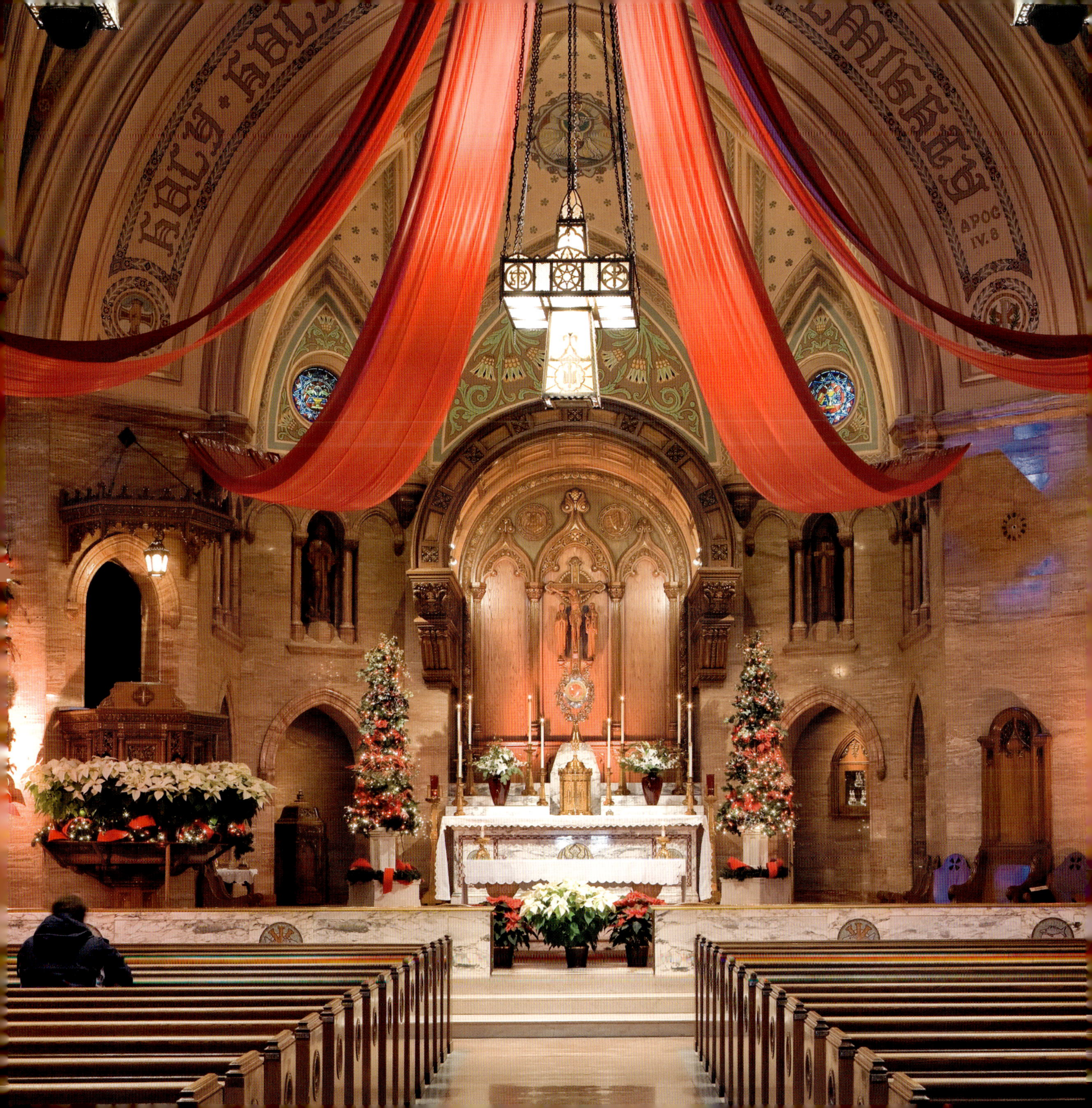
HOLY
APOC
IV.8

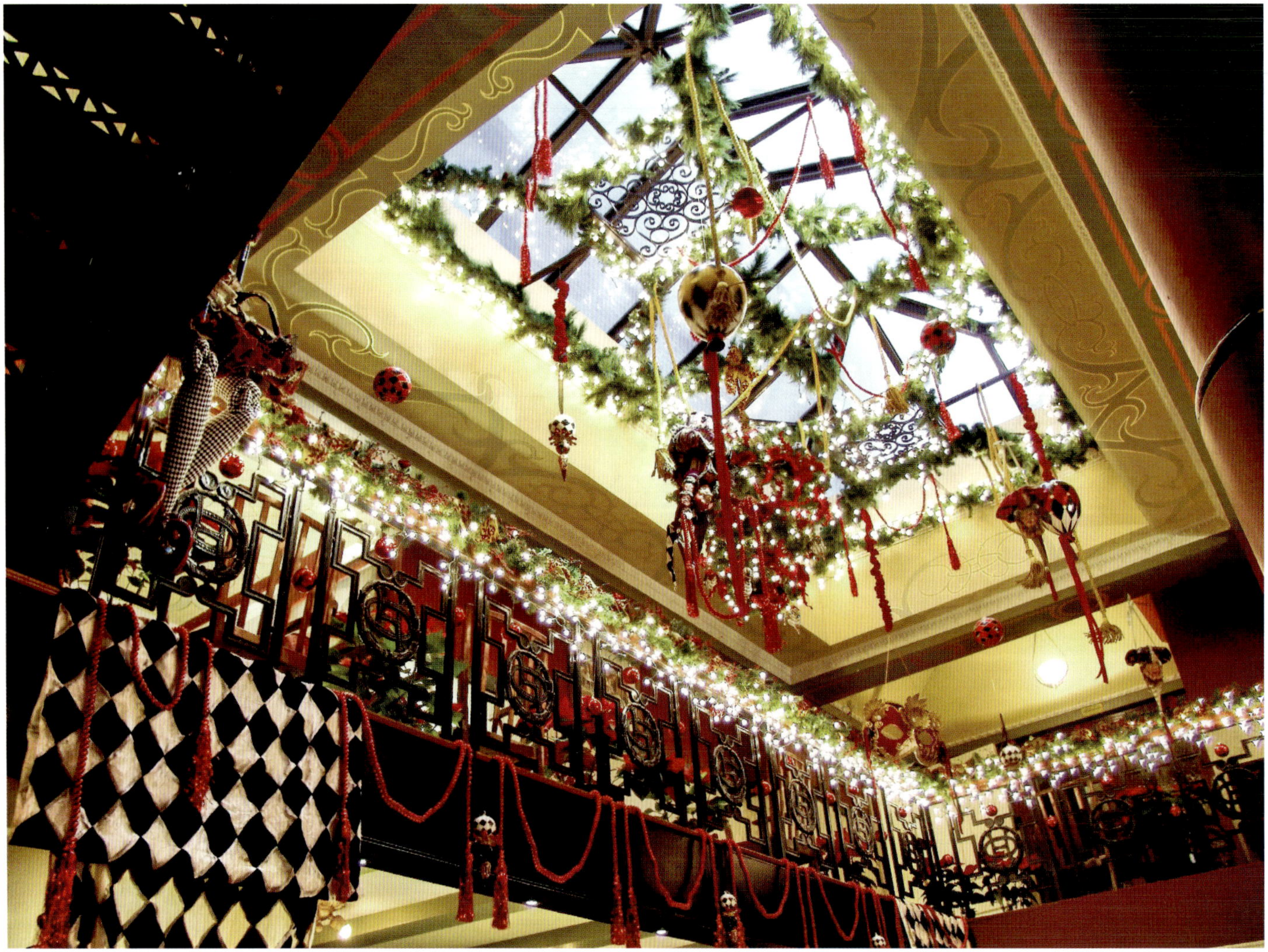

Above: Lavish Christmas decor adorns the skylight above the registration desk of The Oxford Hotel, Denver
Right: The D&F Tower on 16th Street Mall lit for the holidays, Denver

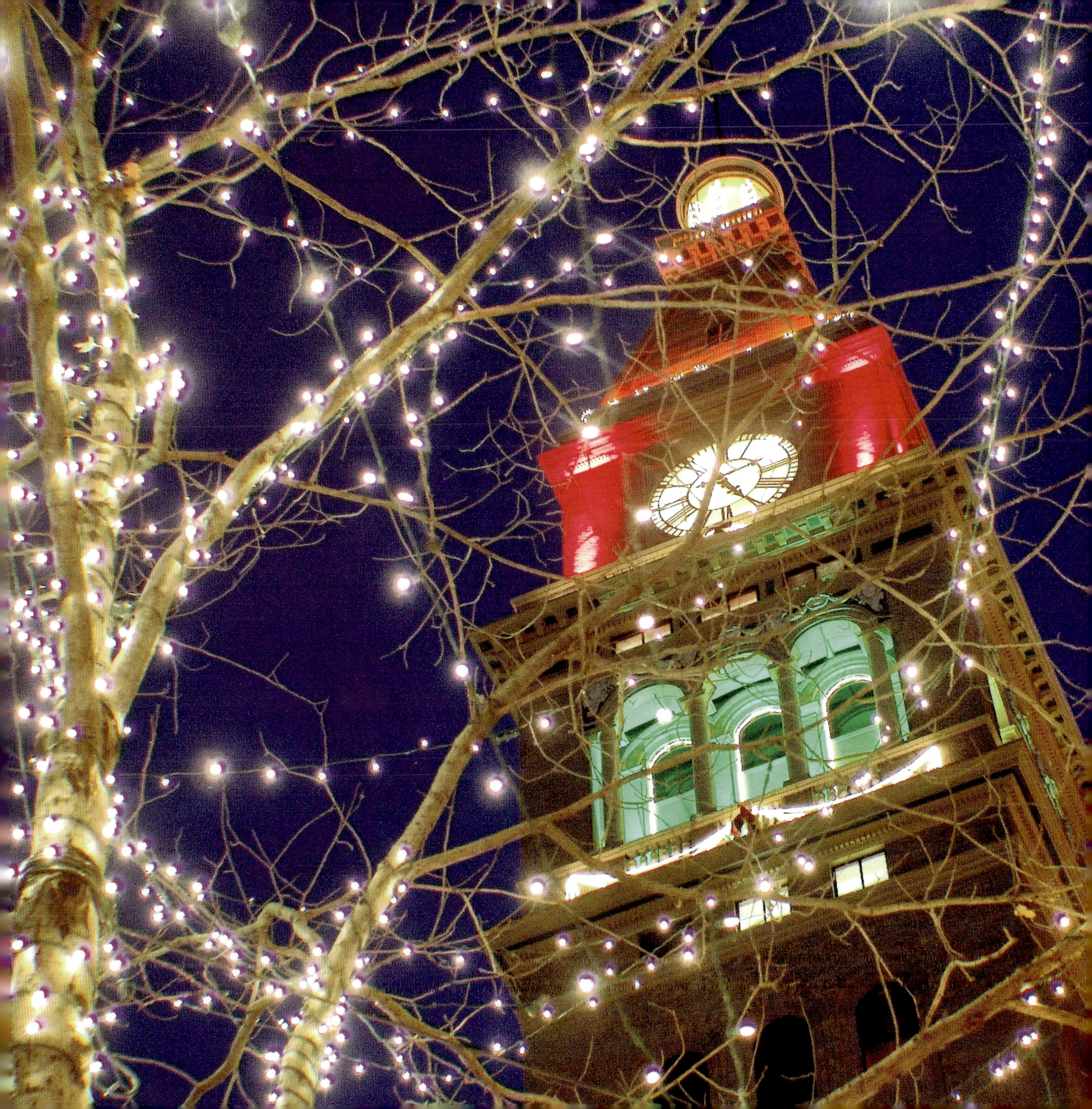

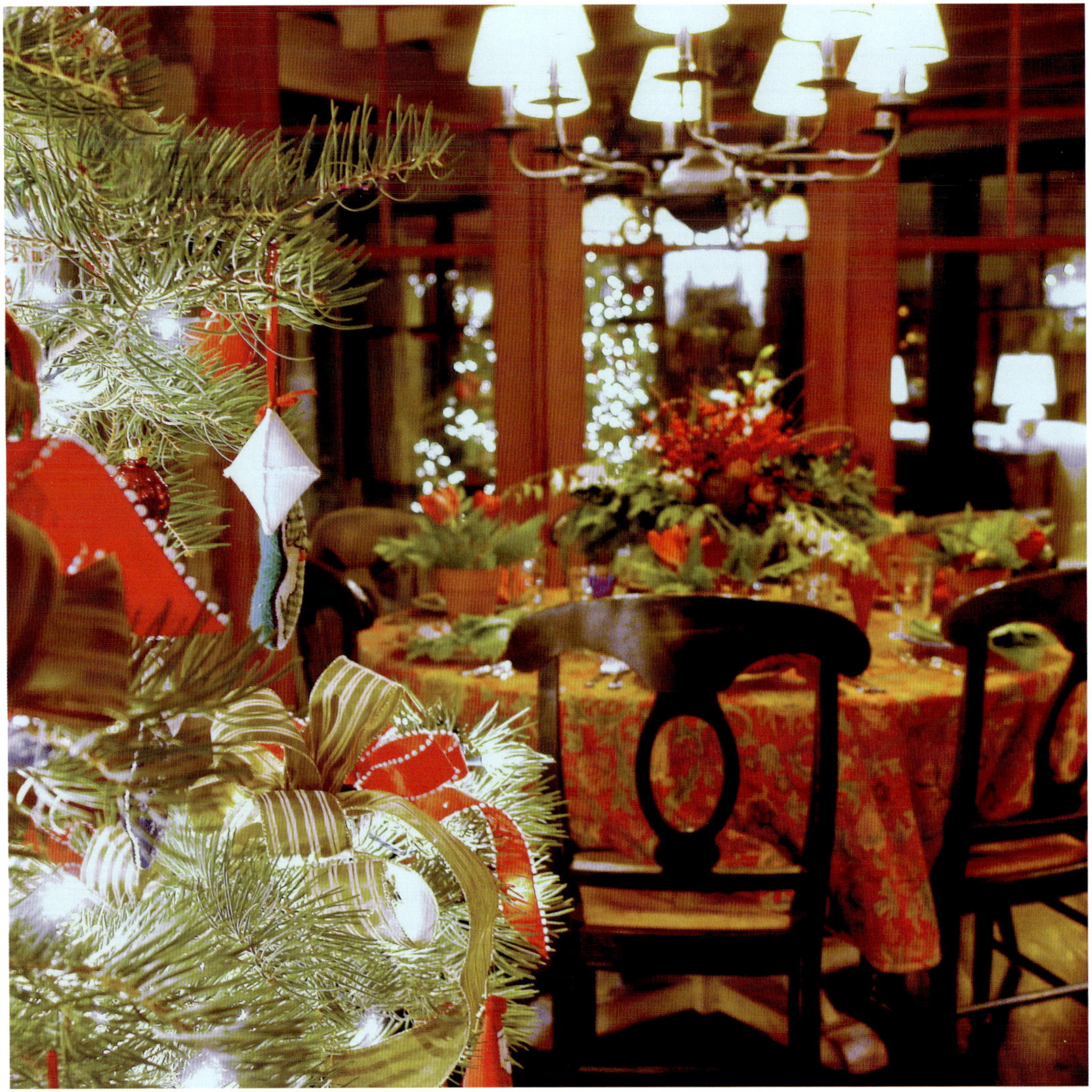

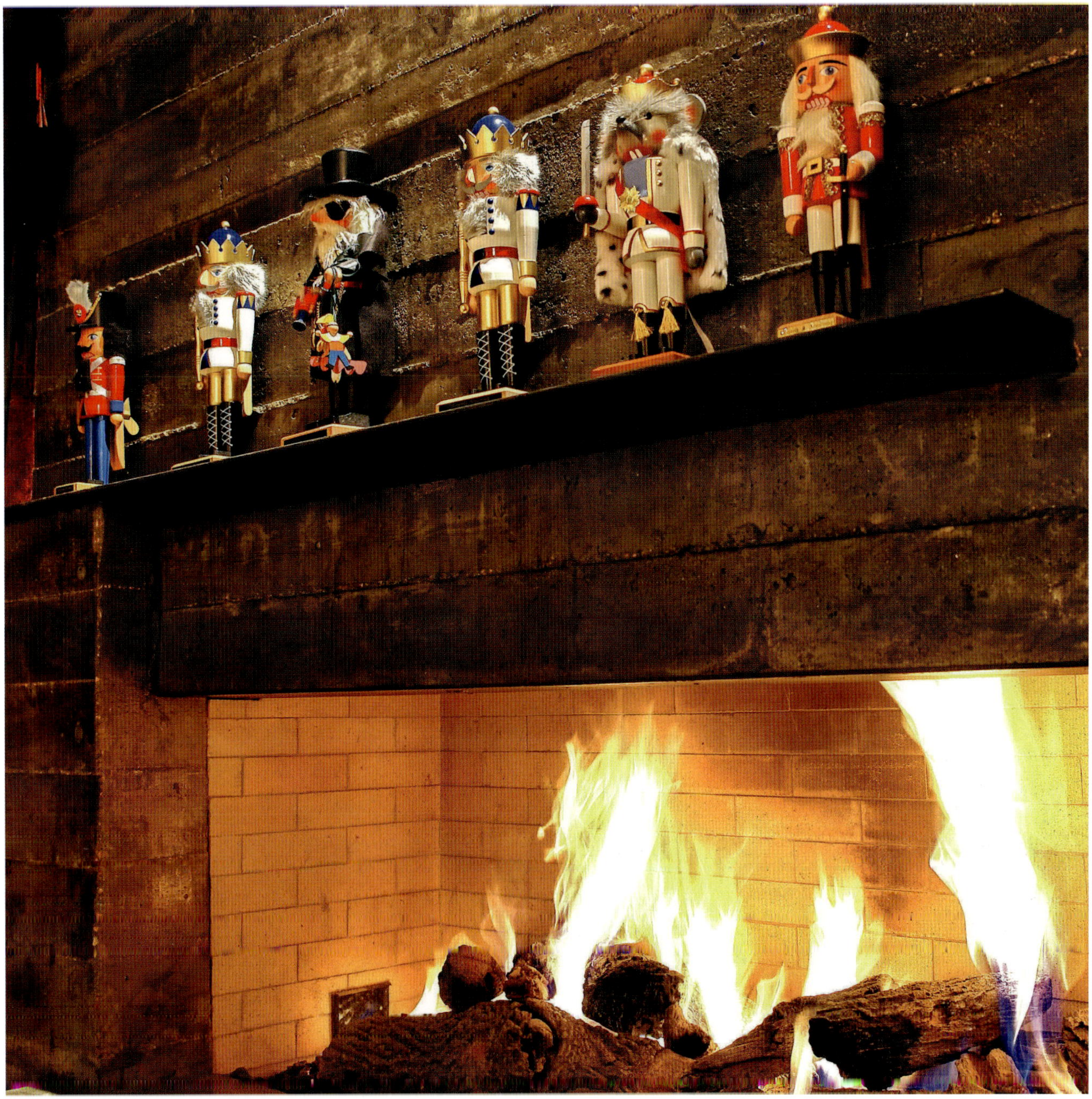

Above: Nutcrackers grace a mantel above a roaring fire, L'Esprit de Noel Holiday Home Tour, Denver
Left: Rich colors and textures in a Christmas tree and table setting, L'Esprit de Noel Holiday Home Tour, Denver

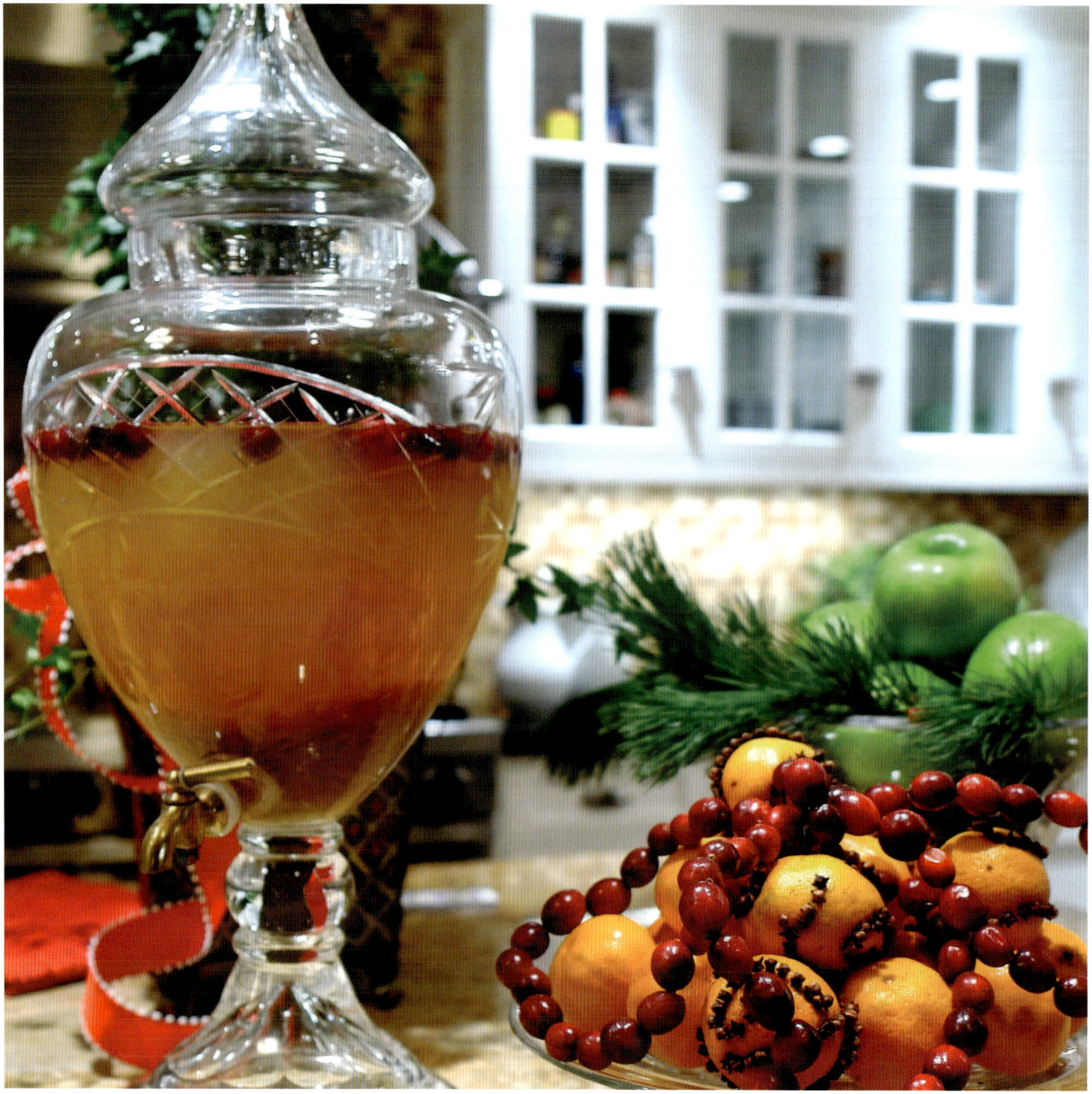

Above: Cranberry beads complement a decanter of wassail, L'Esprit de Noel Holiday Home Tour, Denver
Right: A garland-decked fireplace and living room, L'Esprit de Noel Holiday Home Tour, Denver

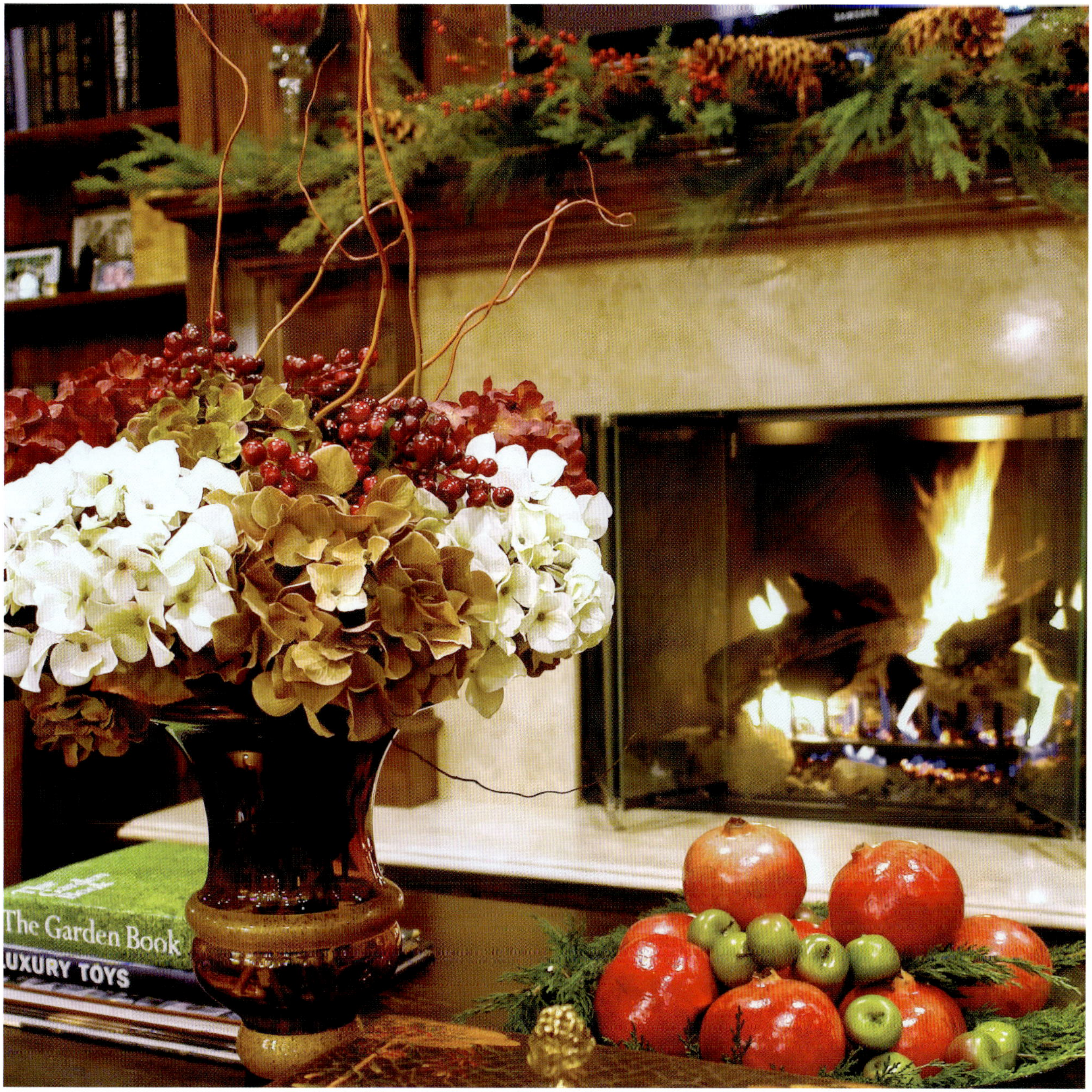
The Garden Book
LUXURY TOYS

Basilica of the Immaculate Conception are truly inspiring.

For a special day downtown, take in Victorian holiday splendor with high tea at The Molly Brown House Museum. The Byers-Evans House Museum, an elegant historic home built in 1883 by *Rocky Mountain News* publisher William Byers, hosts Christmas high teas each year. Or, make reservations early for The Oxford Hotel's Holiday Doll's Tea Party, a lovely parent/child event founded by Frances Melrose, a reporter for the *Rocky Mountain News*. For the ultimate high-tea experience in luxury surroundings, make reservations early for a festive Lobby Tea in The Brown Palace atrium. Be on the lookout for the location and dates of the annual L'Esprit de Noel Holiday Home Tour & Boutique, the profits from which go to benefit the Central City Opera House Association's Education and Community Programs.

As the holiday season winds down, get ready for New Year's Eve. Every year, the Children's Museum of Denver hosts "Noon Year's Eve" for families. And no matter what plans you have, check out the New Year's Eve Fireworks Downtown on the 16th Street Mall, beginning at 9 p.m. with an encore at midnight.

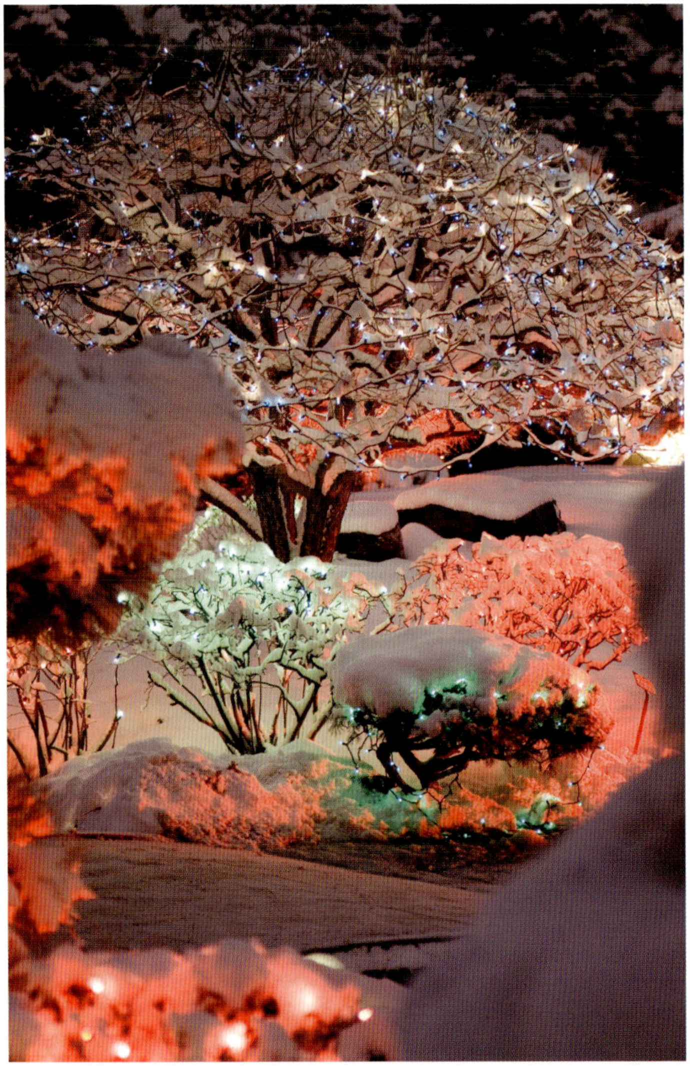

Above: Blossoms of Light, Denver Botanic Gardens, Denver
Right: Annual Candlelight Walk and Tree Lighting, Littleton

Next page: Trees shrouded in lights on Mockingbird Lane, Denver

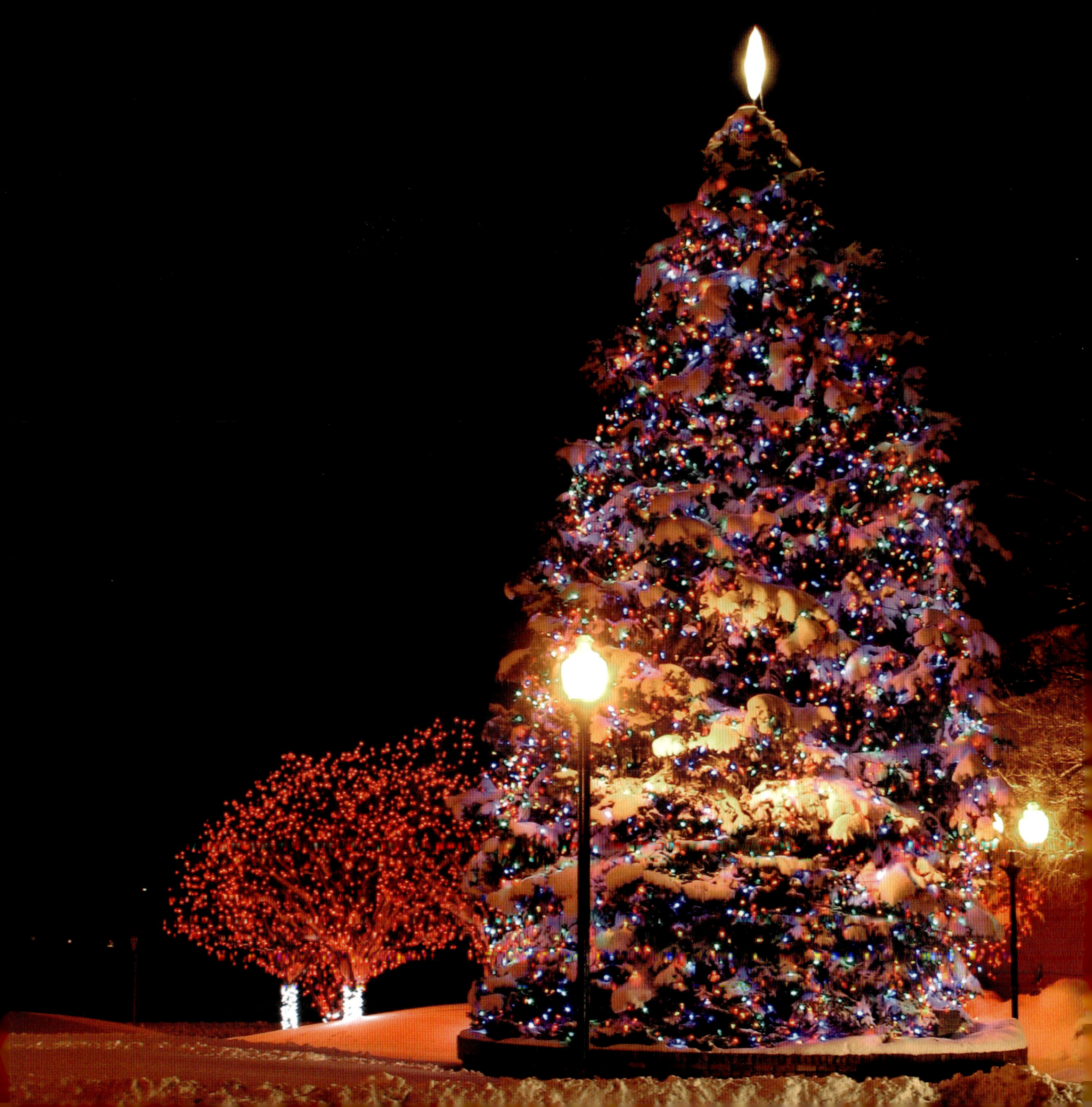

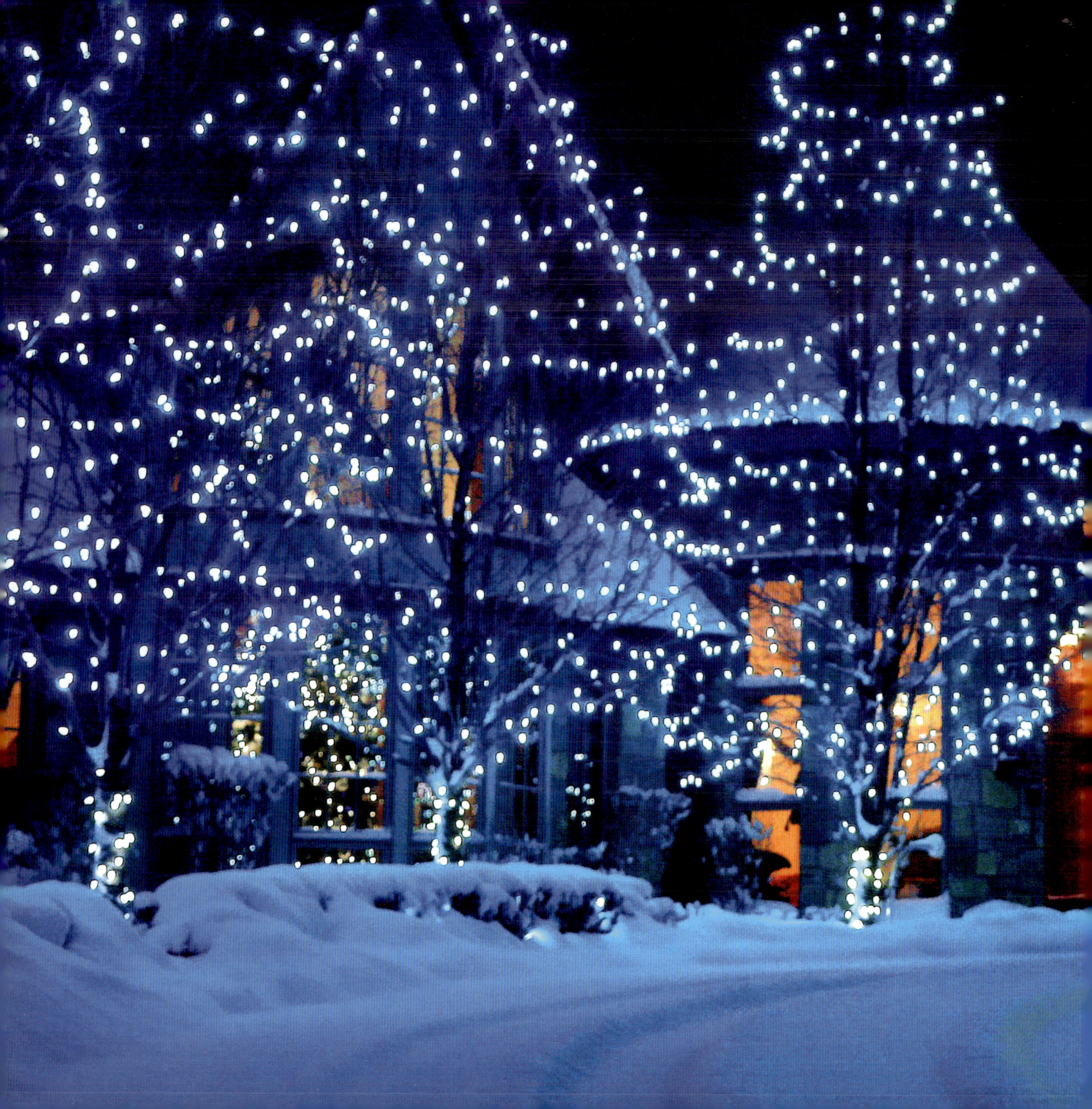

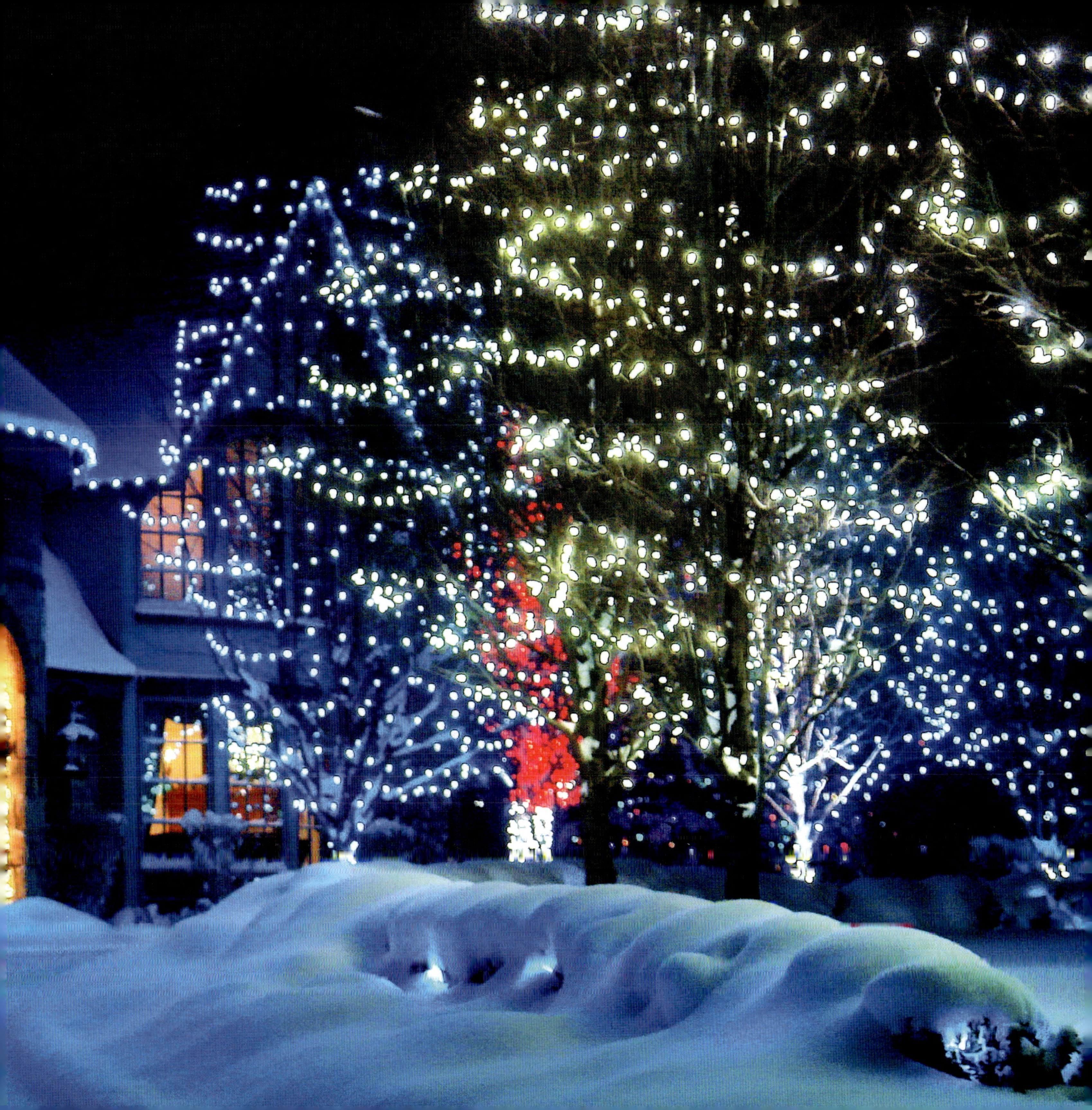

Durango

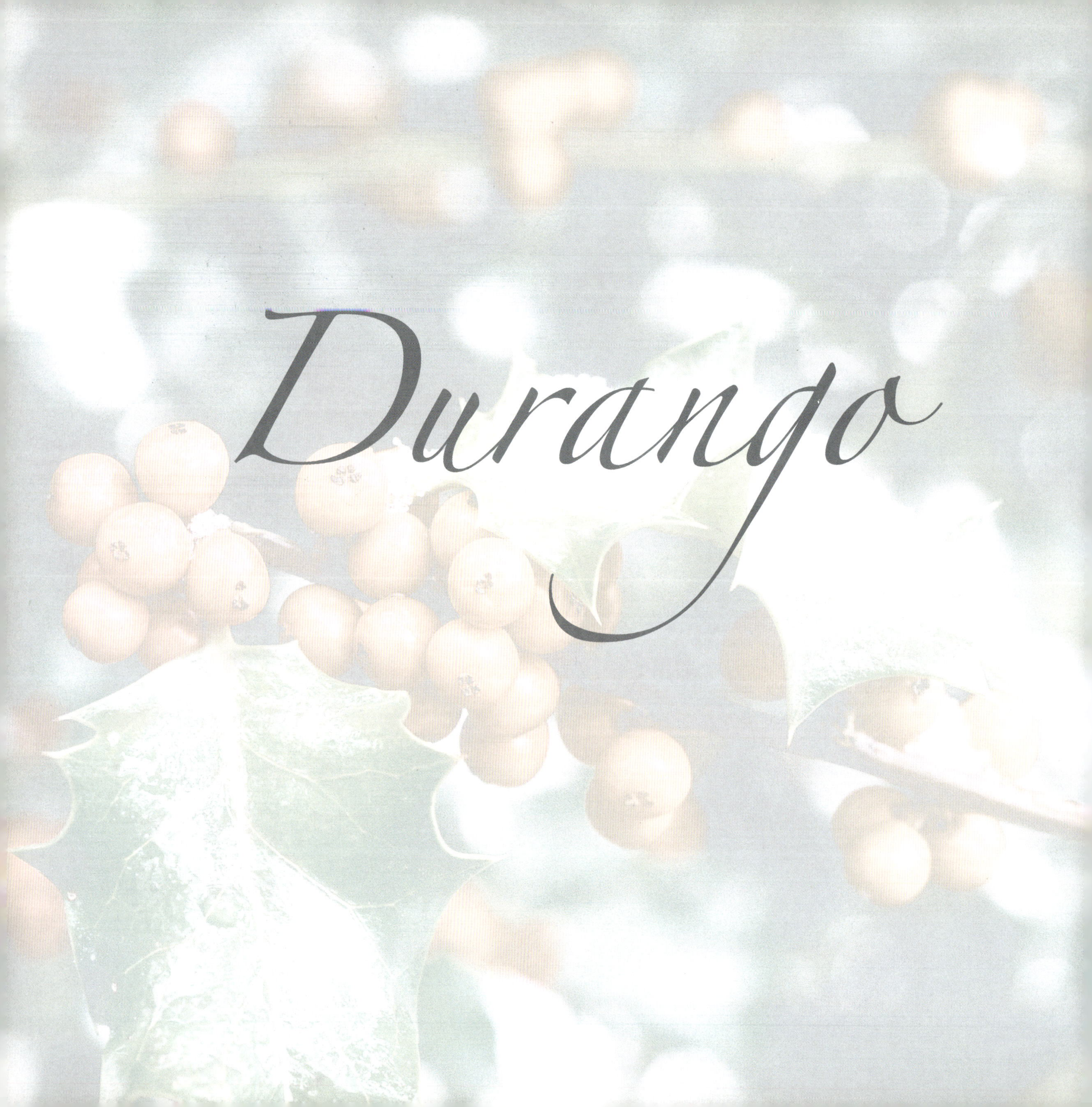

Christmas waves
a magic wand over this
world, and behold,
everything is softer
and more beautiful.

—NORMAN VINCENT PEALE

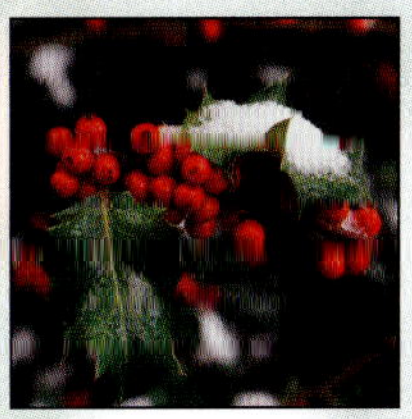

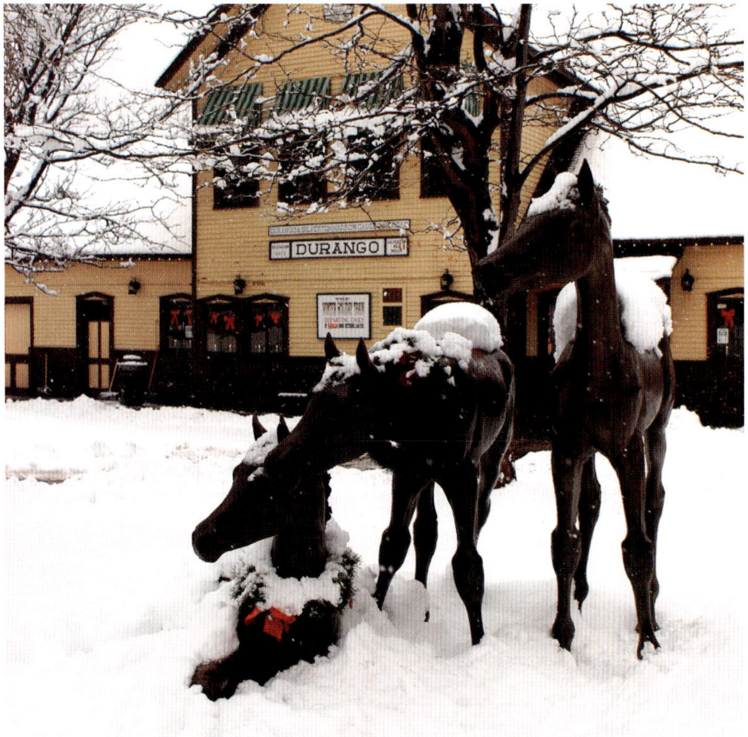

Above: Sculpted horses covered in snow, Durango
Right: Snowdown Light Parade and fireworks, Durango

SNUGGLED INTO THE San Juan Mountains, Durango's red brick buildings and scenic river location make it a place of obvious beauty. Originally settled as a town along the railroad, Durango is still a true train town. In fact, it is still home to a major depot along the Durango & Silverton Narrow Gauge Railroad. And though the Wild West may be a distant afterthought in most mountain towns, in Durango cowboy hats and big belt buckles live on. The Western tradition is alive and kicking in this Colorado town.

Taking the town back to its roots, a special holiday train chugs into the Durango Depot every weekend in December. Dubbed the "Polar Express," it offers exciting rides to the North Pole to pick up Santa. Carolers, hot chocolate, and games for kids await at the depot when you return! And don't forget to head back to the depot later in the month for a ride on the special New Year's Eve train.

Get a jump start on your holiday shopping during Noel Night in downtown Durango. All the local boutiques are open late, so you can shop 'til you drop while the kids enjoy listening to live music and hanging out with Santa Claus just down the road.

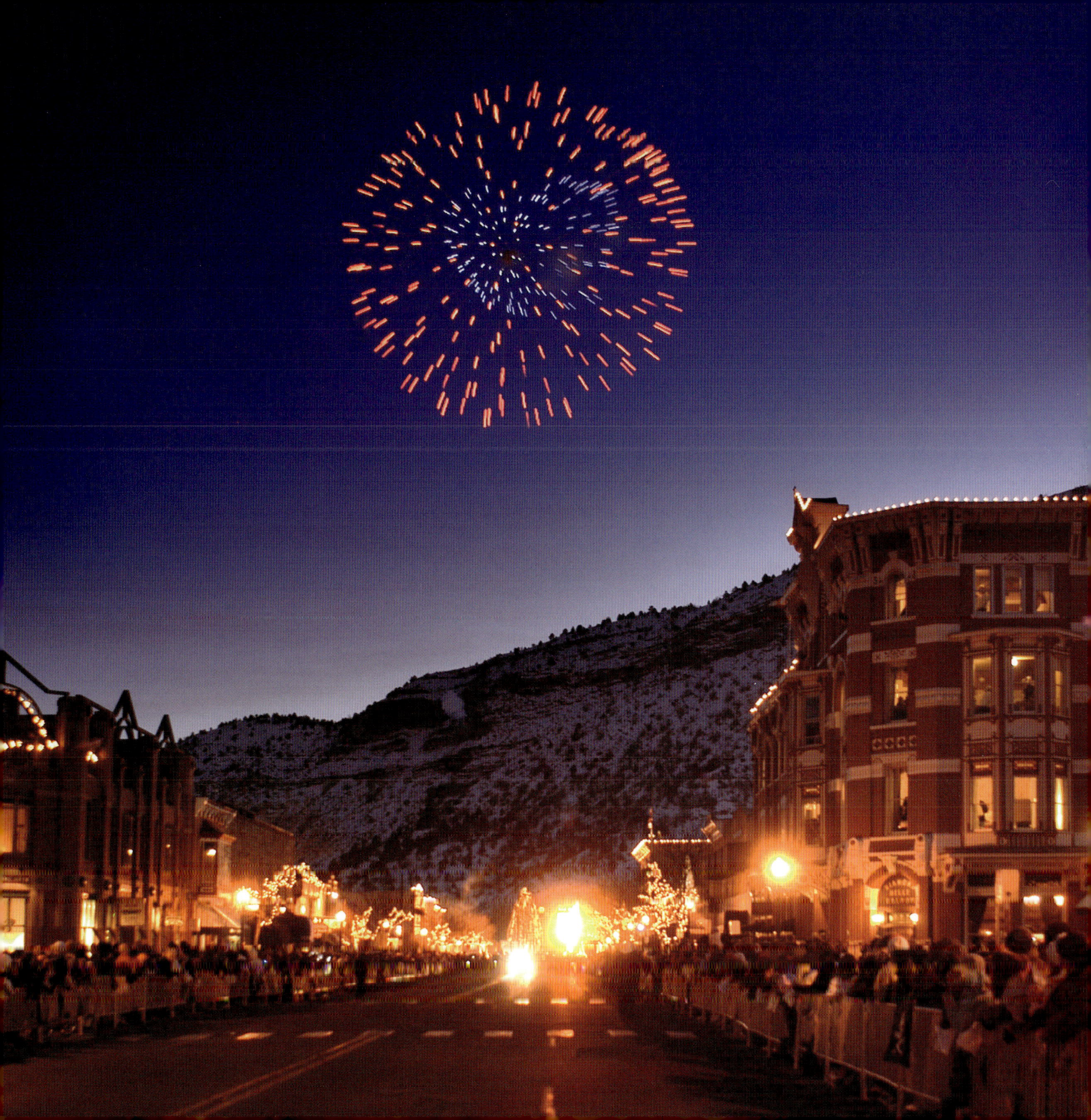

A true highlight of the holiday season for anyone Western at heart is the Durango Formal Cowboy Christmas. A night of boots, spurs, and Stetson hats, this dance is sure to bring down the house. With holiday treats and entertainment, the local Diamond Belle Saloon in the Strater Hotel is the real smokin' gun to the Durango holiday season.

A more family-friendly Western holiday bash is the Bar D Wranglers Christmas Jubilee at the Community Concert Hall. A holiday-themed play that inspires morals in a Western tradition, this family show is for everyone.

The La Plata County Fairgrounds hosts two annual holiday events: the Holiday Arts and Crafts Festival and the Festival of Trees. During early December, find one-of-a-kind gifts for trimming the tree and unique arts and crafts to ring in the season. Later in the month, decorate trees and wreaths in a warm community setting. Neighbors and friends alike support peers who perform in the three-choir Traditional Family Christmas and Holiday Gala at the Community Concert Hall at Fort Lewis College. With a holiday performance, silent auction, and ever-cheery voices, this area event is sure to get any Scrooge into the holiday spirit.

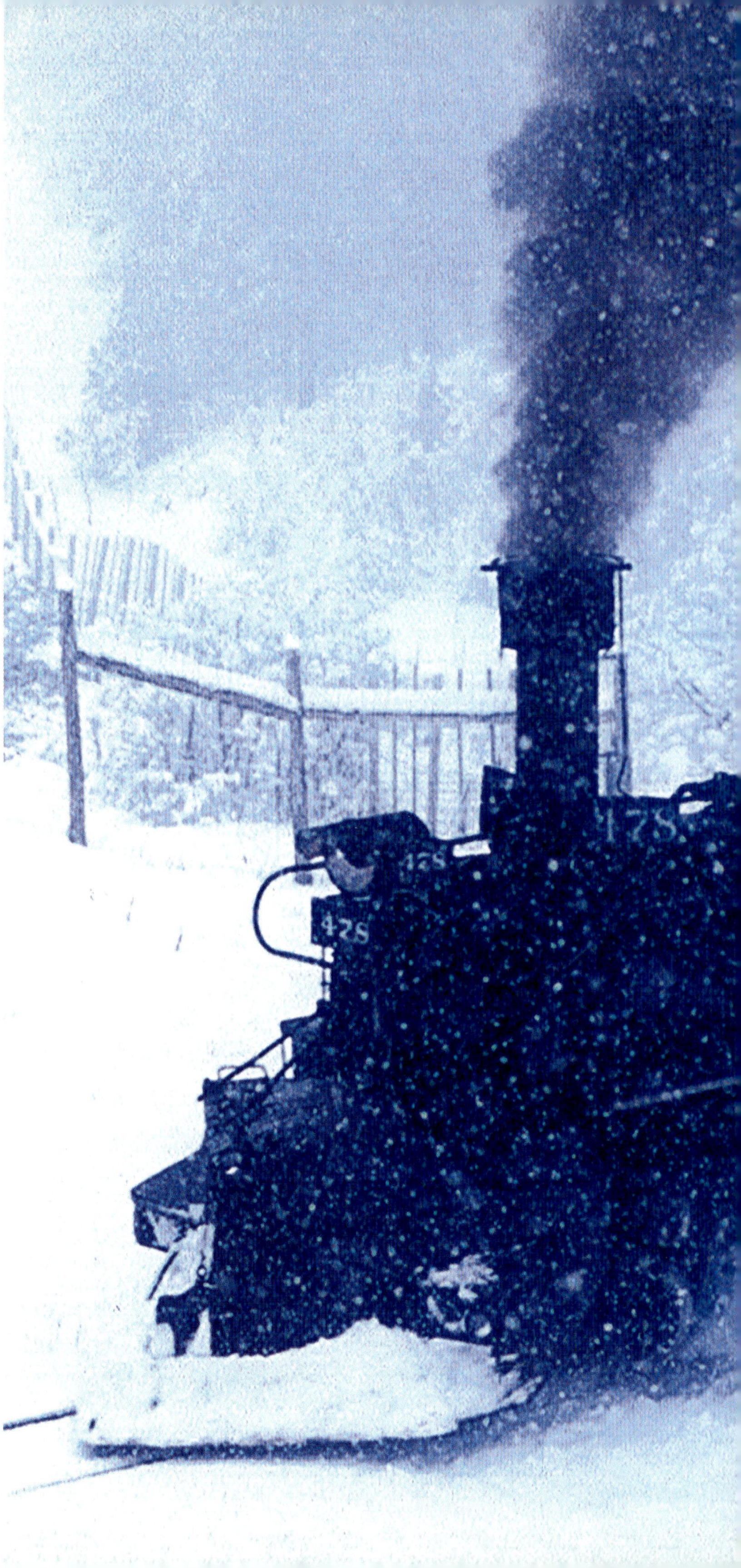

Durango & Silverton narrow gauge train blasts through snow

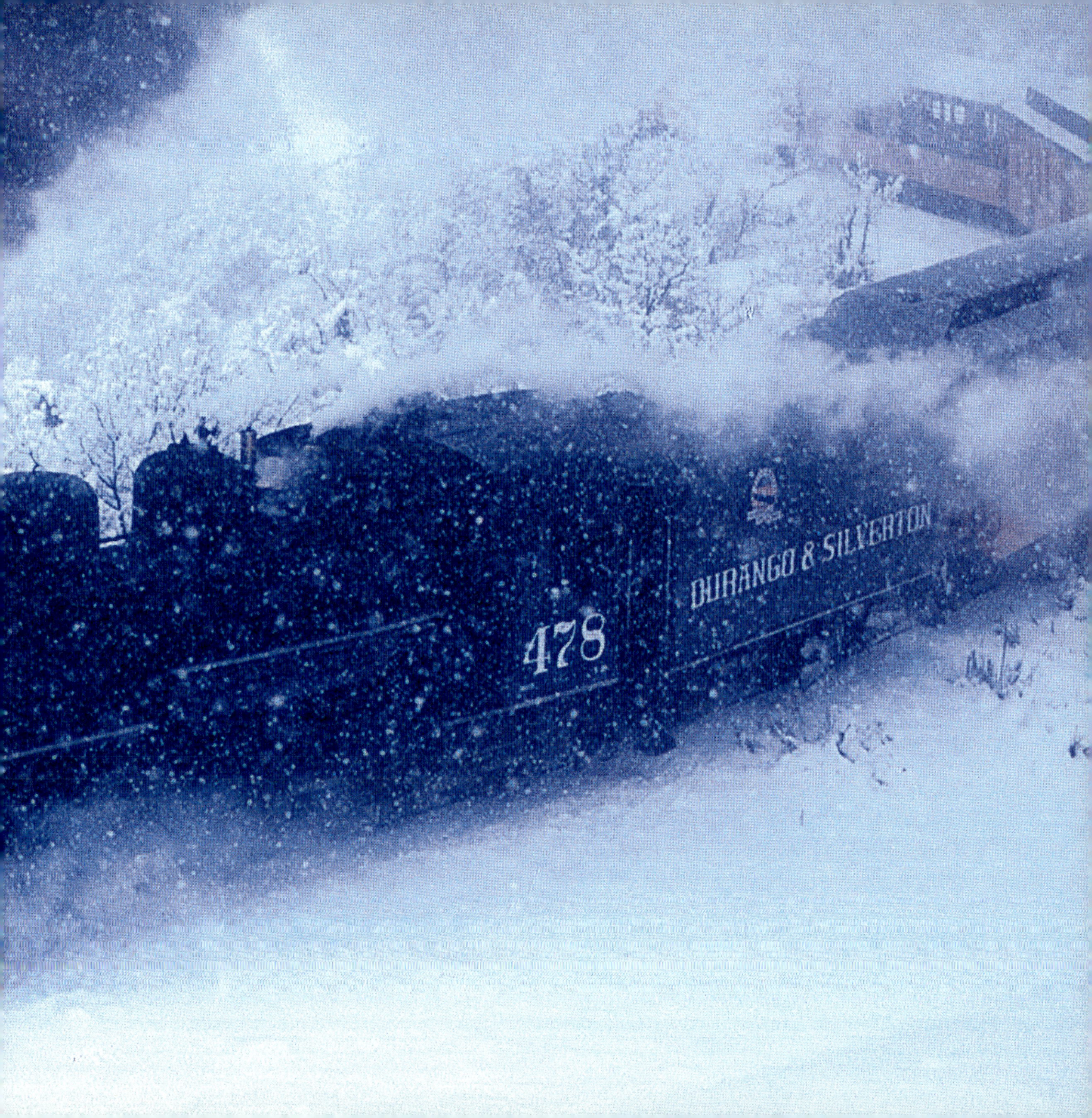
DURANGO & SILVERTON
478

Estes Park

& GRAND LAKE

The perfect

Christmas tree?

All Christmas trees

are perfect!

—CHARLES M. BARNARD

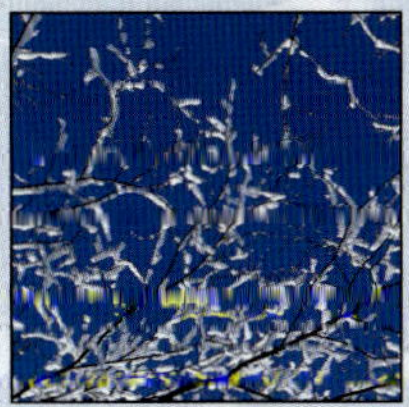

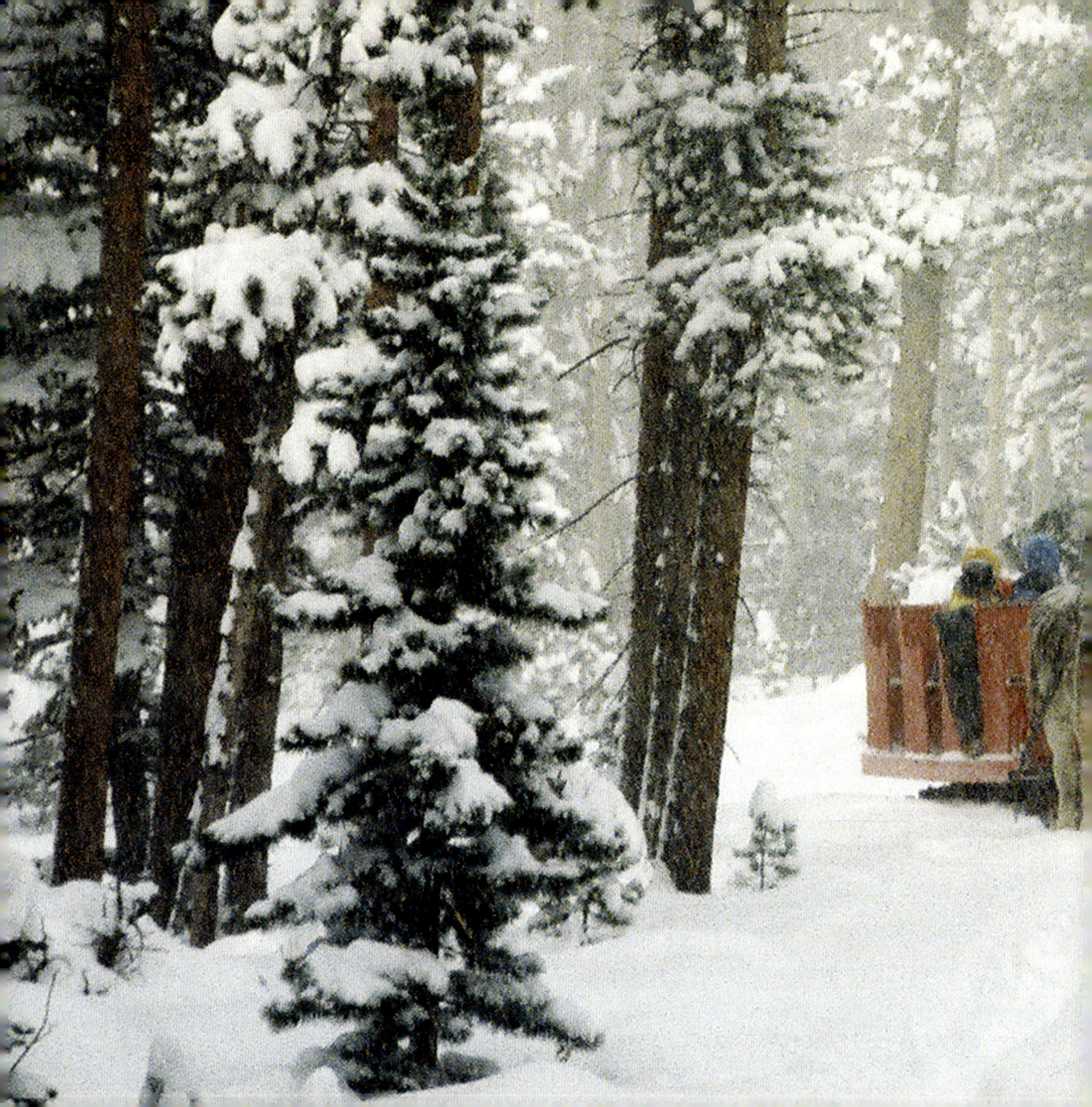

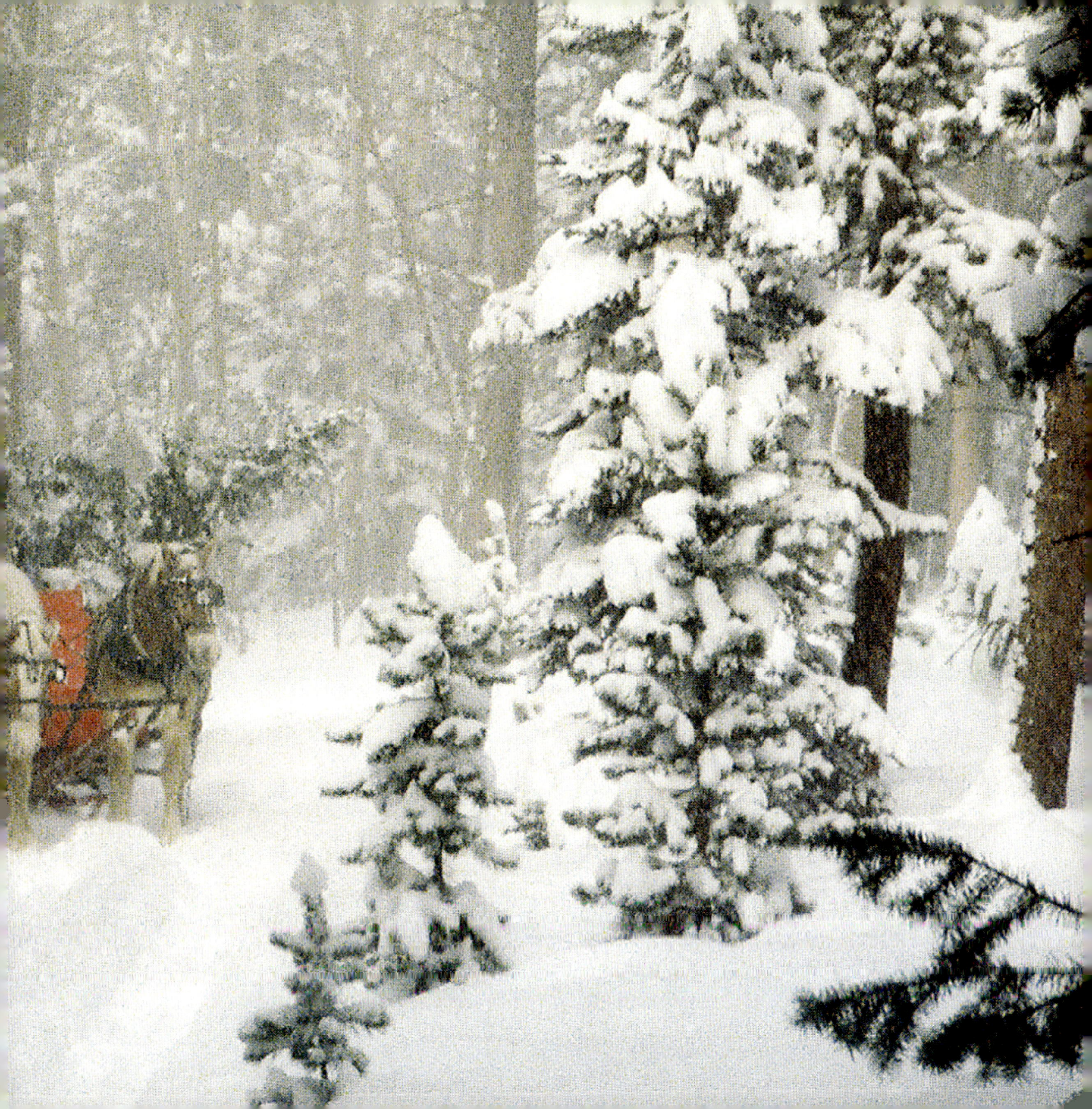

LOCATED ON THE OUTSKIRTS of magical Rocky Mountain National Park, the town of Estes Park climbs from the valley up the surrounding mountains to create a picturesque scene. Wildlife, blankets of snow, and a warm community all make Estes Park a truly enchanting place to be for the holidays.

The holiday season begins early in Estes Park, with the Come Catch the Glow festival the day after Thanksgiving. All day long, Elkhorn Avenue is transformed into a bustling center of activity. Featuring pony rides, adorable walking holiday characters, and Santa, the day is fun for the entire family. When the sun sets, the Parade of Lights will proceed down the street and thousands of tiny lights will illuminate the town. Fairytale floats, swaying dancers, and white glowing lights everywhere make this truly one of the most gorgeous holiday parades in Colorado.

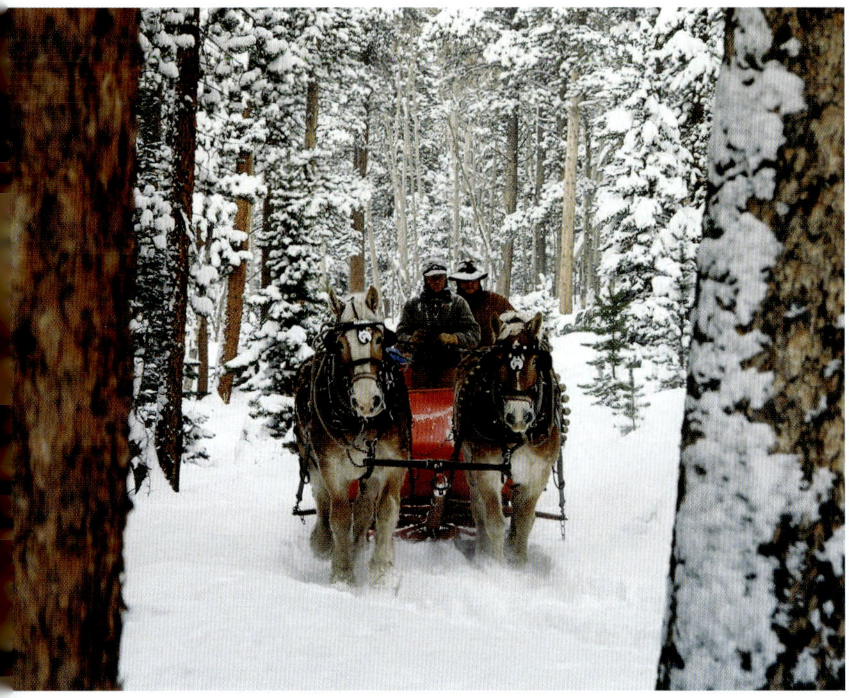

Above: Sleigh rides through the forest, Estes Park
Right: Christmas tree lighting up the town, Grand Lake
Previous page: Hauling a Christmas tree by sleigh, Estes Park

Any weekend in December, take a tour of the town in a romantic horse-driven sleigh. If you are in the mood for some forest scenery, take a Full Moon Walk led by a park ranger in Rocky Mountain National Park for an experience in the area's natural nightlife. Back in town, take the annual Holiday Home Tour, which showcases gorgeous mountain homes lavishly decorated for the holidays.

By far the most famous building in Estes Park is the legendary Stanley Hotel. Built in 1909, the Stanley sports breathtaking views in every direction. For Christmas, the hotel lights up with the sound of music as the Estes Park Music Festival Winter Concert Series takes over. Having featured such bands as the Kings

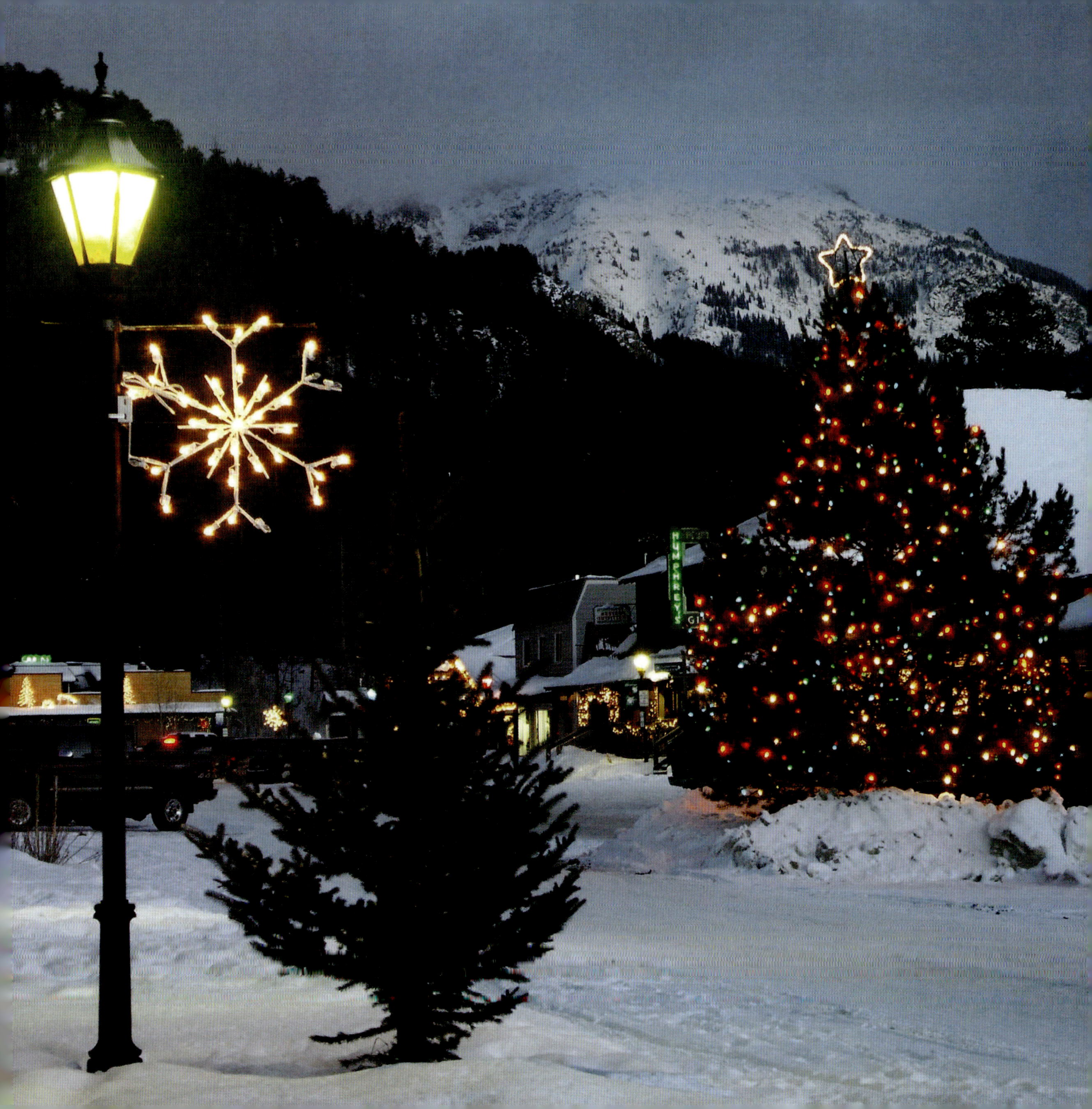
HUMPHREYS

of Swing, the music festival draws a large and enthusiastic crowd every year. The festival's biannual Fantasy Ball makes the holiday celebrations even more black-tie and beautiful.

Another Estes Park hotel making Christmas waves is Marys Lake Lodge and Resort, which offers an incredible selection of holiday dinners, all beginning with baked brie, fresh berries, and an olive bar. A holiday experience truly unique to Estes Park is the Estes Valley Handbell Ensemble's annual performance of The Bells of Christmas. Jingle your way into the Christmas spirit at the Rocky Mountain Church with this fabulous concert.

Finish your stay in Estes Park by strolling from gallery to gallery on the Holiday Art Walk, a trail of art sure to leave an impression. Take this self-guided tour of the galleries and studios in town and see paintings, sculptures, statues, and other handcrafted wonders exemplary of the beauty of Estes Park.

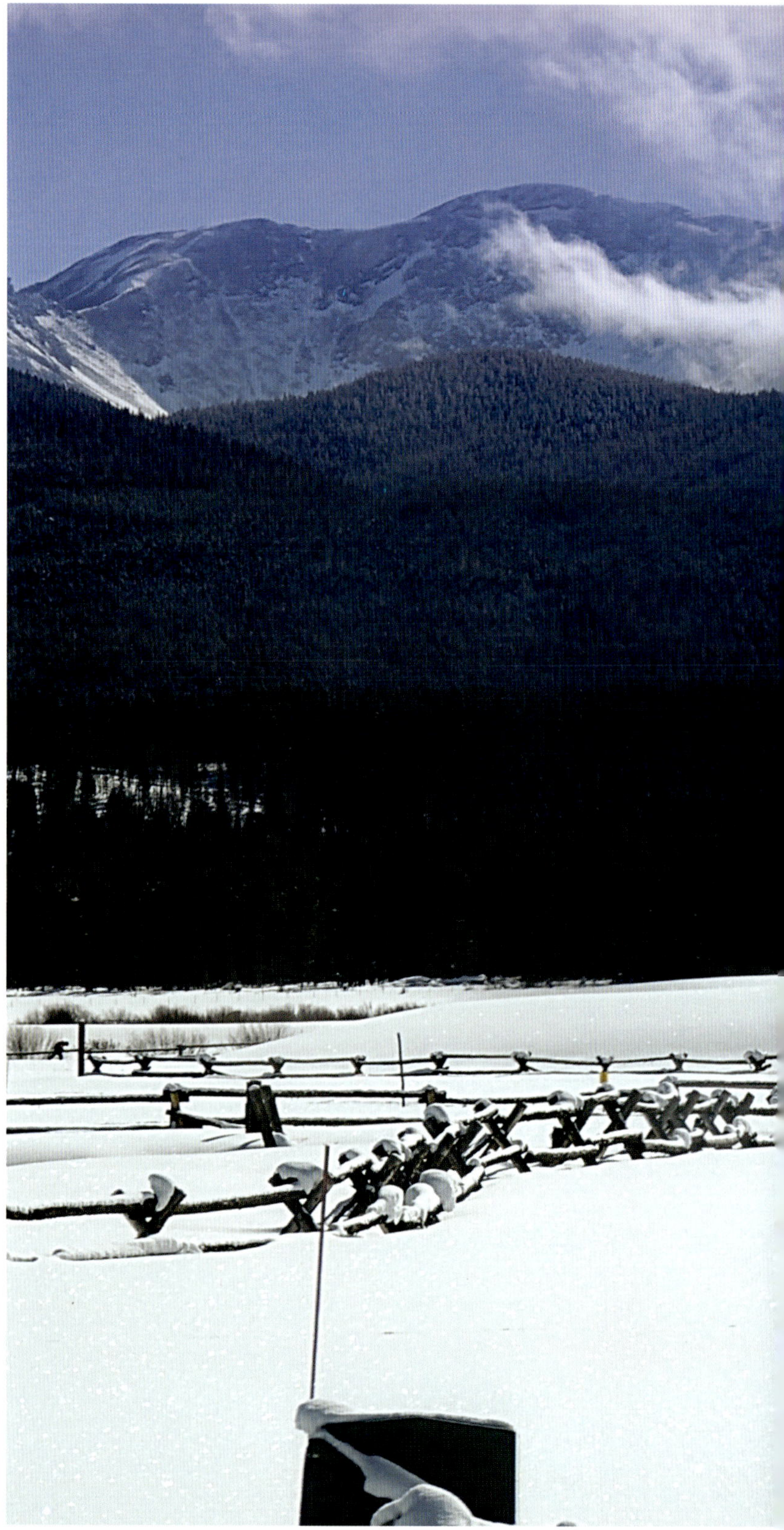

Nordic skiing, between Winter Park and Granby

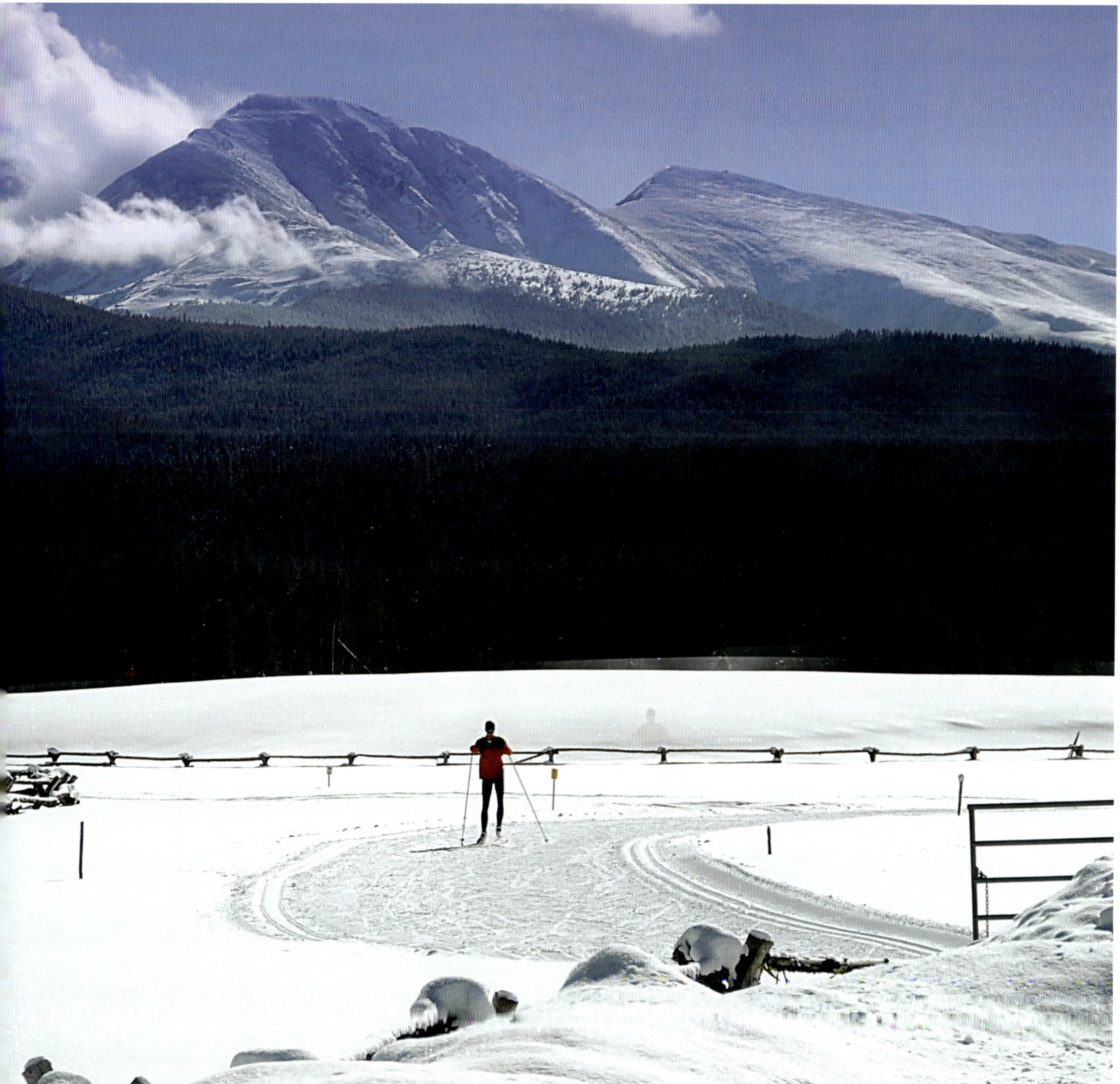

Grand Lake is the largest lake in Colorado, making the town of Grand Lake one of the most enchanting places to visit in the Colorado Rockies. Next to Shadow Mountain and Rocky Mountain National Park, with just 67 miles of highway between it and the Mile High City, Grand Lake is the ideal location for a small-town getaway. It's also the snowmobile capital of Colorado, not to mention a great place for snow sports such as skiing, tubing, and dogsledding.

A major highlight of the holiday season is the Olde Fashioned Holiday Bazaar at Grand Lake Elementary School. With unique handcrafted gifts and fabulous creative ornaments and decorations, this is the perfect place to begin a winter-long celebration in the town of Grand Lake and immerse yourself in the local social scene.

The Community House just off the main road is a major venue for a variety of holiday events throughout the season. First, the Grand Chorale performs Christmas classics to ring in the festive season. Then, the annual Christmas pageant rings through the hall, followed by a live nativity scene acted out in Town Square.

The city glows during the town Christmas Tree Lighting in front of Town Park in the middle of Grand Avenue. Holiday lights and sparkling windows charm visitors. Evenings in December are gloriously peaceful, so listen closely for the Christmas Music Festival at St. Anne's Church. With a beautiful candlelight caroling ceremony, the church serenades the town, which is often covered in a cozy blanket of snow.

During the nights just before Christmas, explore Rocky Mountain National Park at the annual full moon ski and skate, a picturesque

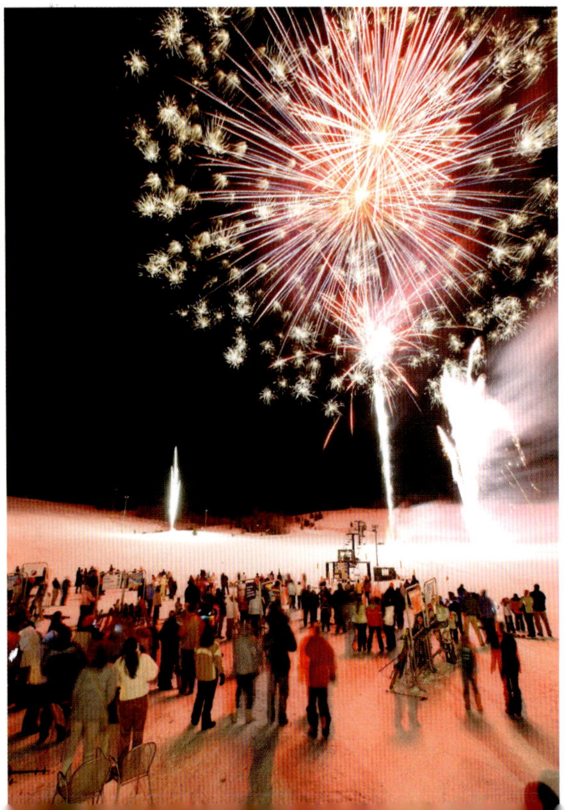

Fireworks over Granby Ranch, Granby

moonlit experience. Skate lakeside while light snowflakes float through the starry night. Following your evening on snow or ice, sit around a bonfire with hot cocoa and s'mores. Once you've felt the magic of the holidays in Grand Lake, appreciate those of previous years by paying a visit to the Historic Kauffman House Museum Holiday Open House, where you can see documentation of the enchanting holiday traditions that have evolved in this town over the years.

Following Christmas, the Holiday Melodrama—a different hilarious show each year at the Grand Lake Community House—offers loads of heartwarming performances by local actors and actresses. Then, fireworks pop, sparkle, and reflect in the lake at midnight on New Year's Eve at the annual Diamonds in the Sky celebration, a picture-perfect way to ring in the New Year.

In mid-January, Grand Lake comes to life again with a Winter Carnival. Participants

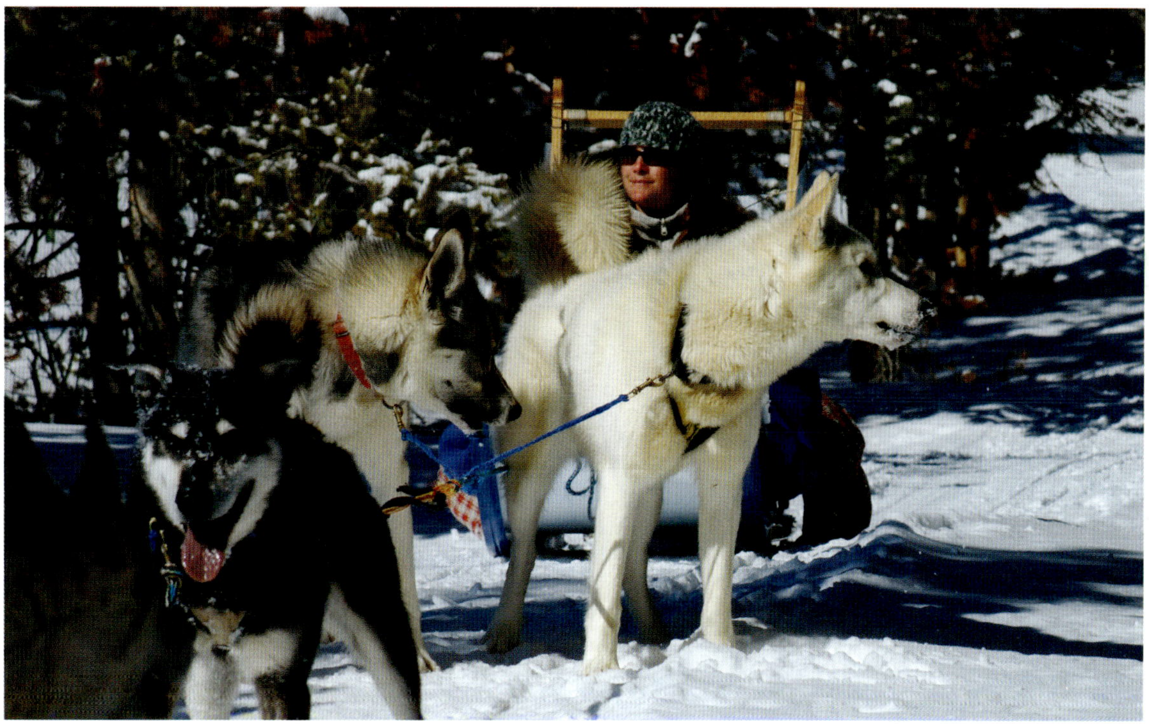

Dogsled rides afford stunning views, Grand Lake

compete in wacky, fun contests such as a bobsled racing, human bowling, and snowman building. With a parade down Grand Avenue, ice sculptures scattered throughout town, and mini-golf in the snow, this is one winter celebration you can't miss. The weekend culminates with a dance on Saturday night honoring Western heroes Buffalo Bill and Annie Oakley.

Just down the road from the winter wonderland of Grand Lake, the town of Granby also puts on quite the Christmas celebration. A holiday parade followed by a neighborhood lunch with Santa at the Community Center and the Independent Sports Center Gala are both major events that kick off a celebration well worth the drive to the Rockies.

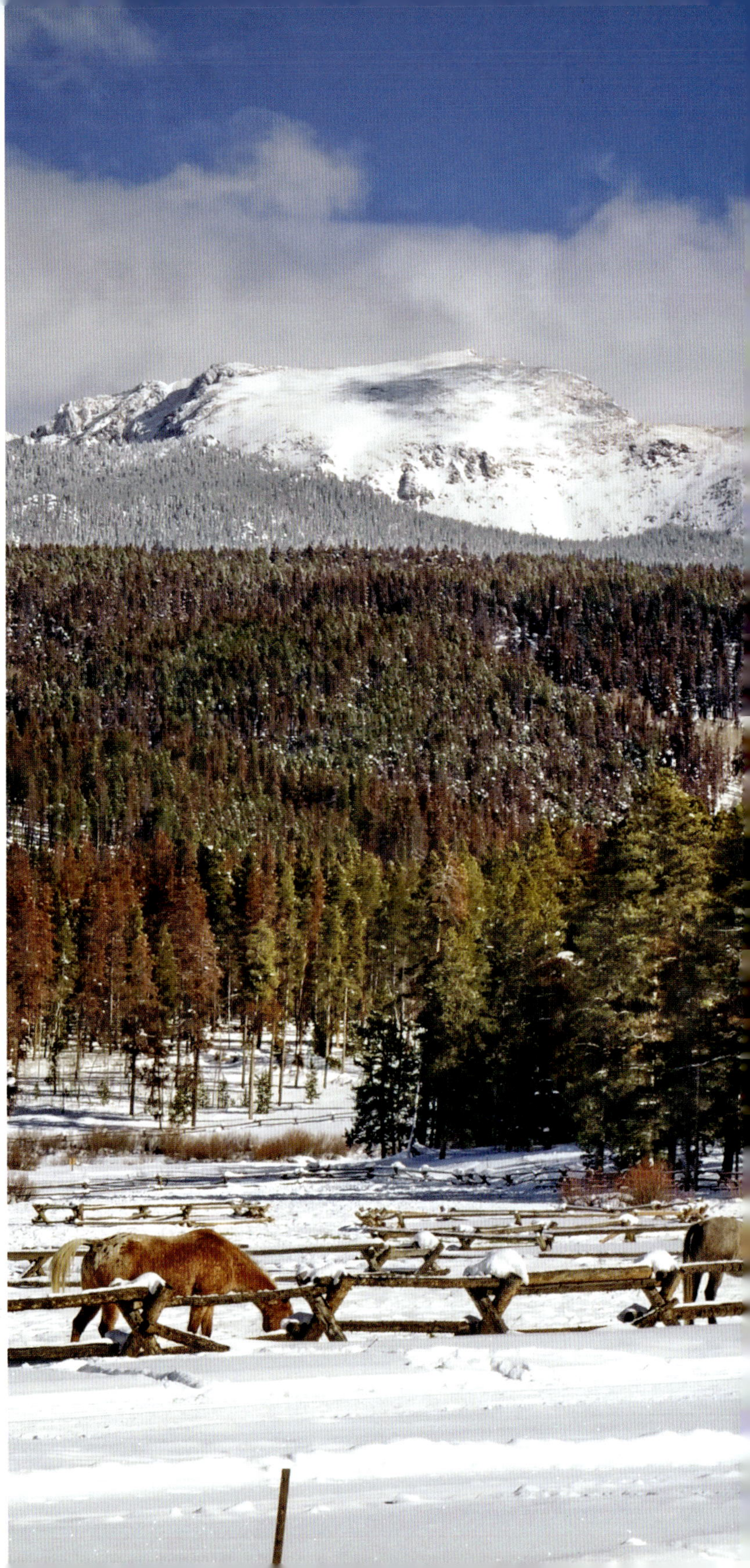

Mountains, trees, and horses punctuate this winter scene, between Winter Park and Grand Lake

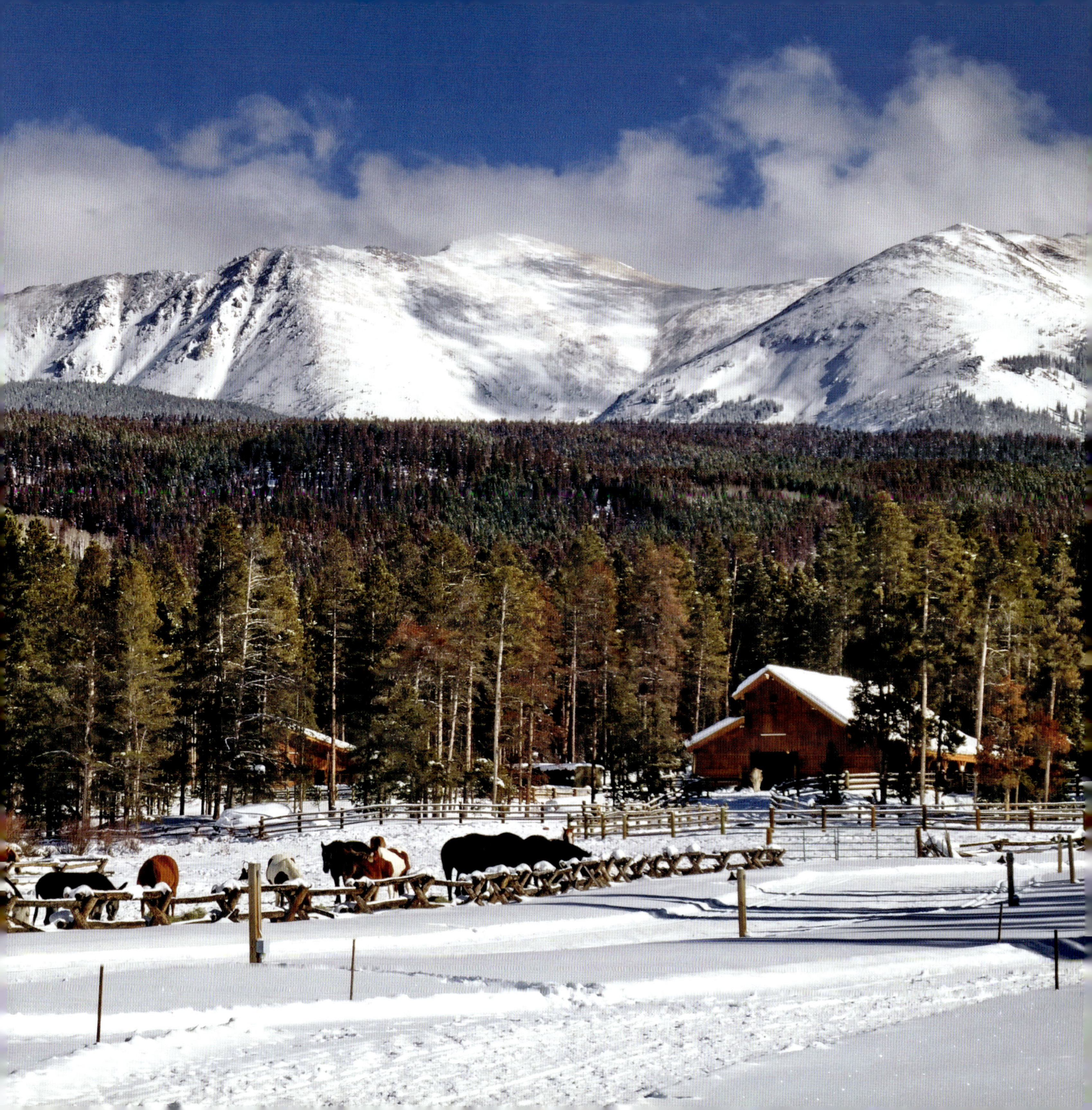

Georgetown

DILLON & KEYSTONE

I will honor

Christmas

in my heart,

and try to keep it

all the year.

—CHARLES DICKENS

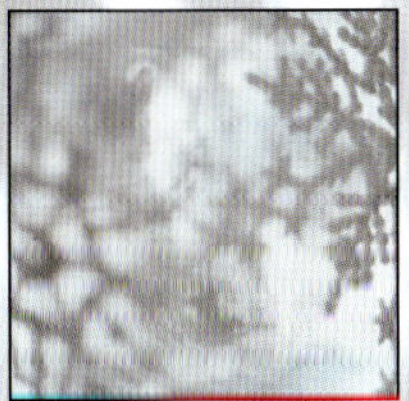

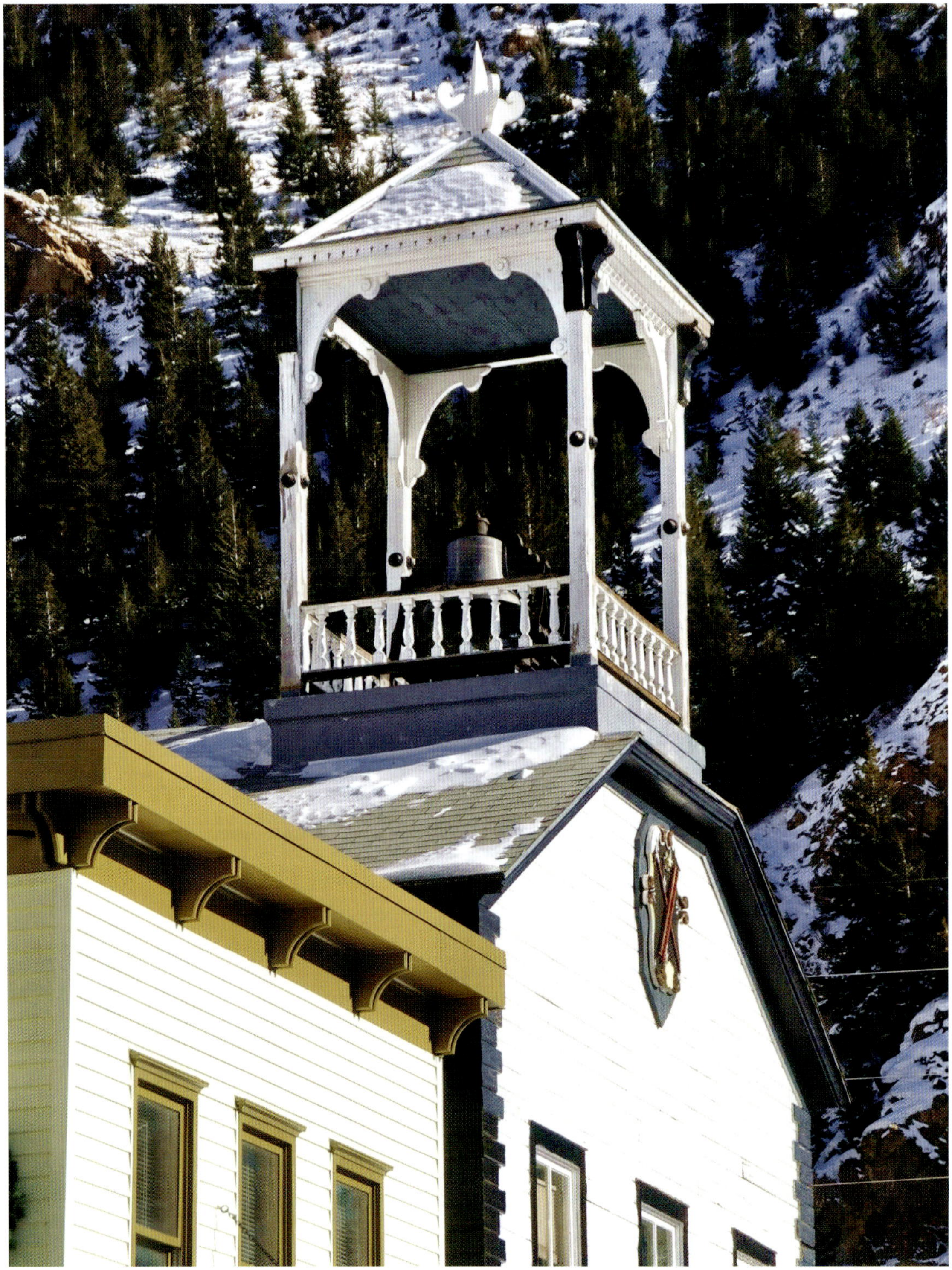

Bell tower, Georgetown

ESTABLISHED DURING THE PIKES PEAK Gold Rush in 1859, Georgetown shines so brightly during the holidays that it glows like gold. Just off I-70 and bordering Clear Creek, the town is surrounded by green-blue mountains and reflective pools of crystal-clear mountain water.

Begin your visit to this charming town with the traditional Georgetown Christmas Market. Enjoy the aroma and delightful taste of seasonal chestnuts while strolling the streets of downtown. Step into shops and pick out gifts for yourself and family and friends. If you're tired of walking the sidewalks toting loads of shopping bags, indulge in a wagon ride through the snowy streets and take solace in the scenery. Keep your ears and eyes open for the soothing sound and sight of carolers dressed in Victorian costume. Then, watch the procession of the Santa Lucia, performed daily during the first two weeks of December.

Once your home is overflowing with gifts and joy, take a day-trip with the Georgetown Museum and Historic Sites Tour. Begin your tour at the famous, beautifully constructed Hamill House Museum. Next, head over to the Hotel de Paris Museum, where you'll find artifacts and

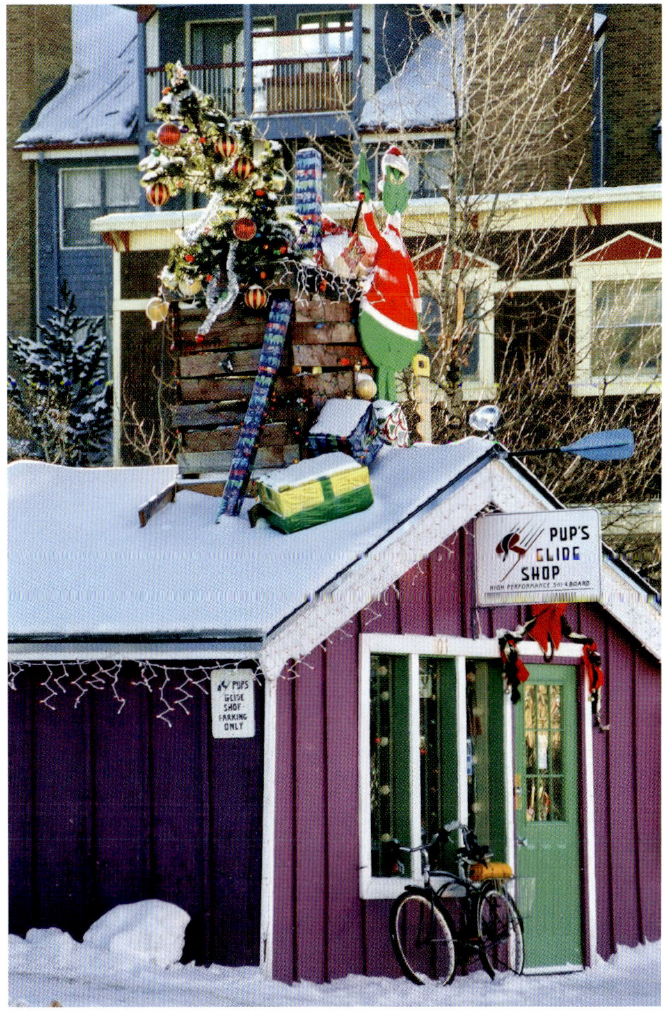

The Grinch atop a ski shop, Georgetown

an enchanting house designed by Louis Dupay. After warming up to the cozy interior designs of this little piece of France, progress on to tour the Georgetown Energy Museum, an operational hydroelectric generating plant. See the evolution of lights and then take them in at the Grace Episcopal Church, elegantly decorated for the festive season. Finish your tour at the Snetzer Building, an historic tailoring building that showcases shopping experiences of the past.

Decadence and decorations come together in high fashion at Grace Hall. Attend an afternoon high tea for a cultural adventure in the Rockies. Sip on tea and nibble delectable scones in the impeccably decorated historical house.

Finally, feast your eyes on a perfectly prepared meal at the Hamill House. Enjoy their truly festive Christmas celebration, featuring a traditional Victorian tree and live music. Listen to harmonious singing as you enjoy a delicious and memorable holiday dinner. Engage in readings of your favorite Christmas stories or let the live bands and orchestras serenade you as you dine in style. The wassail, caroling, and enchanting decor at the Hamill House dinner are sure to light your heart.

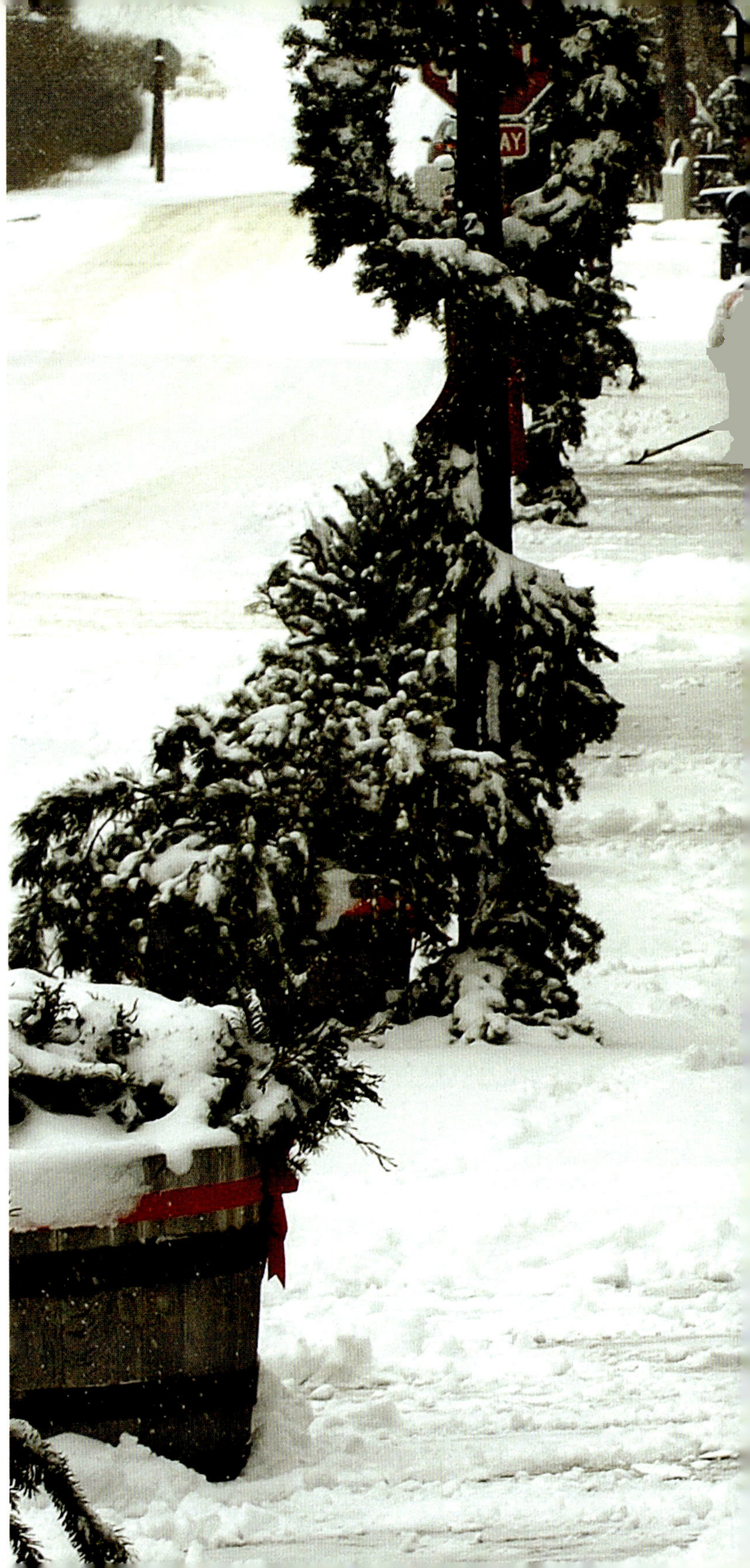

Shopkeepers shoveling snow, Georgetown

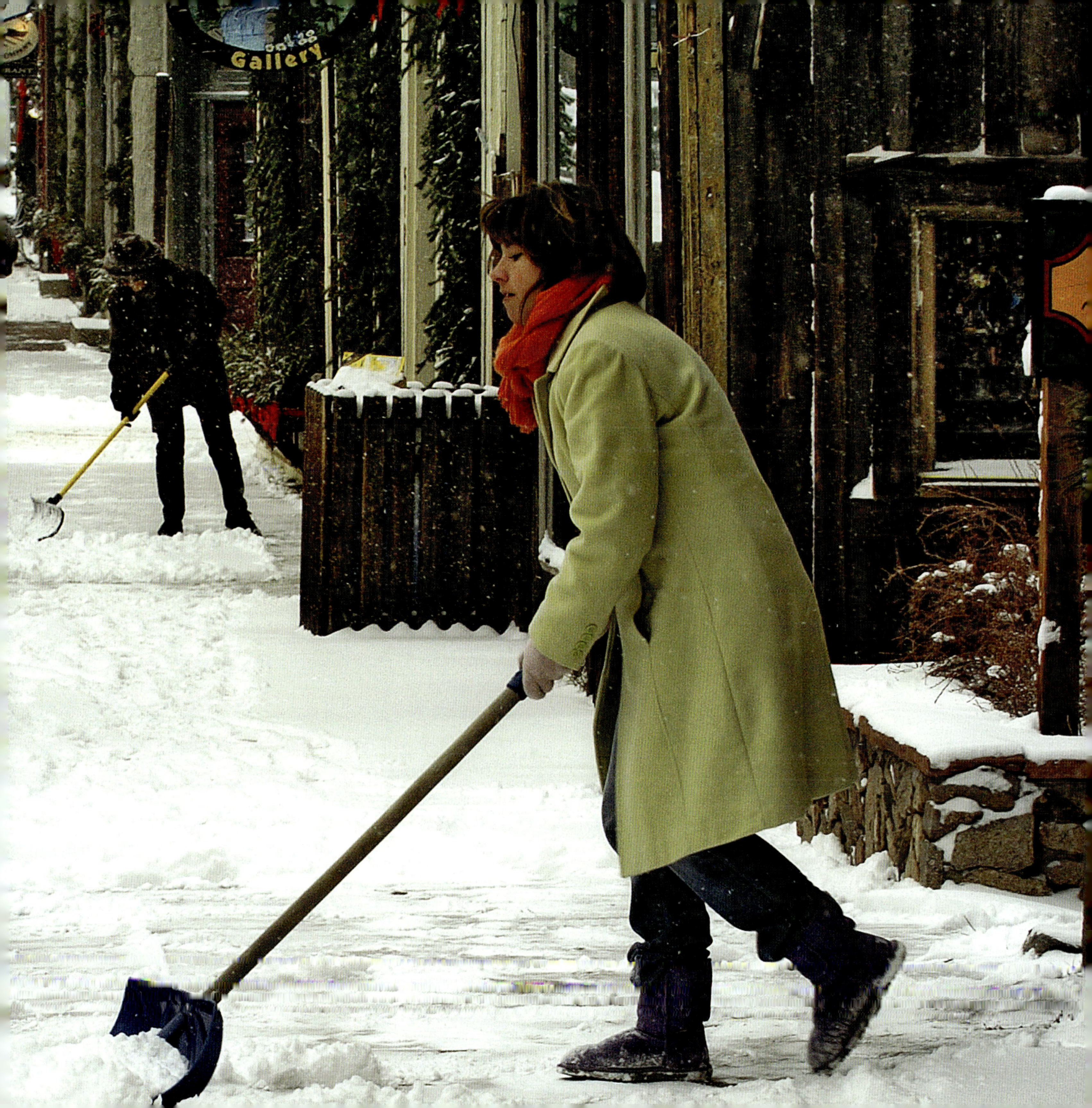
Gallery

Picture this: A large frozen lake set against a backdrop of mountains, a bustling ski area blanketed with fresh powder, and an automated chocolate village inside a luxury hotel. This image is not imaginary; it's that of Keystone during the holiday season.

Located a mere 6 miles down the road from Keystone is the tiny town of Dillon, complete with its famous brewery and nearby outlet shops. Dillon's holiday season gets off to a grand mountain start with the Holiday Wonderland, an open vendor market held at the Dillon Tech Center. Local artists and shop owners set up tables and sell handmade gift baskets, pieces of art, and unique gifts made from recycled products. Throughout the day, children relish the magic of the holidays while listening to various story readings and creating crafts. Carolers and a special visit from Santa complete the day and ring in the holiday spirit.

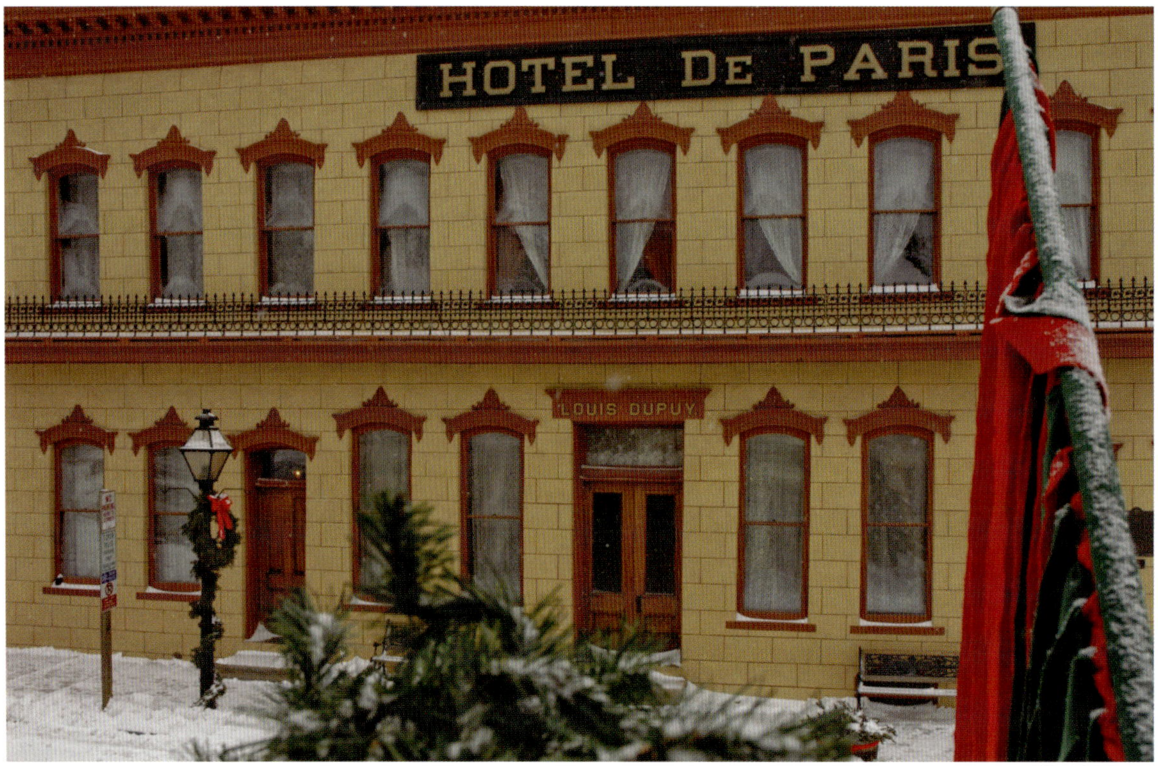

Hotel de Paris Museum, Georgetown

As they stroll down the street and sip warm beverages, shoppers can visit with Santa and his reindeer during the holiday Lighting of Dillon. Once the lights are strung and sparkling, leave Dillon and drive down the road to Keystone, a resort village with personality.

Keystone kicks off its Winterfall festival in late November or early December with 36 Hours of Keystone, an event that invites participants to ski for 36 hours straight. Open to the public, this event includes multiple other competitions with fabulous rewards as well as music and plenty of caffeinated beverages. The next big event of the season is the Keystone Demo Days. Test out the newest equipment on Keystone's slopes and prepare yourself for the powder that's sure to fall the rest of the season.

With an enchanting lighted tree growing in the middle of the ice, Keystone Lake is the ideal place to skate through the holidays. Between turns around the ice and hockey at the back rink, warm yourself with hot chocolate in the wooden hut built just for skate rentals. If you're in need of some inspiration, watch for a visit from the Denver Figure Skating Club, a group of skaters who dress in their shiny holiday best and jingle around to

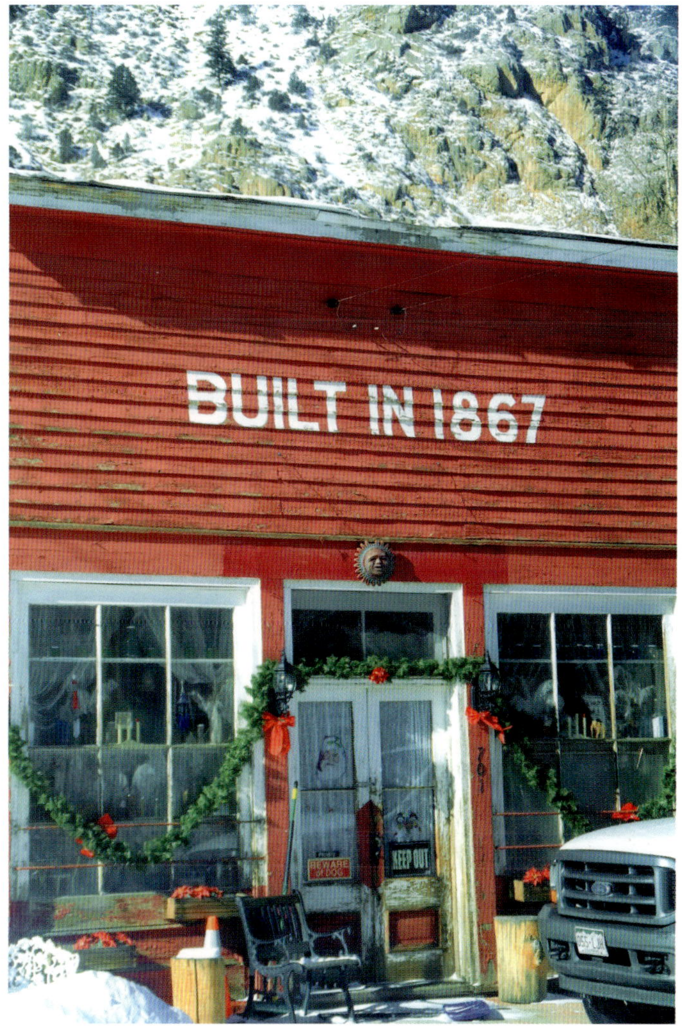

Above: A shop downtown, Georgetown

Next page: The lake outside Keystone Lodge & Spa, Keystone

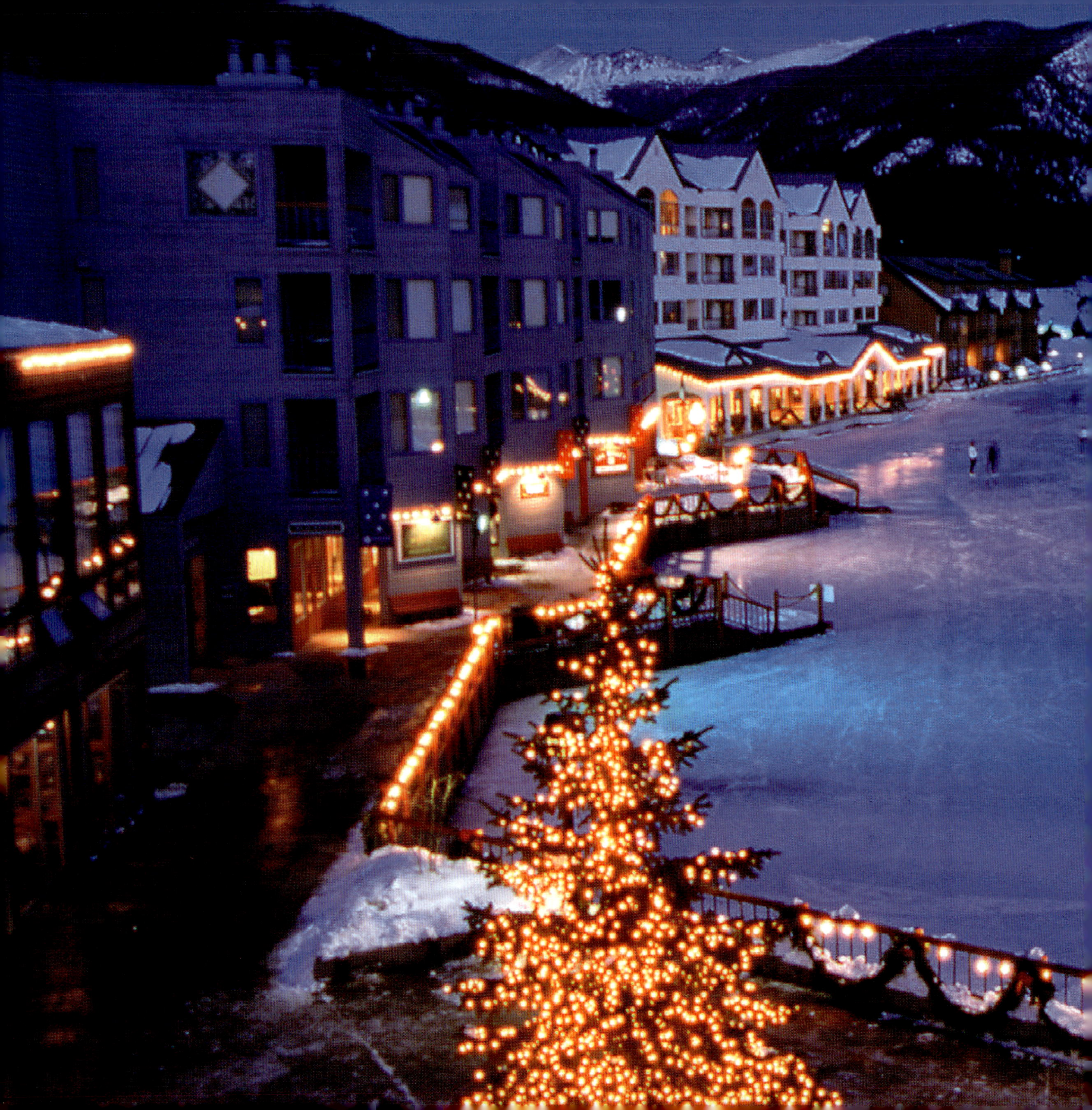

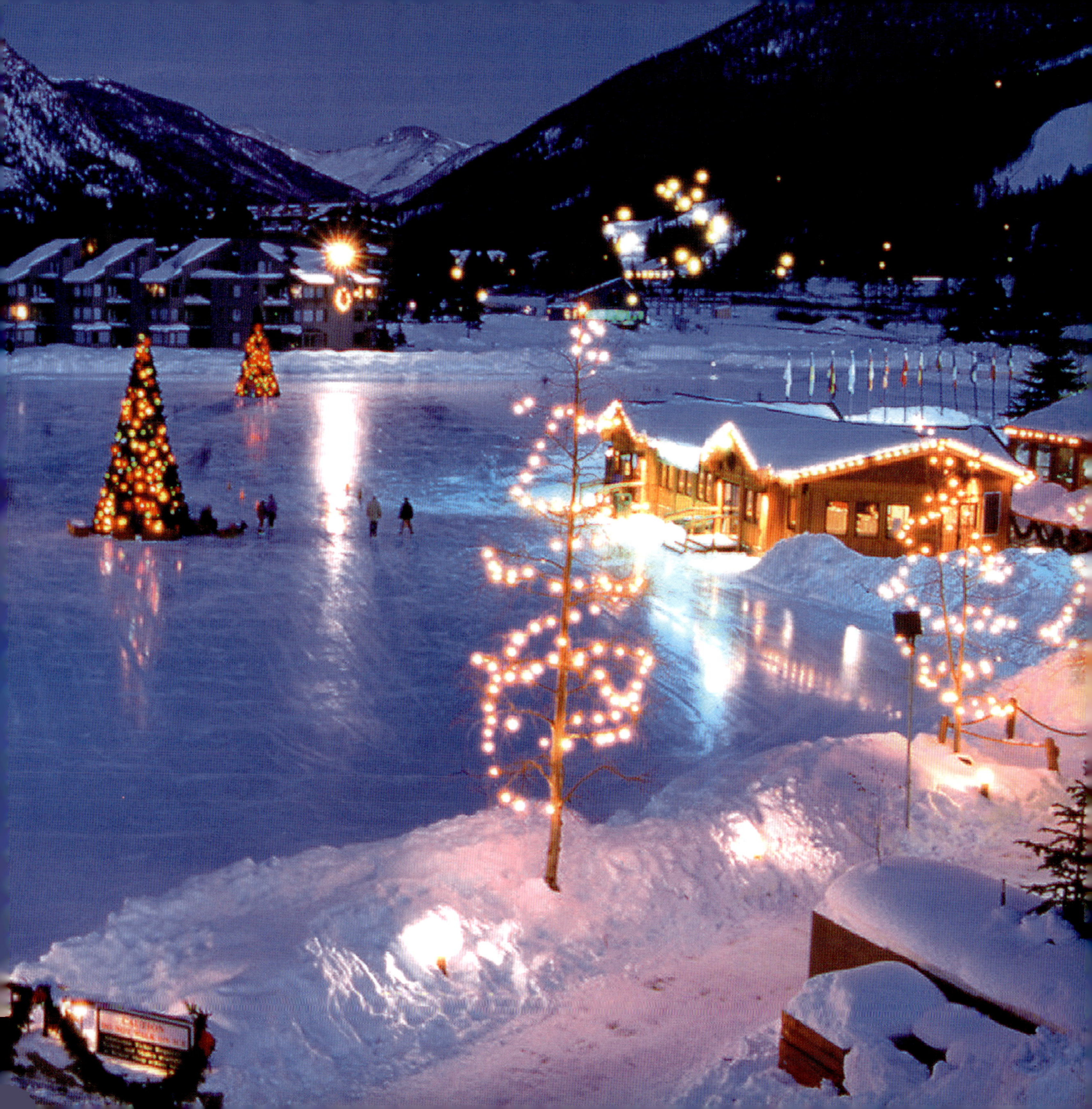

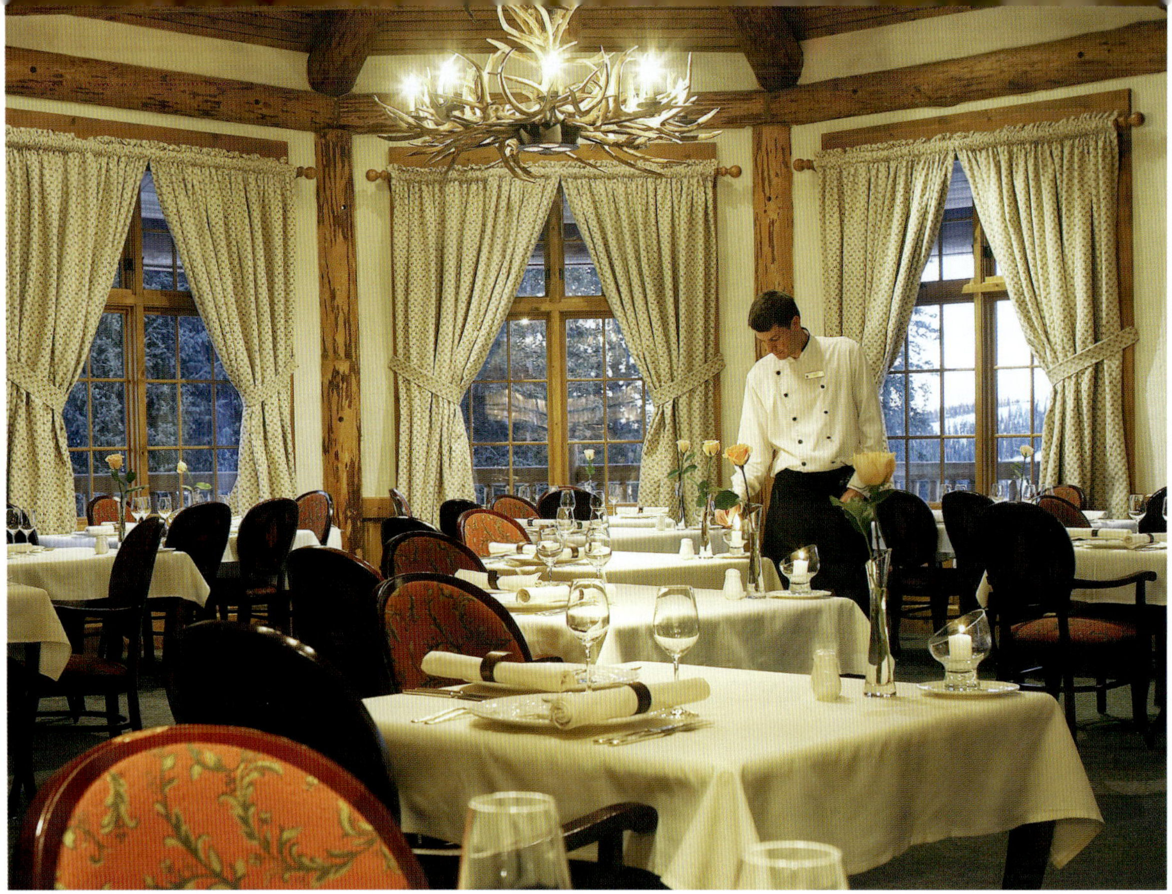

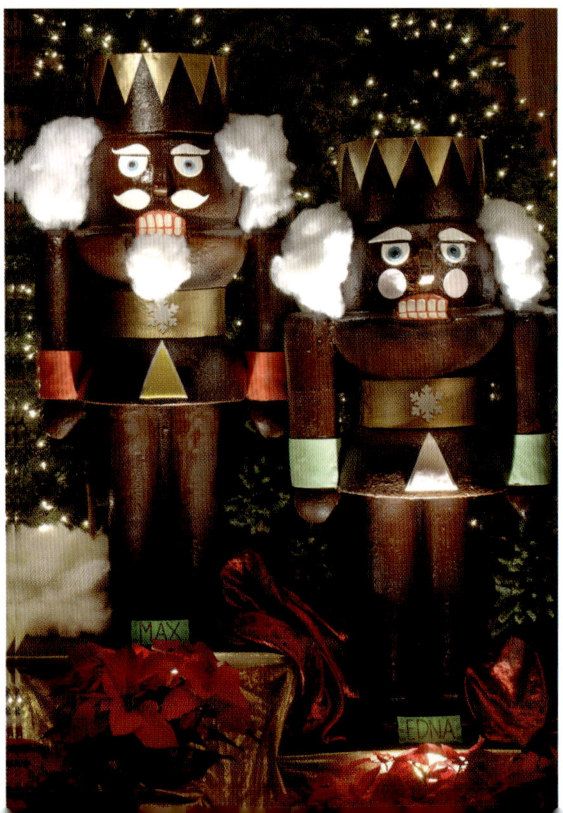

holiday tunes. If you're not gliding gracefully in a pair of blades, walk around the lake to take in the holiday ice sculptures, including one of Santa, reindeer, and an enchanting, detailed sleigh, perfect for photo ops. Charming, locally owned shops surround the lake, offering chances to warm up and finish your shopping.

Perhaps Keystone's most exuberant holiday event is Chef Ned Archibald's automated chocolate village, on display in the lobby of

Top: Alpenglow Stube restaurant, Keystone
Left: Nutcrackers in the Chocolate Village at Keystone Lodge & Spa, Keystone

the Keystone Lodge & Spa. Though you can't eat the marvel, it's worth a visit just to see the working gondola carved of pure chocolate as well as a chocolate waterfall and a 6-foot white chocolate Christmas tree.

If you want to feel as if you're inside an L.L. Bean photo shoot, reserve the 7,700-square-foot Keystone Ranch, a luxury vacation rental on the 12th hole of the Keystone Ranch Golf Course. The nine-bedroom, eight-bathroom home was actually used for the clothing company's winter 2007–2008 catalog. And no trip to Keystone is complete without a gondola ride up to the Alpenglow Stube restaurant for old-world food and service complemented by stunning views.

Spend your last days of the holiday season ringing in the New Year in River Run Village, where you can watch or take part in a torchlight parade and take in breathlessly colorful fireworks, an explosively fun entrance into the next year.

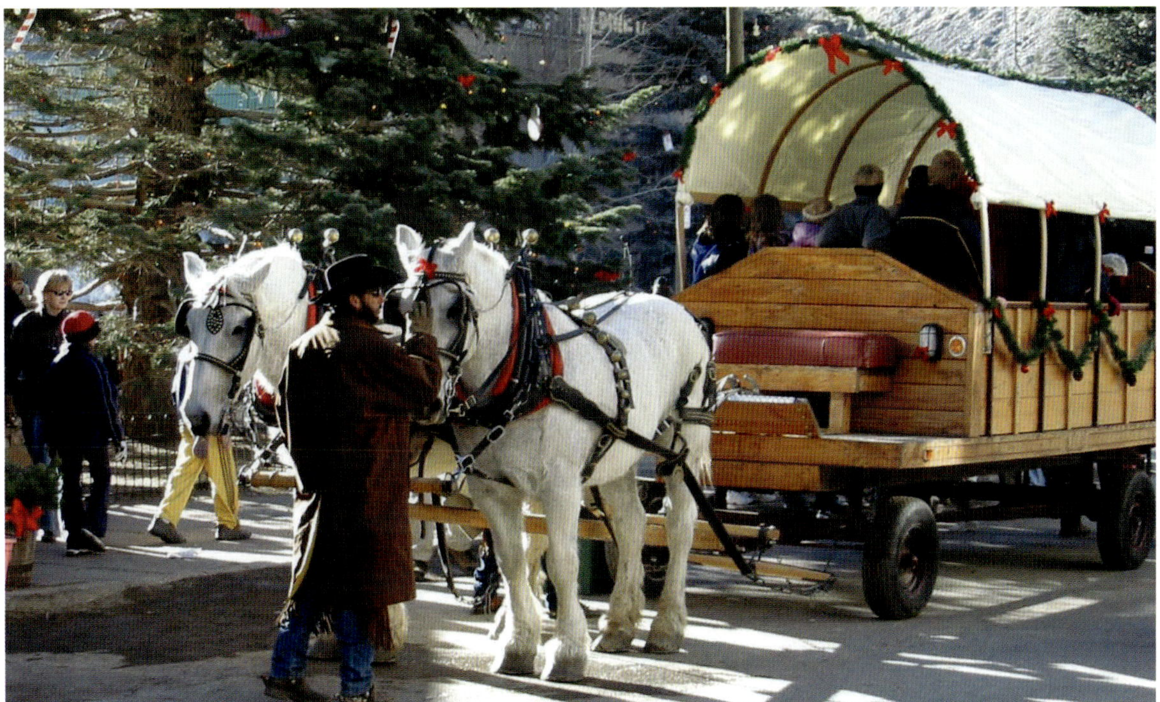

Horse-drawn covered-wagon rides during the Christmas Market, Georgetown

Glenwood Springs

& GRAND JUNCTION

May the spirit of Christmas

bring you peace,

The gladness of Christmas

give you hope,

The warmth of Christmas

grant you love.

—UNKNOWN

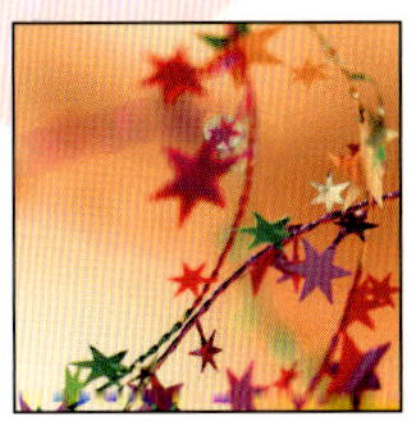

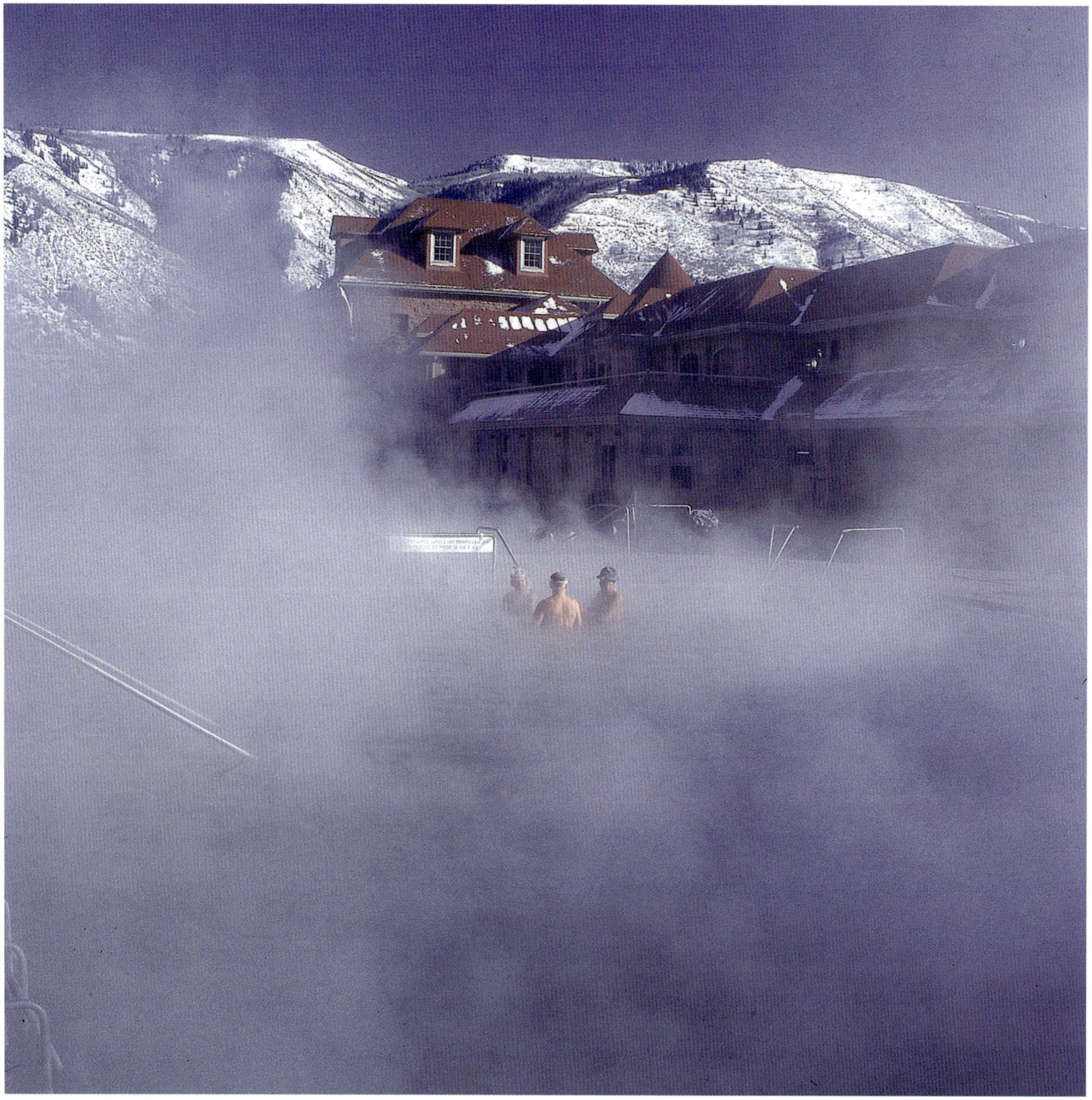

Glenwood Hot Springs Pool, Glenwood Springs

NEXT TO THE COLORADO RIVER, in a scenic valley 160 miles west of Denver, Glenwood Springs lights up for the holidays. In this refreshingly relaxed and gorgeous environment, the days and nights come alive with outdoor activities, endearing traditions, lights, shopping, and truly great scenery.

Begin your stay in the springs by selecting and cutting down your own tree in the White River National Forest—be sure to obtain a permit first. Trim the tree in your suite at the Sunlight Mountain Inn, a perfect place to spend the holiday season. Or, book a room at the historic Hotel Colorado, a replica of the 16th-century Villa de Medici, which sits across the street from the Hot Springs Pool. With holiday breakfast leading up to planned outdoor activities and cookies by the fire every afternoon, you're sure to have a Christmas to remember. Spend your days skiing, snowshoeing, and snowmobiling, then come back for delectable feasts. On Christmas Day, settle down with friends and family to the annual Holiday Candlelit Buffet, a spread of food so beautiful that devouring it is almost a shame.

While you're in the area, pay a visit to the Glenwood Fairy Caves, a glorious natural display of lighted caves full of stalagmites and

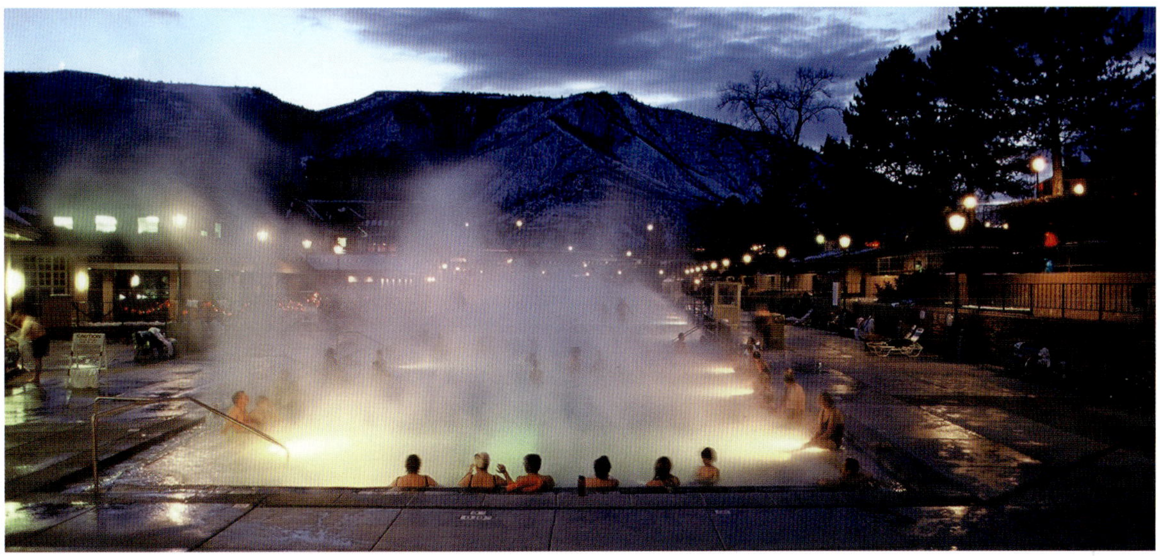

Mountain views from the Glenwood Hot Springs Pool at twilight, Glenwood Springs

stalactites, God's own holiday decorations. Named for how they look when reflecting light, this natural wonder is the pride of Glenwood and a must-see sight.

In town, musical and cultural options abound. Attend the Mountain Madrigal Singers annual performance of A Perfect Christmas—truly a standup show. The United Methodist Church lights up with the synchronized sounds of a holy choir. Experience a traditional Victorian Christmas celebration at the Holiday Open House at the Frontier Historical Museum. Enjoy decorations while browsing the museum, just off Colorado Avenue downtown. While perusing artifacts, enjoy appetizers and hot cider for the holiday season.

A true high spot of the Glenwood Springs winter season is the Grand Holiday, a downtown festival of lights. In mid-December, the town literally lights up with dazzling, glistening lights on every tree and shop window. Carolers walk up and down the streets and Santa and his reindeer are sure to make an appearance. Shop and take pleasure in the live entertainment, then take a cart ride around downtown and taste award-winning soup and chili from the Grand Holiday's annual contest.

Highlight your Glenwood journey with a dip in the soothing hot springs. Open on Christmas Eve, Christmas Day, and New Year's Eve, this landmark Colorado venue allows you to soak up minerals and relaxation during this special time of year. Imagine ringing in the New Year in the peaceful hot springs, where you can finish the countdown at midnight in the pool.

If the pool isn't your cup of tea, attend the New Year's Eve Celebration at Rivers Restaurant, where you'll dine on a six-course meal followed by classic, sparkling, and spectacular champagnes. Then, countdown to midnight with live music and dancing, Glenwood Springs style.

GRAND JUNCTION & PALISADE

On the Western Slope of the Columbine state, Grand Junction livens up a valley of peaceful natural scenery. Almost 200 miles west of Denver and on the north side of the Colorado River, this town is set against a backdrop of mountains, water, and gorgeous plateaus.

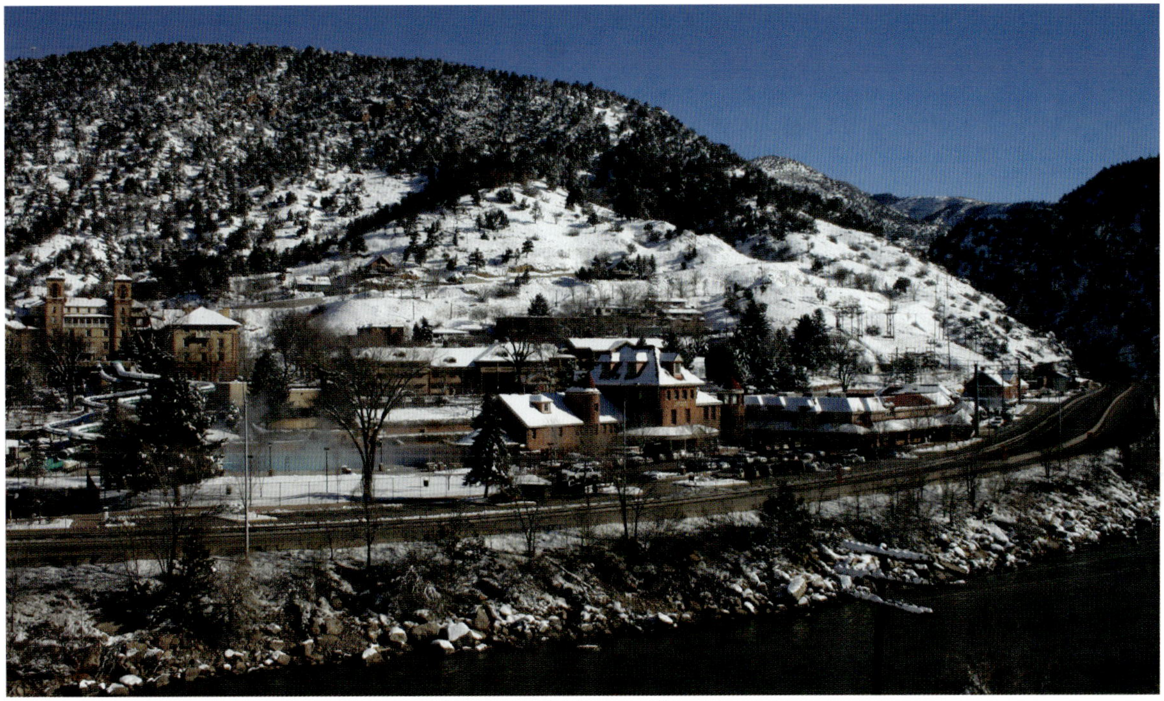

The town of Glenwood Springs

For the Grand Junction community, Christmas begins the day after Thanksgiving, otherwise known as Black Friday. But in this sweet town, there's nothing black about this Friday except, perhaps, the delicious coffee from Main Street Bagels. Better yet, try their specialty Polar Express Hot Chocolate—inspired by the children's holiday story—and get ready for a full day of activities.

During the day, browse shop windows and vote your winner for the annual window decorating contest. Then, listen to local school groups and musicians serenade you with holiday songs in the Qwest Holiday Sounds Concert Series, musical bliss that continues every Saturday in December. Visit the Heiden Homes Realty Winter Festival, where local nonprofits set up booths and sell drinks and goodies. When the sun sets, the Parade of Lights commences from Fourth and Main streets, making downtown glisten with colorful lights that wind through the trees. For about two hours, watch as dancers, singers, more than 100 floats, and Santa Claus ride into town, bringing with them holiday cheer and spirit.

Head back downtown in mid-December for the Holiday Chocolate Walk—a fascinating guided tour of downtown complete with a commemorative mug of hot chocolate, coffee, or cider. That same night, meander through the streets in the Spirit of Christmas Walk. Enjoy twinkling holiday lights as you pass a strolling Santa and observe live entertainment all night.

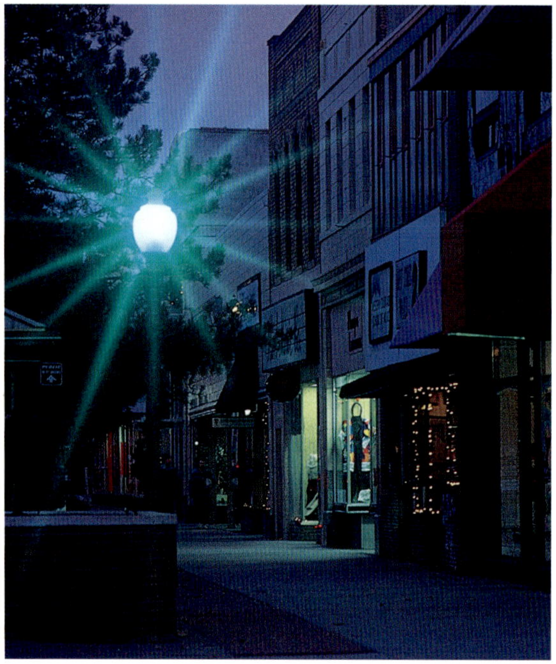

Downtown decked for the holidays, Grand Junction

Just a few miles from Grand Junction, the town of Palisade plays host to an Olde Fashioned Christmas in early December. For a nostalgic, dreamlike holiday experience, this is the place to go. The vineyard capital of Colorado, Palisade produces more than 75 percent of Colorado's wine, and the holidays augment the fruitful economy of the area. Attend complimentary wine tastings and sip the rich flavors of the season. Then, get to know the history of the area as you tour Victorian homes, participate in gingerbread house building contests, and scoop up some love at the Fire Department's annual chili cook-off.

As you walk through beautiful downtown Palisade, wave hello to the carolers and beloved holiday characters that stroll the streets to welcome visitors. Children giggle and bask in mountain pleasure as they ride the train and create crafts in the Olde Town Marketplace. Stay around town for the holiday lighting parade, presided over by the Peach Queen, who illuminates the town just after nightfall. Sure to enchant you, this vineyard capital of the Wild West offers a high-class holiday in old-fashioned form.

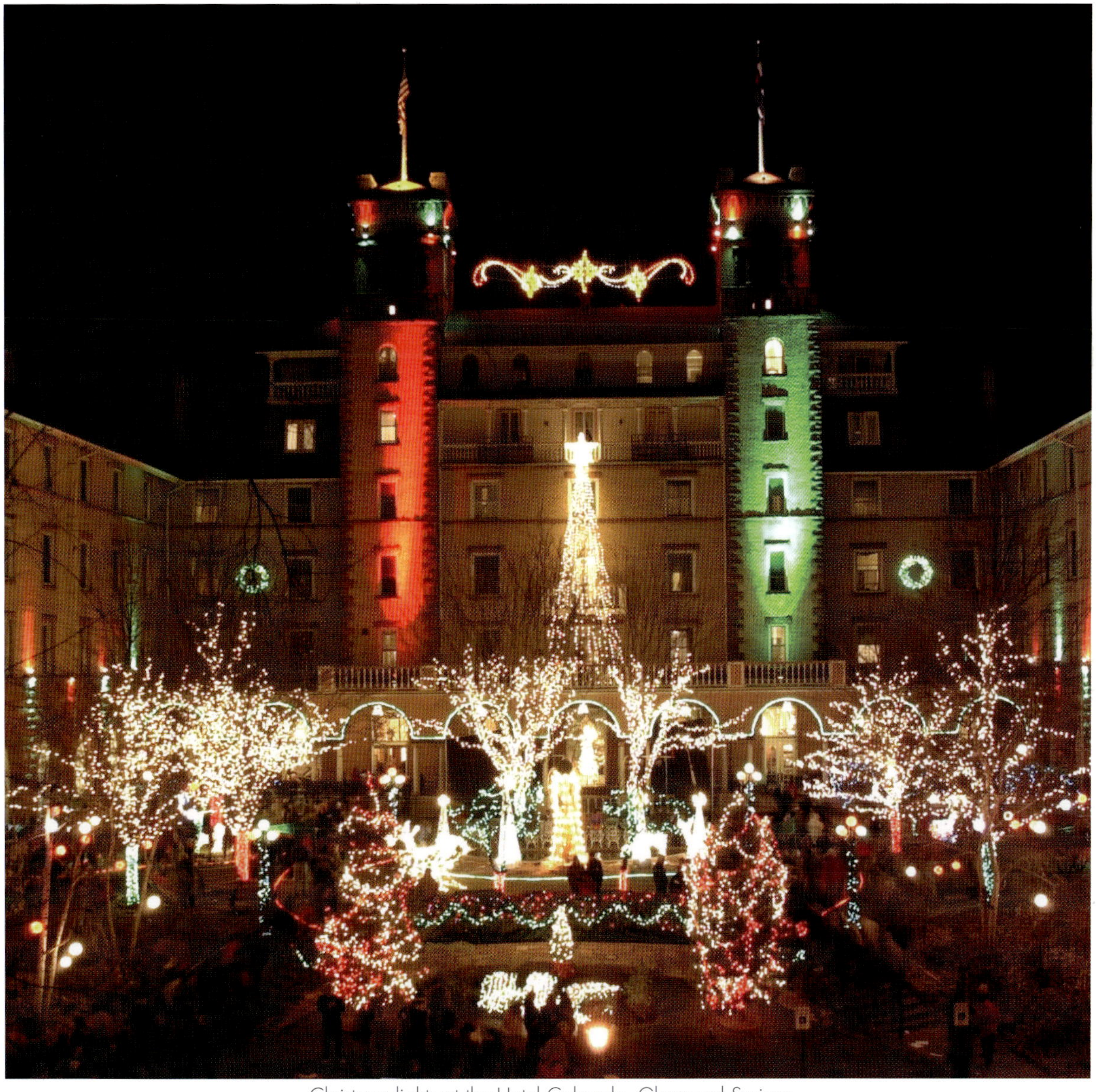

Christmas lights at the Hotel Colorado, Glenwood Springs

Leadville

At Christmas play
and make good cheer,
For Christmas comes
but once a year.

—THOMAS TUSSER

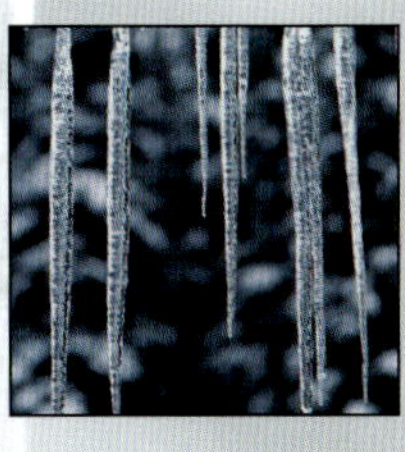

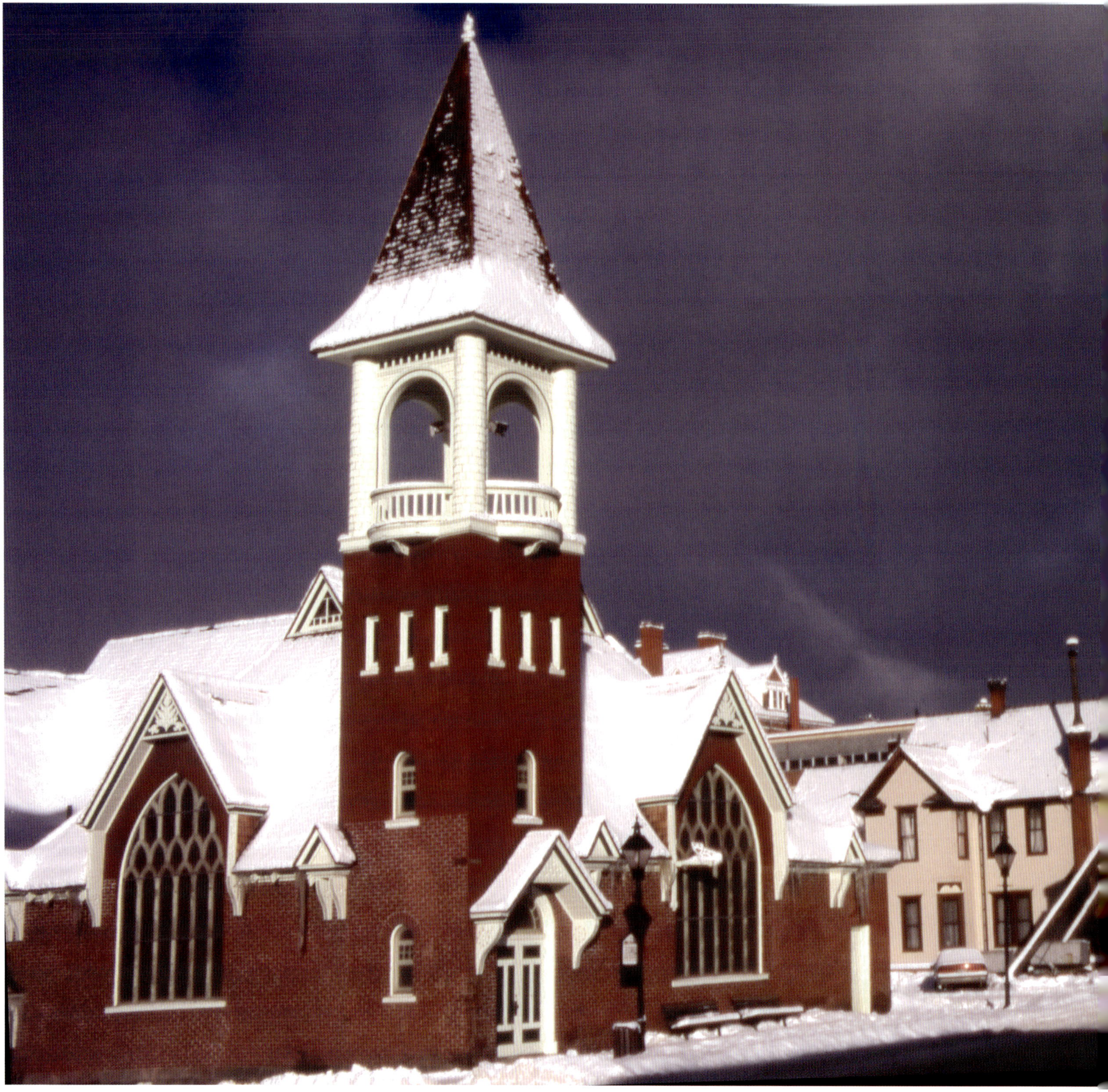

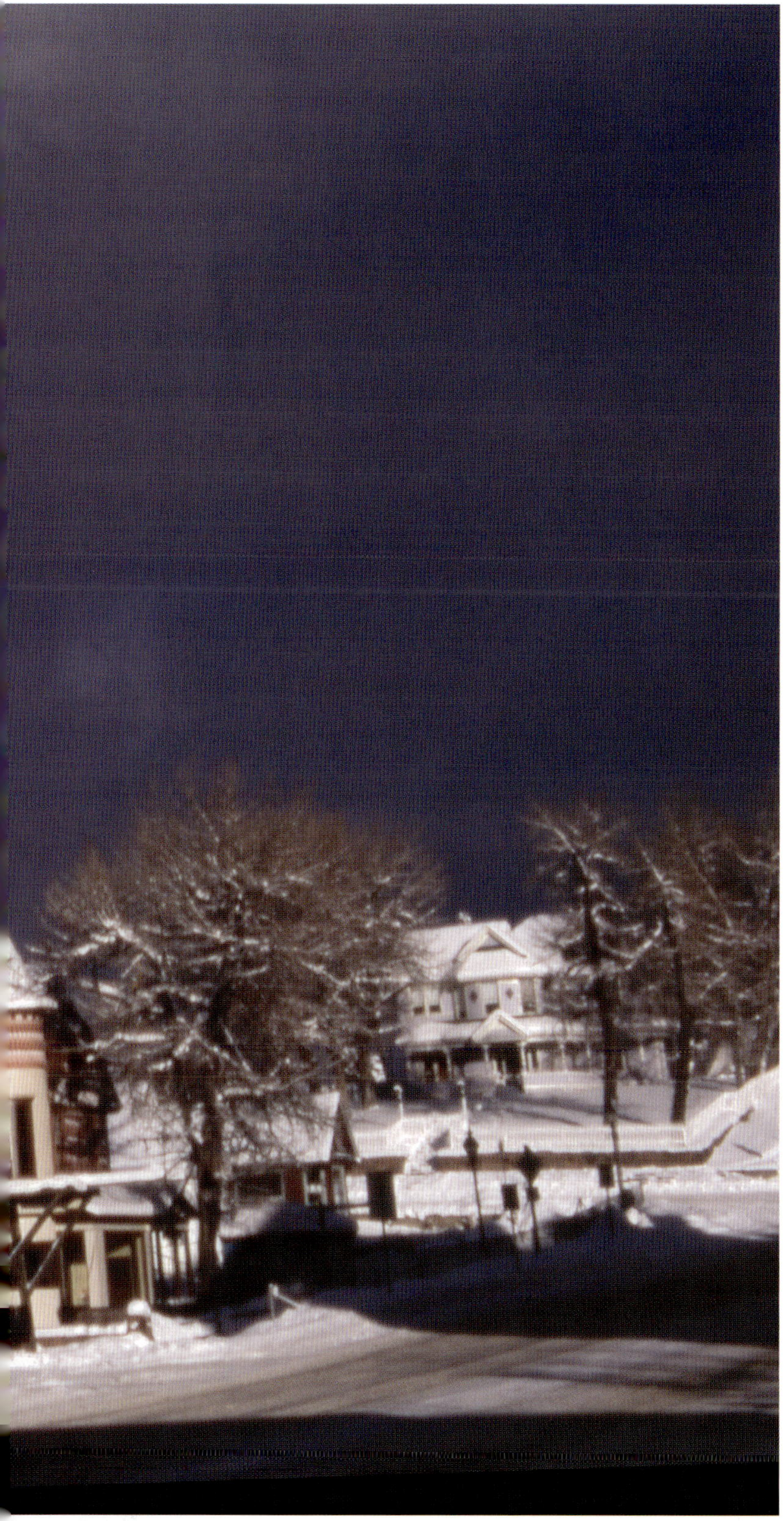

FIRST SETTLED IN 1860 during the Pike's Peak Gold Rush, Leadville has quite the history. It was known as Cloud City until 1878, when it was given its current name. Though little gold was discovered in the city, settlers found another aspect of the town to boast about—the altitude. Commonly regarded as the highest city in the country, 10,430-foot Leadville rests atop mountains of natural resources—mostly zinc and, of course, lead.

As in many mountain towns, the holiday season in Leadville commences with a holiday craft show. Odd Fellows Hall is guaranteed to be packed full of homemade crafts, goods, decorations, and candy, and all proceeds go to charity. Stay for a community lunch with family and friends. In early December, the holiday spirit truly takes over the city as the Parade of Lights illuminates the Victorian architecture and rustic beauty of the old mining village. Trees throughout the city shimmer as carolers stroll through the center of town. As you watch, take a peek in all the shop windows, decked out with snowflakes, detailed

"Old Church," a Presbyterian church on Harrison Avenue, Leadville

Christmas ornaments, and carefully crafted winter decorations. The true spirit of Christmas is said to appear as the picturesque Courthouse Christmas Tree is decked in thousands of tiny lights.

In the spirit of its founding, Leadville hosts an annual Victorian Days Weekend. Participants in the Victorian Fashion Show parade large and stylish hats and dresses through the city, inspiring you to don your own Victorian attire and enjoy traditional holiday tea. Take the Victorian Home Tour showcasing the historic architecture of the city, adorned for the holiday season with twinkling lights hung from roofs, trees, and bushes. Follow the tour with a festive dinner and a surrey ride through this enchanting city. In the morning, settle in for a champagne brunch at the National Mining Hall of Fame and Heritage Museum, the only nonprofit federally chartered mining museum in the country and a true tribute to Leadville history.

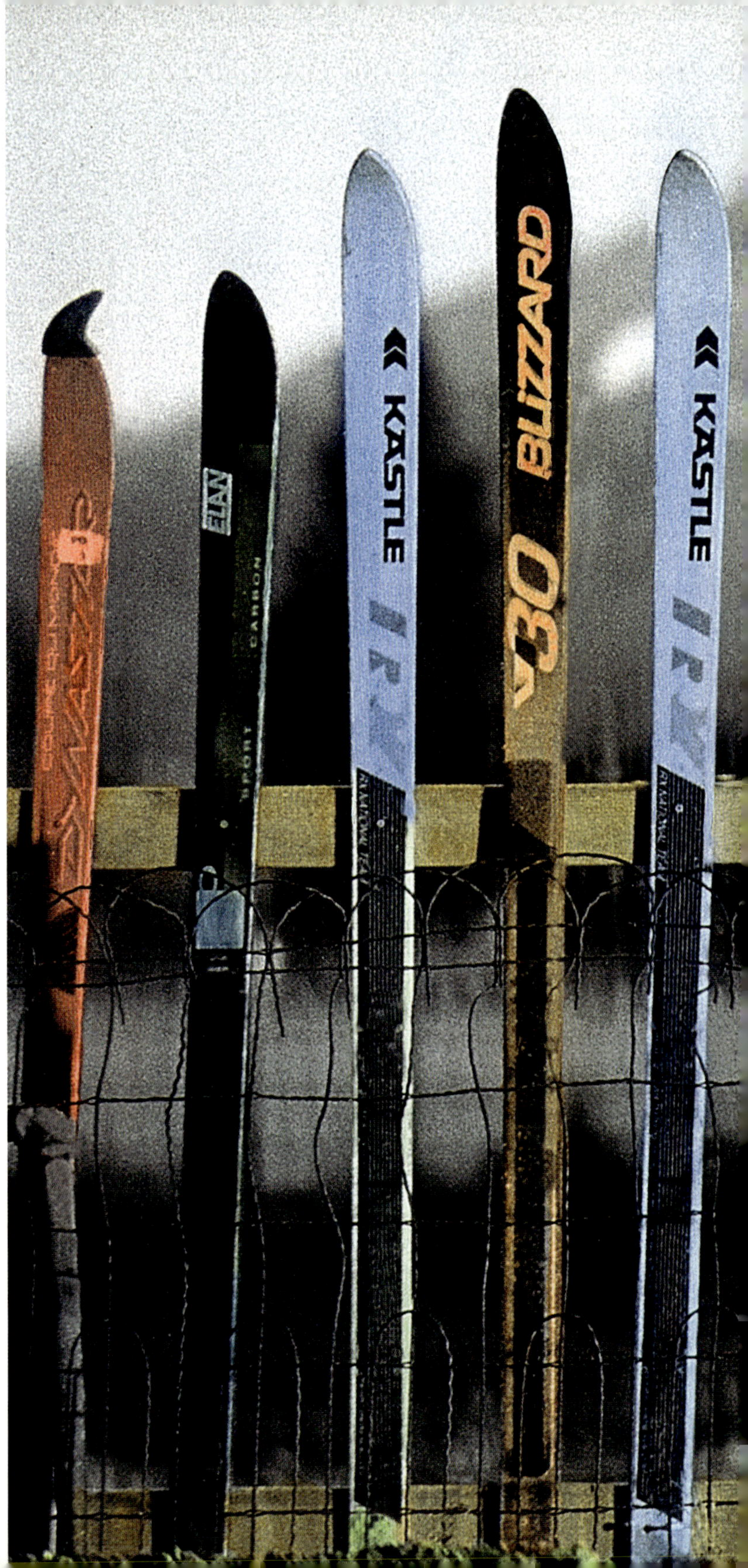

Sustainable fence made of skis, Leadville

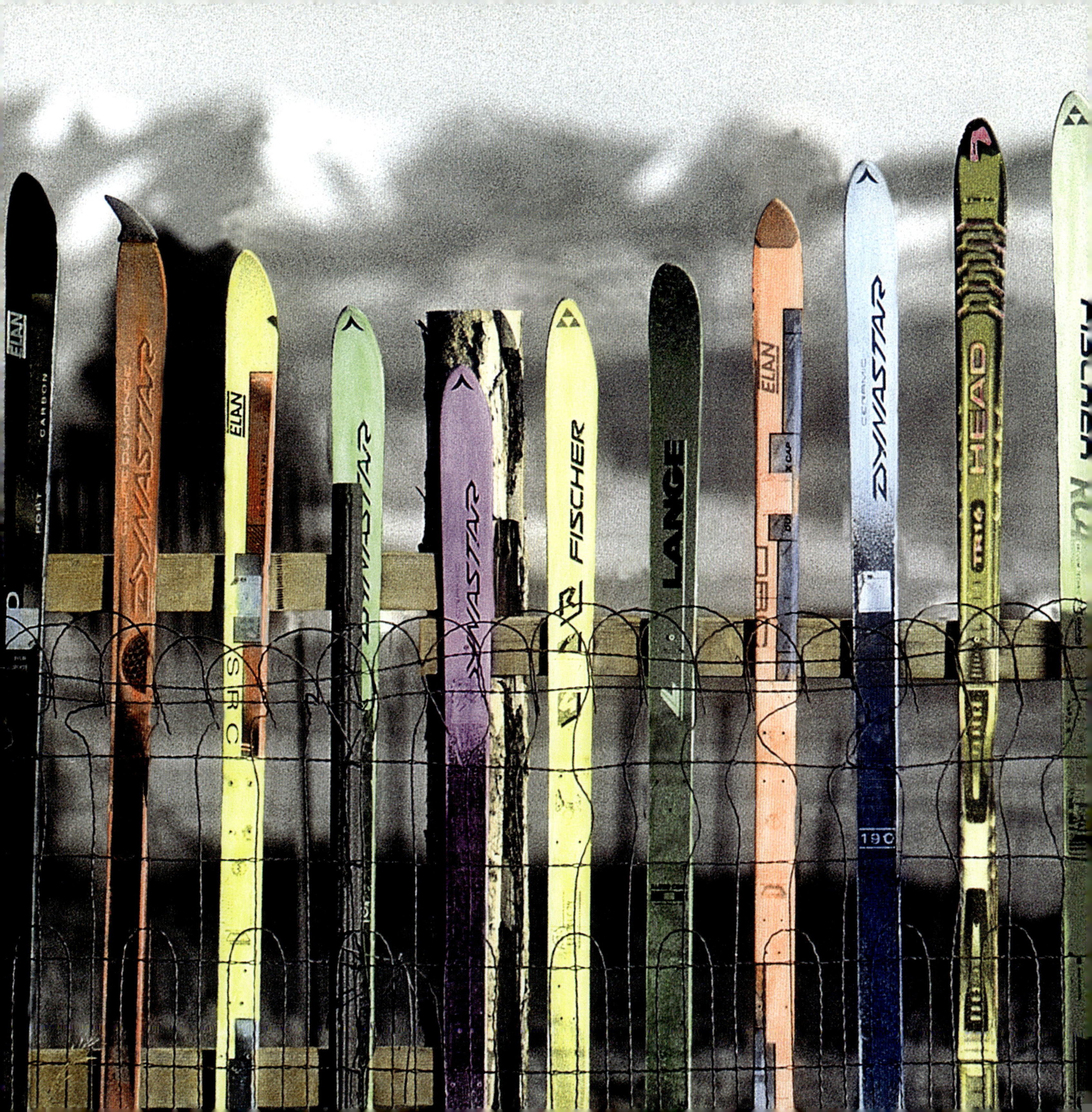
ELAN
CARBON
DYNASTAR
ELAN
SRC
DYNASTAR
DYNASTAR
FISCHER
LANGE
ELAN
CERAMIC
DYNASTAR
190
HEAD
FISCHER

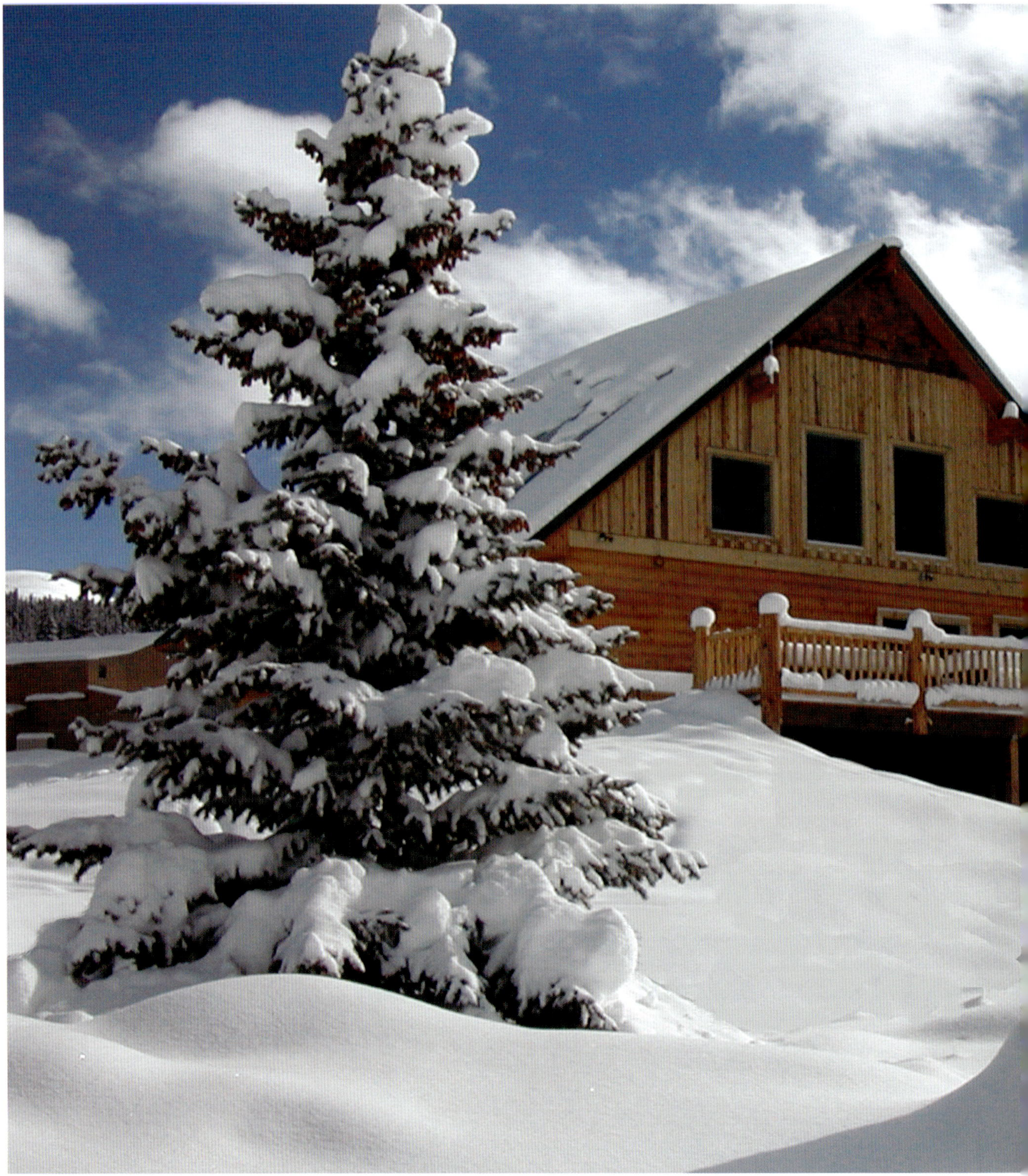

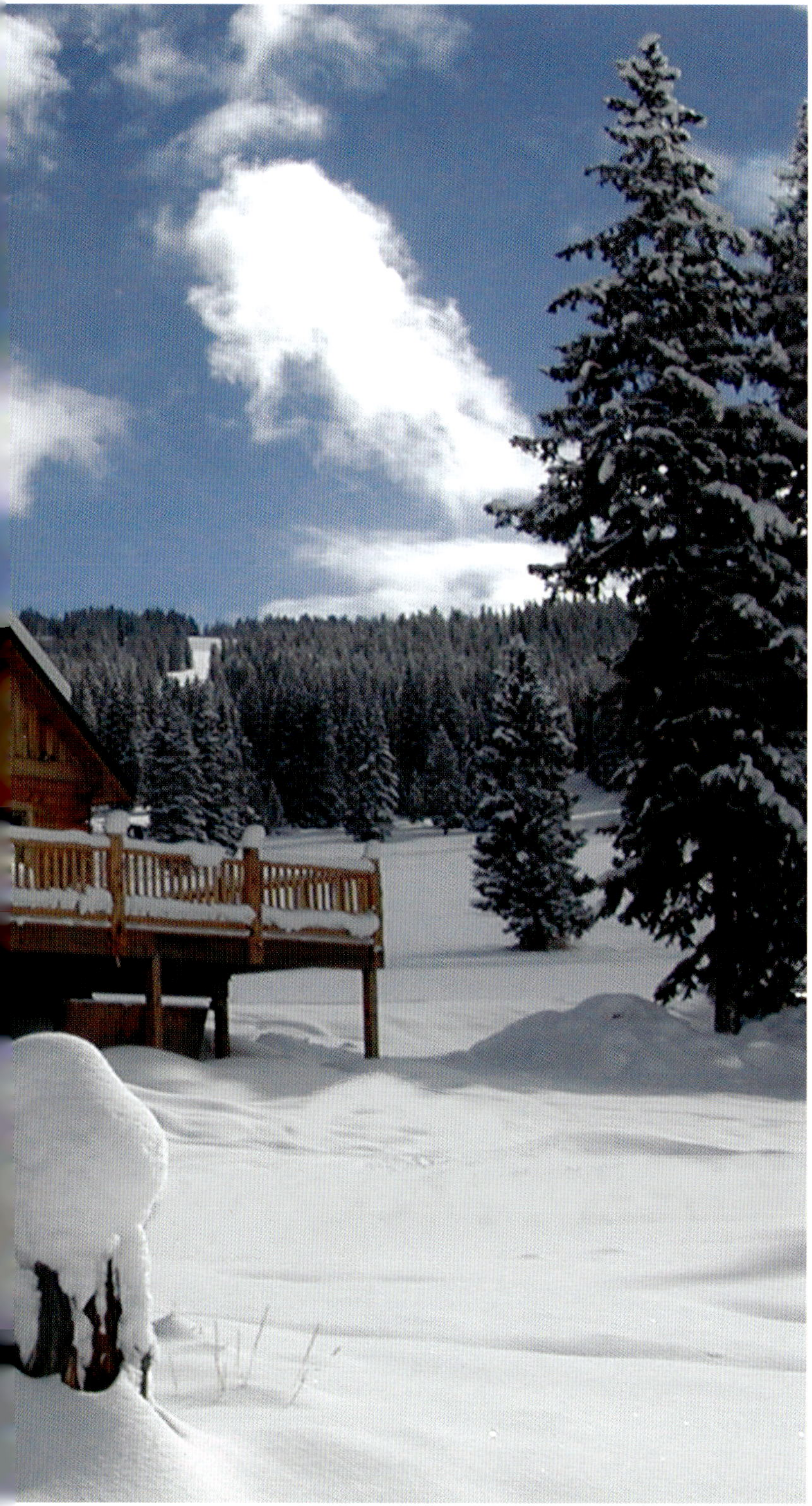

When the holidays are over, the Crystal Carnival makes its home in Leadville. Each weekend from January to March, take part in a different exciting activity. One weekend, crowds climb high for an ice-fishing derby. Another weekend, it's a parade and snowshoeing. Later, cross-country skiing takes center stage. Ski joring and snowmobile races round out the season, all making Leadville a spectacular place to spend your winter vacation.

Piney Creek Nordic Center, Leadville

Steamboat Springs

Great little One!

Whose all-embracing birth

Lifts Earth to Heaven,

stoops Heaven to Earth.

—RICHARD CRASHAW

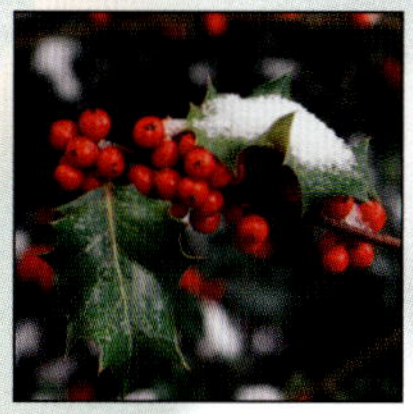

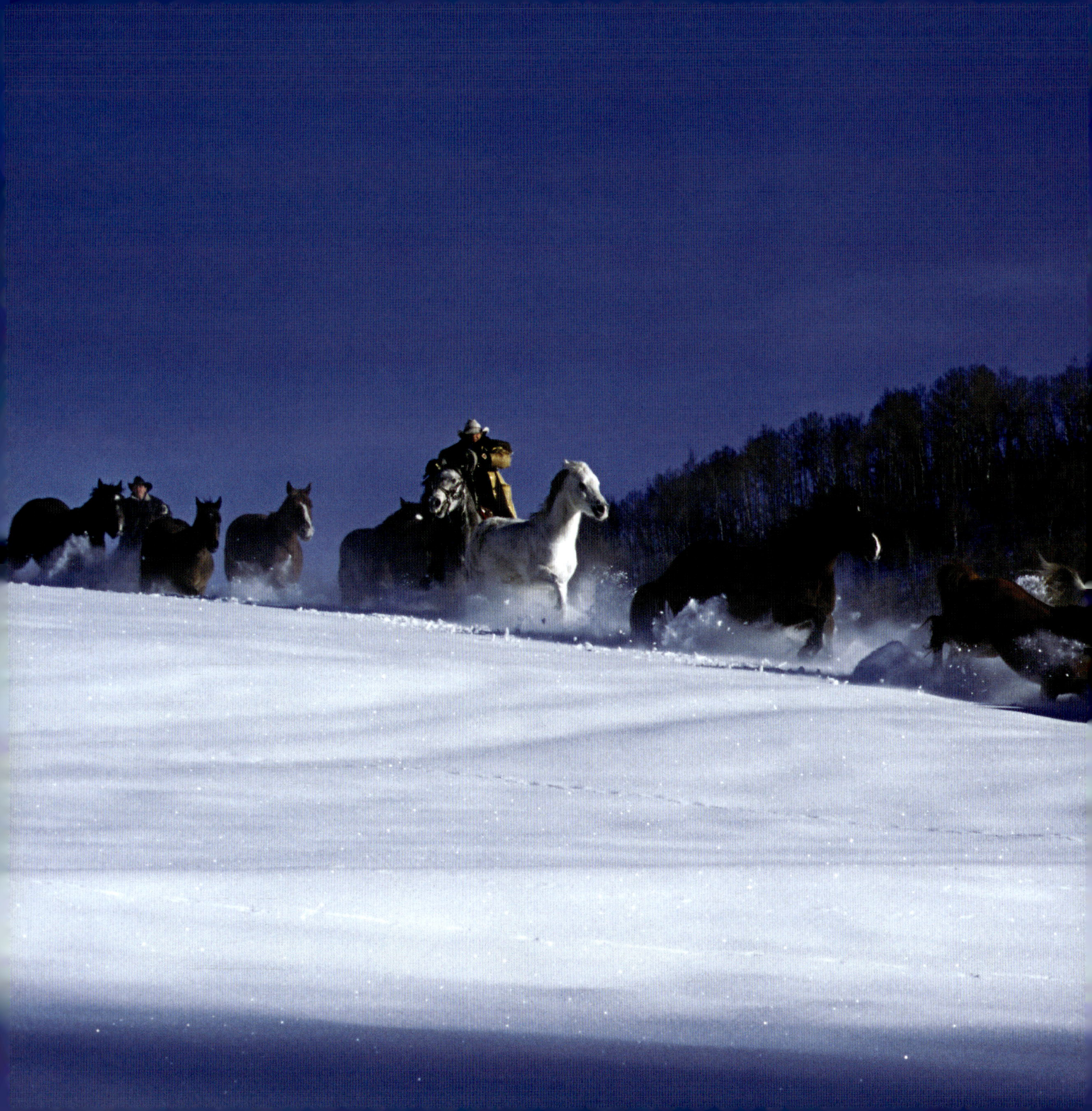

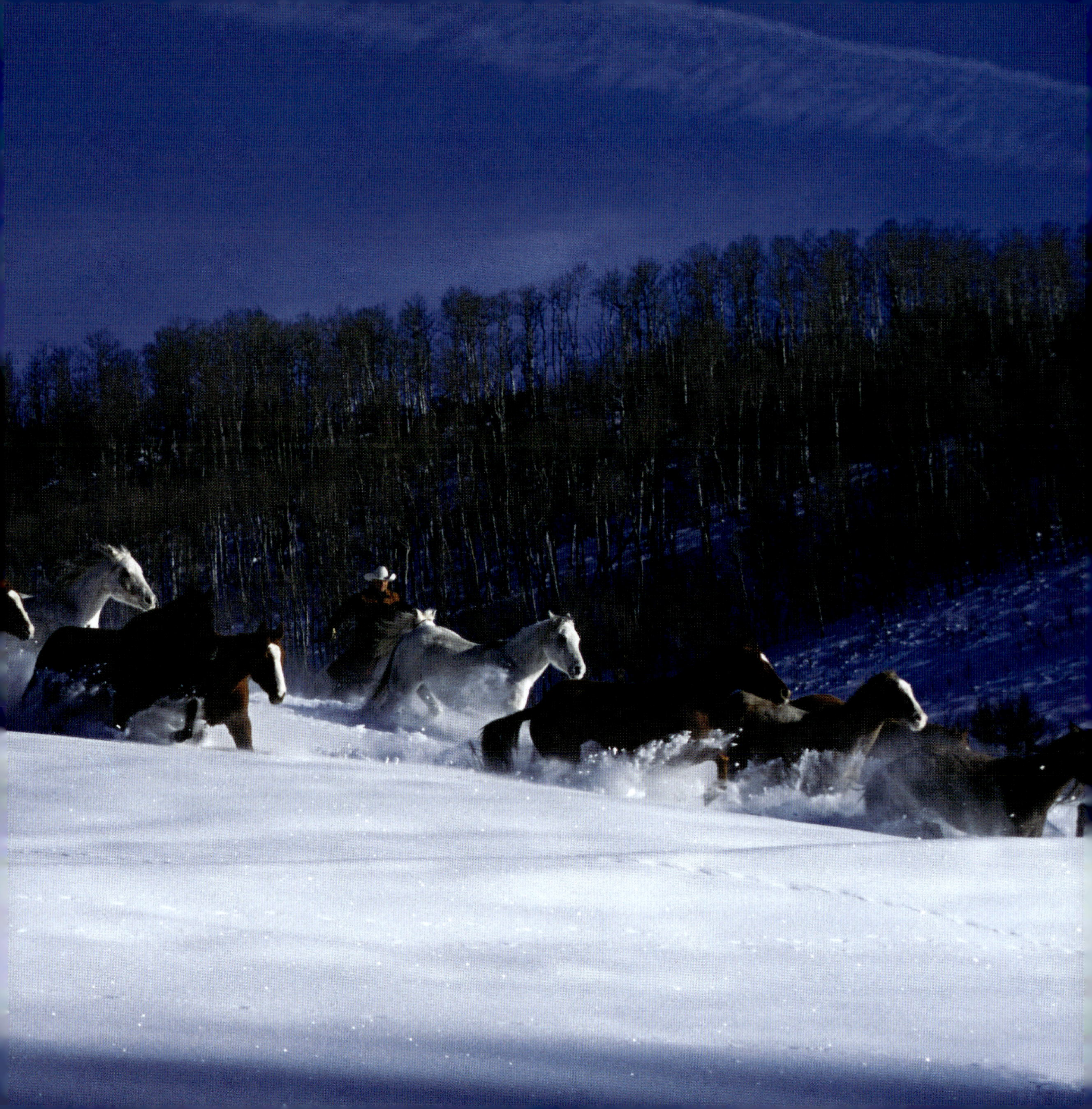

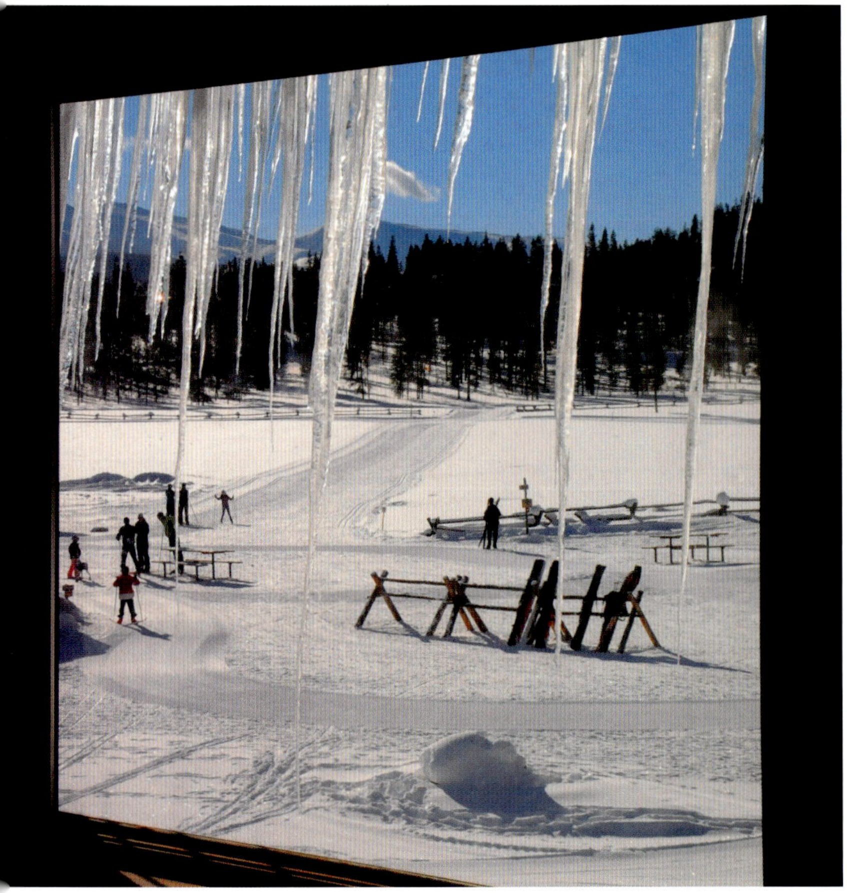

Above: Cross-country skiers enjoy fresh snow
Right: Bird's-eye view of Steamboat

Previous page: Horses running through snow, Steamboat

COMMONLY REFERRED TO AS "Ski Town USA," Steamboat is a town of multiples—multiple ski areas, multiple winter activities, and, of course, multiple holiday celebrations. Spend your Christmas living like a Steamboat native by participating in local traditions and community programs.

Decorate your pad with a purchase from the Lions Club Christmas Tree Sale, an annual event whose proceeds go to great causes. Then, explore the artistic side of Steamboat at the Artisan Market, a setup sporting 50 vendors of creative and beautiful jewelry, fine arts, and decorative creations. Steamboat offers so many activities, it's worthwhile to visit the annual Winter Activity Fair to get some help figuring out the best way to spend your time there. It's free, so take advantage of the opportunity to meet and greet and discover all the best fun in the Yampa Valley.

On a warm day in the valley, venture into the mountain skies on a hot air balloon ride. It isn't rare for the skies of Steamboat, one of the premier ballooning towns in the country, to appear pink, purple, and polka-dotted due to the plethora of colorful balloons flying

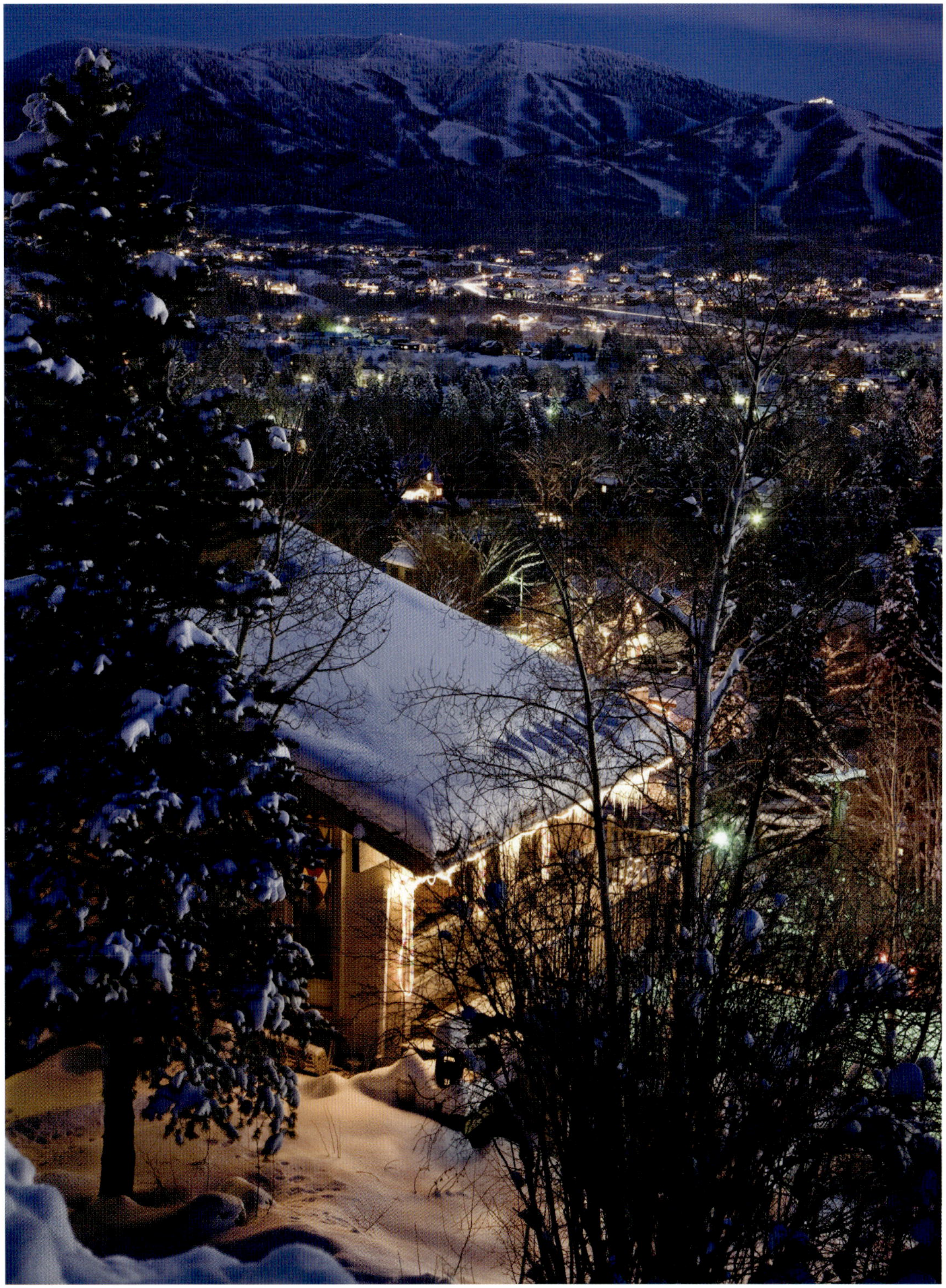

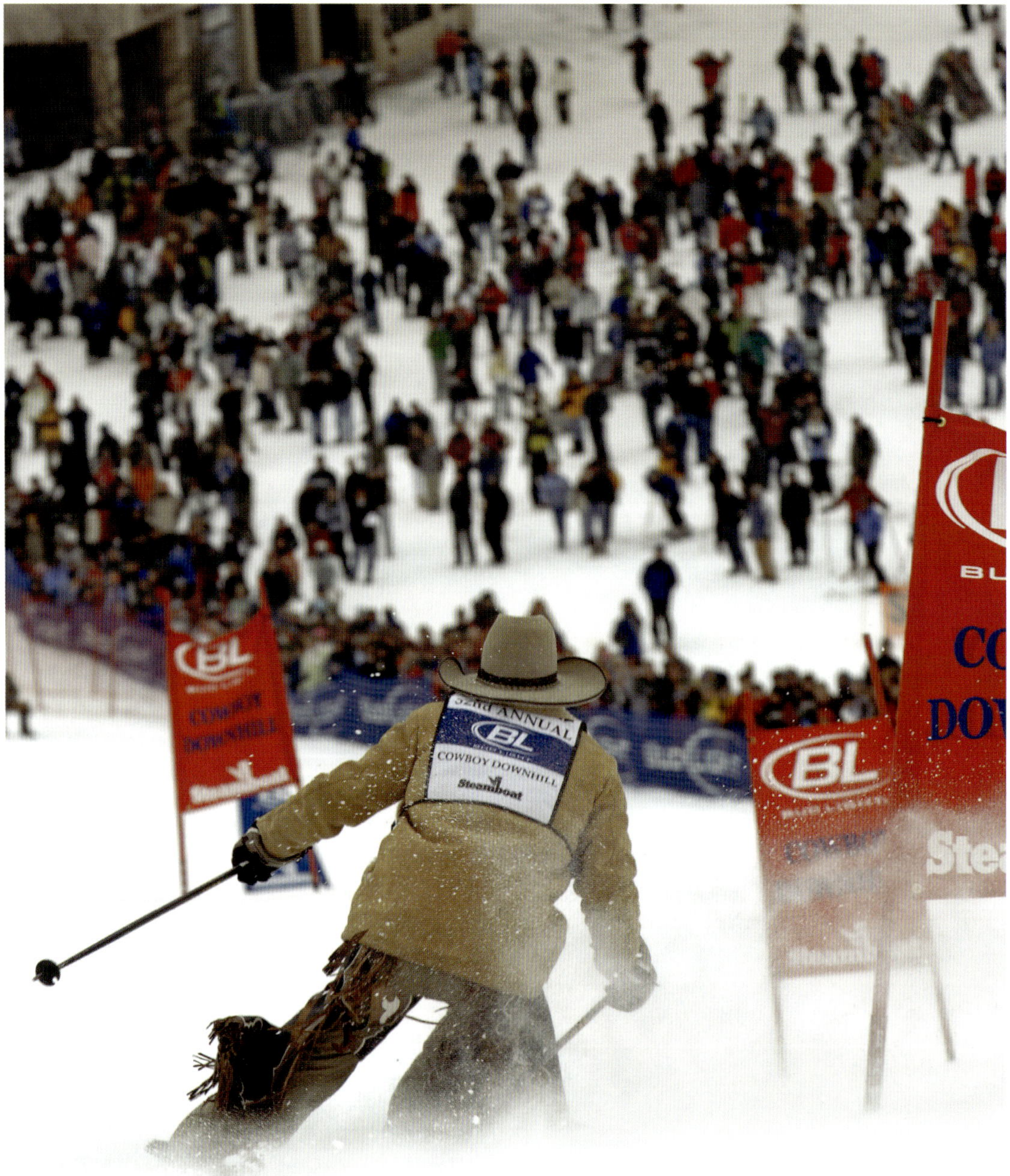

Skier competing in the annual Cowboy Downhill race, Steamboat Springs

high. If you prefer a romantic excursion closer to the ground, indulge in a sleigh ride dinner through town. The combination of nibbles, neighs, and nippy weather is guaranteed to delight.

When snow falls softly on the beckoning slopes, it's only logical to spend your days doing runs on the legendary Howelsen Hill, the oldest continuously running ski area in the country. Skiing this area, which is named after the town's renowned Carl Howelsen, is a raw and necessary experience for all ski lovers. Keep the ski suit on for some mountaintop dining at Hazie's, a restaurant offering an unmatched view.

For a night on the town that's festive in spirit and beauty, see the town's holiday ice show, A Steamboat Christmas. Performed by local skating club members, the show dazzles and excites with bright costumes and enthusiastically choreographed holiday numbers. To benefit the Steamboat Springs Figure Skating Club, there is an annual Holiday Dance Party that includes a silent auction, wine tasting, and delectable three-course meal. With a different location each year, this traveling party is always a night of fun in charity's name.

Spend Christmas Eve watching bright lights soaring down the smooth mountains in the dark of night. The Steamboat Christmas Eve Torchlight Parade showcases the beauty of the Yampa Valley in a gorgeous ceremony of skiers jetting down a mountain lit only by torches. At the end of the Torchlight Parade, watch fireworks explode to ring in Christmas Day.

In mid-January or early February, a tradition first started by Carl Howelsen takes over the town. With spectator sports and cheer galore, the annual Winter Carnival lights up the town. Watch ski racing and jumping competitions at the ski resort, and then head back to town to watch dogsled races and chariot events on Main Street. The night of the festival, watch in amazement as lights travel down Howelsen Hill in a light parade that's unique and breathtaking, like most everything in this town.

Telluride

& OURAY

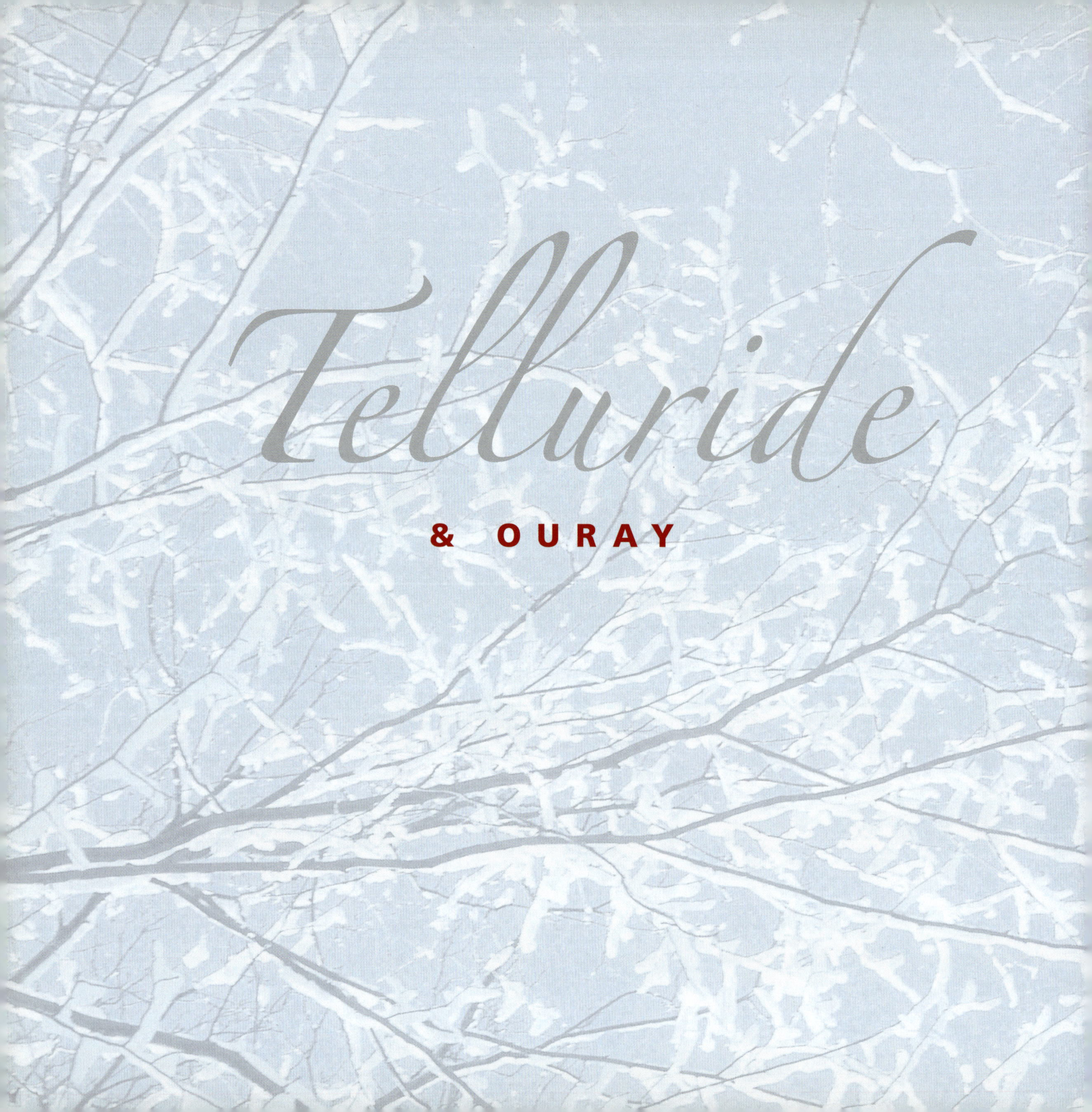

What is Christmas?

It is a fervent wish

that every cup may overflow

with blessings rich and

eternal, and that every path

may lead to peace.

—AGNES M. PHARO

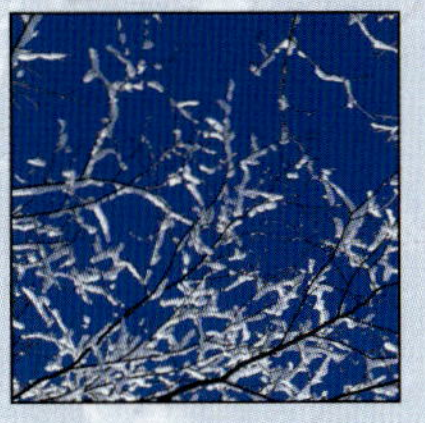

TELLURIDE IS A TOWN THAT INSPIRES songs, and once you see it, you'll understand why. Located 360 miles west of Denver, Telluride is small and picturesque. Once a mining town, the economy is now supported by tourism and skiing. With a Main Street straight out of the movies and sloping mountains on all sides, Telluride becomes a valley of lights during the holiday season.

Graceful as the valley it takes place in, the annual presentation of *The Nutcracker* at the Sheridan Opera House is nothing short of wonderful. This adventurous tale that inspires the spirit is a perfect start to the season. Watch as members of the Telluride Dance Company dazzle in this community performance of a holiday favorite.

As any good small community does, Telluride holds many events that anyone can participate in to get into a grand holiday spirit. The Very Victorian Christmas at the Telluride Historical Museum is just one such event. Create Victorian ornaments and help decorate the museum tree. Then, move on to the Conference Center in Mountain Village—just a gondola ride away—for Sitting with Santa, an opportunity to

Cabin in the woods, off Hwy. 162 in Nathrop, near Ouray

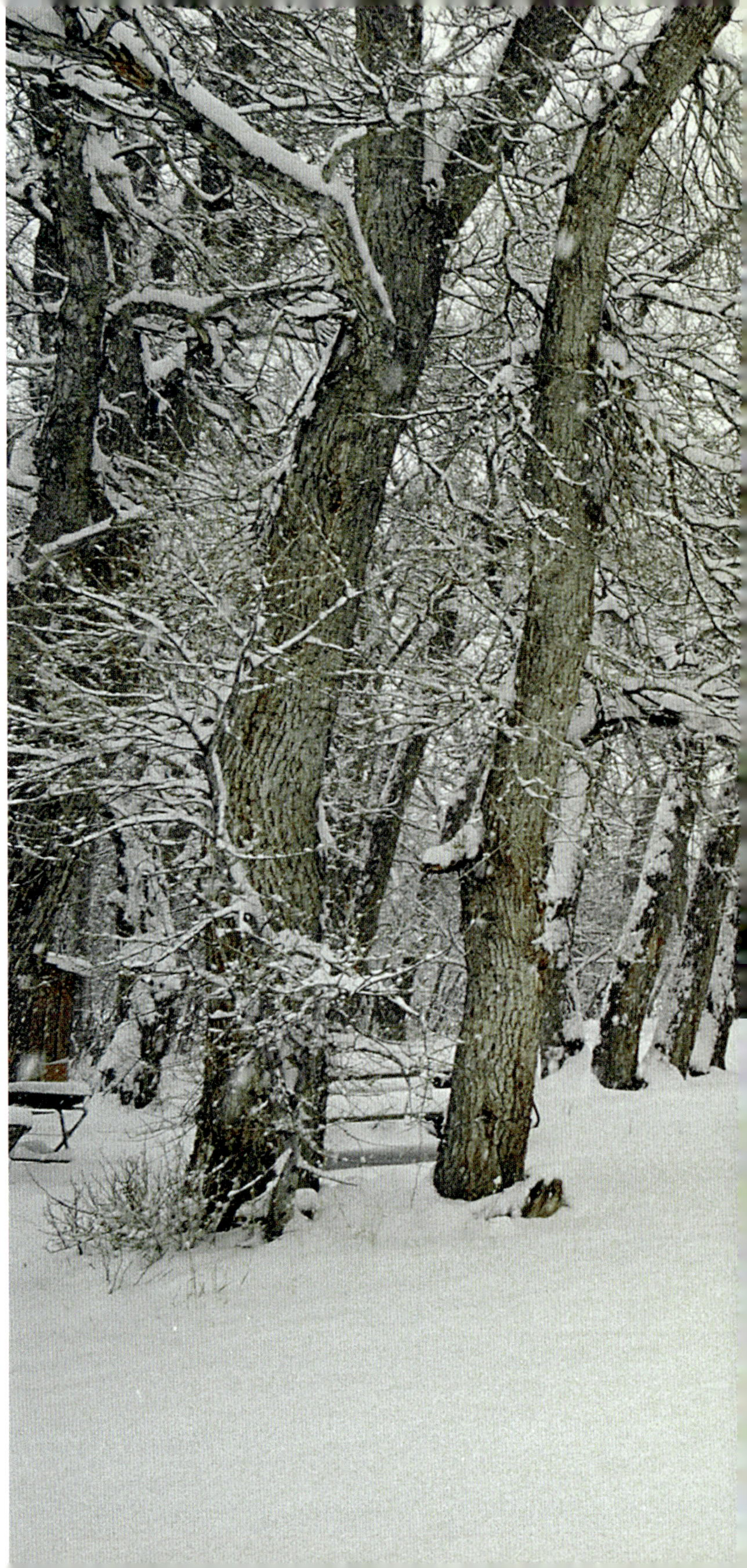

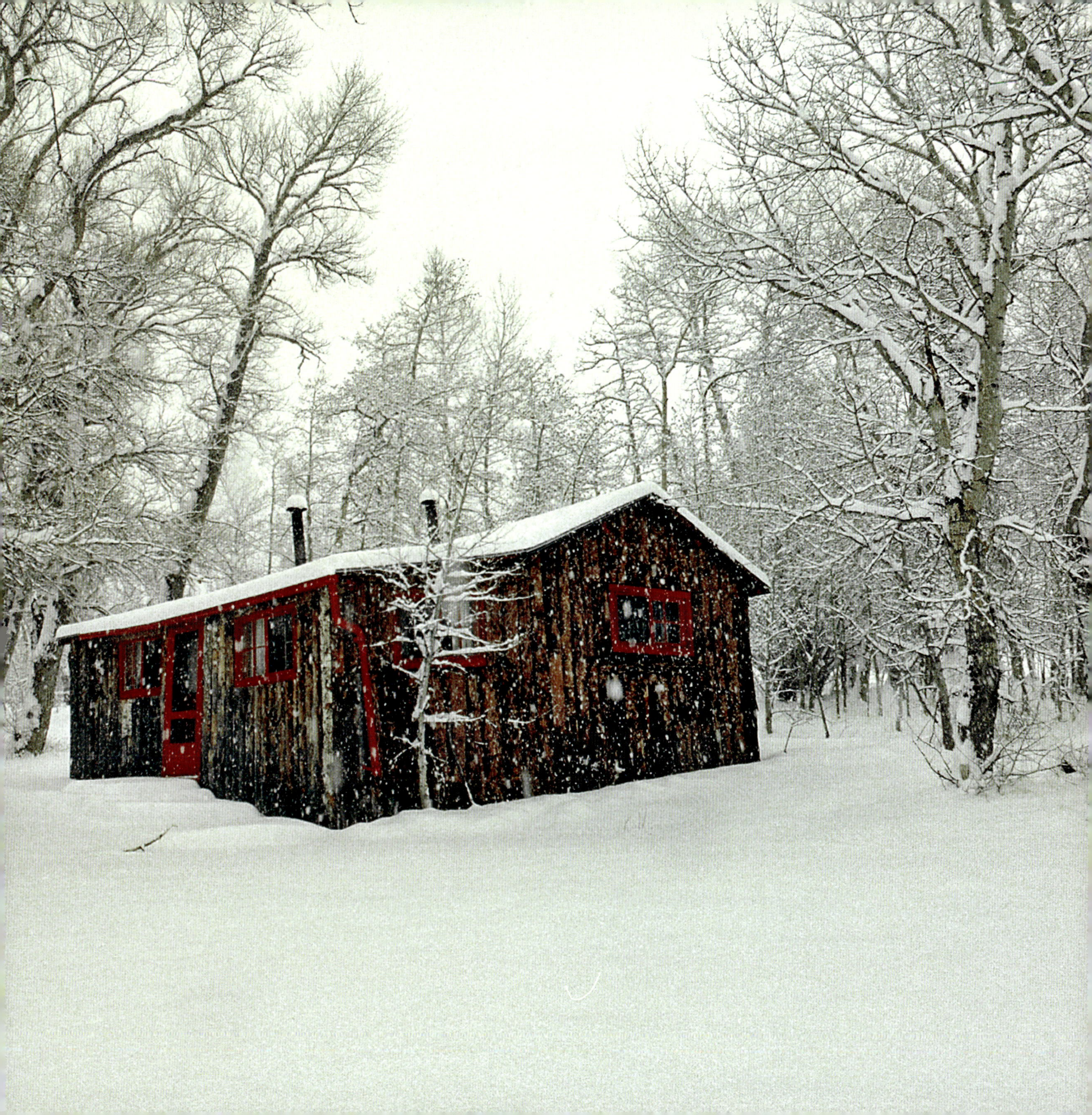

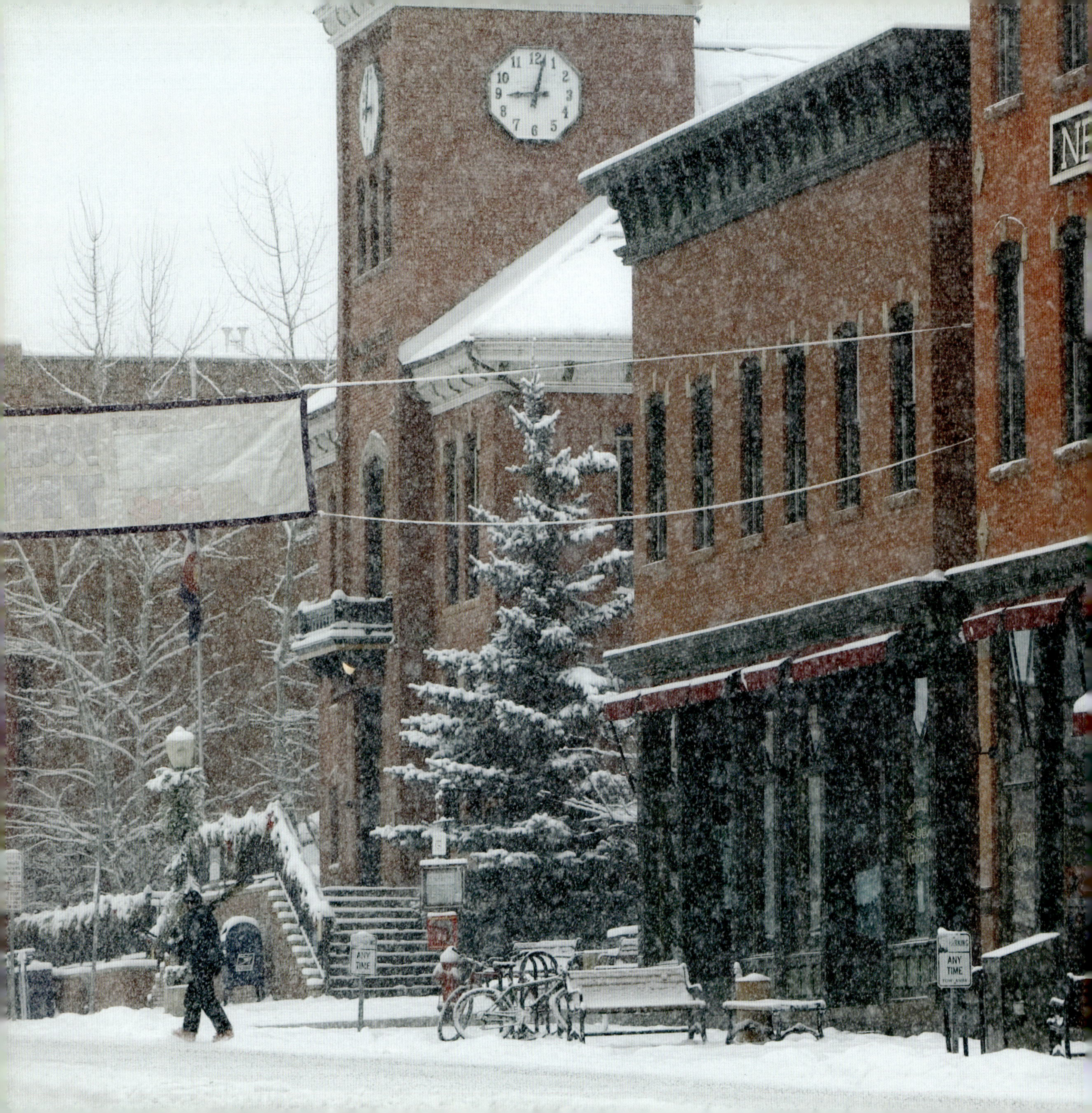
ANY
TIME
ANY
TIME

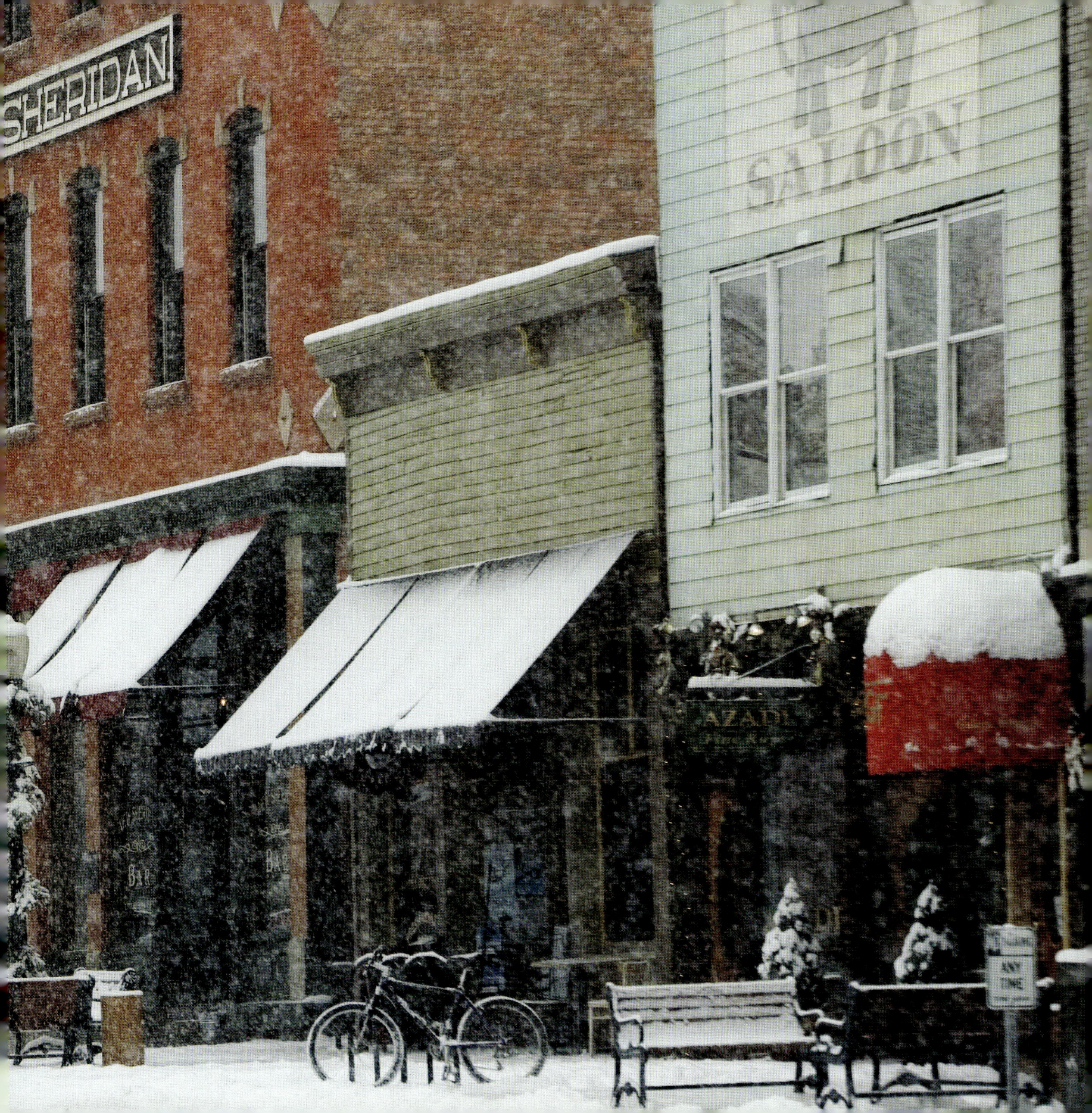
SHERIDAN
SALOON
ANY TIME

meet and greet Santa in an antique sleigh and decorate cookies with his elves.

Head downtown for the annual Jingle Jam, a celebration at Heritage Plaza. Promenade down tree-lit streets, stopping in one-of-a-kind boutiques while sipping a sweet cup of hot chocolate. Browse extravagant gingerbread house displays and snowy store windows for gift ideas while your children meet with Santa.

In early December, Noel Night brings carolers, one-night holiday discounts, and delicious snack stands to the town. For more gift ideas, the TAG Holiday Bazaar is full of creativity and original presents. Find jewelry, ceramics, fine art, bath products, and food all made and sold by local vendors. Held over an early weekend in December at Telluride High School, the event is always bustling with life and locals.

On Christmas Eve, watch in awe as the Torchlight Parade lights up one of the most famous mountains in Colorado. Skiers with torches create sparkling dots that zoom through moguls and trees in intricate patterns, a breathless sight from below. If the parade pleases your fancy, return for a second helping on New Year's Eve. Another spectacular venue for New Year's is the Sheridan Opera House. With a live popular band, hors d'oeuvres, and a champagne toast at midnight, it's the perfect place to dance the night away.

Make sure to enjoy the winter snow sports, including dogsledding, snowmobiling, Nordic and downhill skiing, and heliskiing. As powder piles up in January, head out to the Winter Snow Fest Carnival. Exciting, original activities such as snow sculpting and nighttime snowshoe racing spark interest and intrigue in all viewers. Rock out at concerts that take place on the mountain. Finish your stay in Telluride at the festival of lights, which illuminates the valley as well as your heart.

OURAY

Secluded in the San Juan Mountains nearly 350 miles from Denver, Ouray is a diamond in the rough. With less than 900 year-round residents, the town's entire economy is based on tourism. Drawn by outdoor activities, homey getaways, and breathtaking views, tourists head to this sweet, peaceful town that lights up for the holidays.

Right: A view of the town and ski resort, Telluride

Previous page: The town's main street, West Colorado Avenue, Telluride

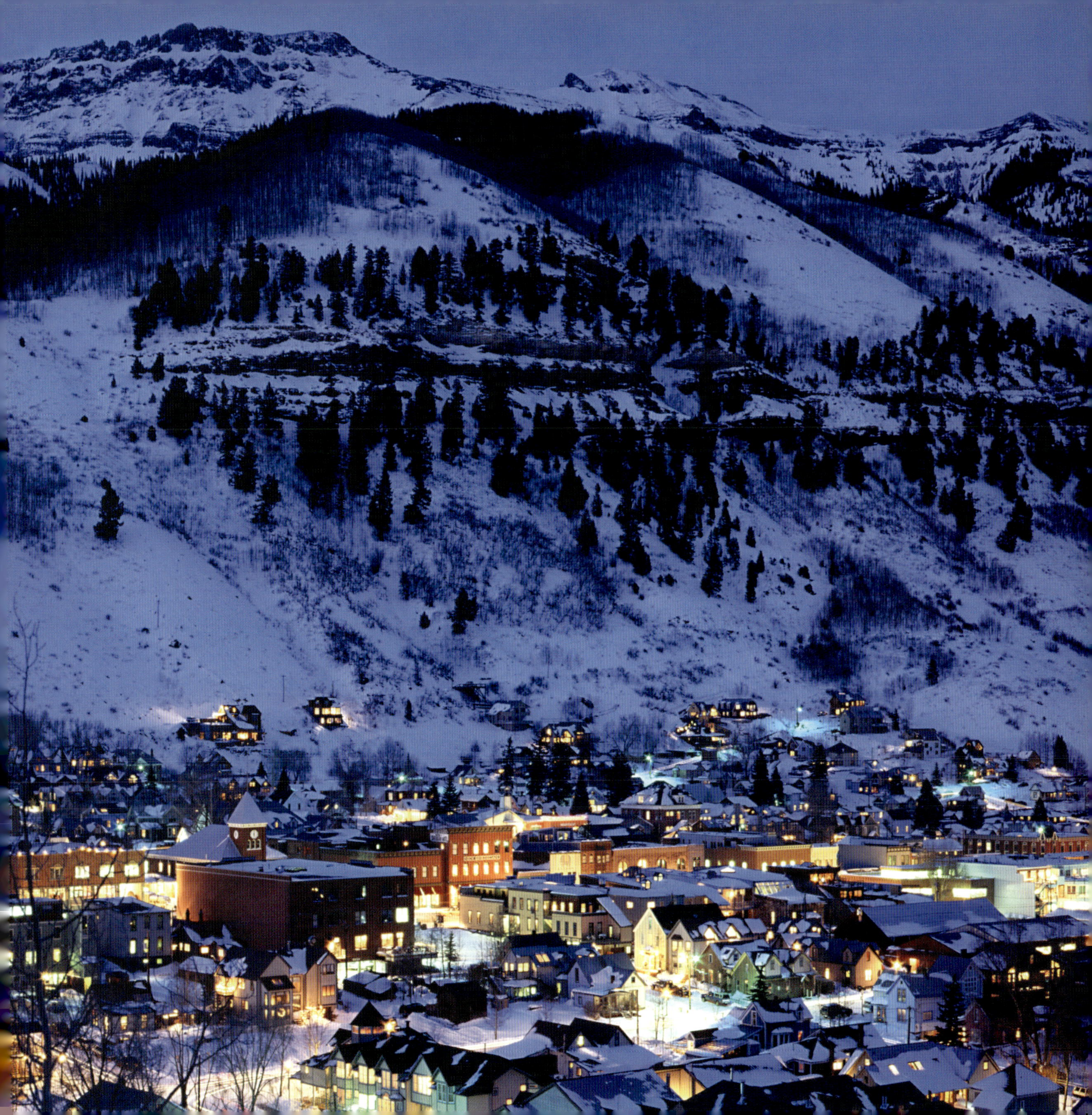

The perfect place to stay during your holiday getaway is the Christmas House Bed and Breakfast, a small inn with just five gorgeous guest suites. Romantic fireplaces, antiques, spa tubs, saunas, and all the usual amenities make this B&B the place to be, especially for Christmas. If you can pry yourself away from your home away from home, watch the entire town light up the day after Thanksgiving, as all businesses and residences turn on their trees, outdoor exhibition lights, and fun holiday decorations.

A few nights later, the official Christmas welcome in Ouray occurs—Yule Night. A Parade of Lights brightens up the San Juan Mountains with floats and smiles. Then, a live nativity scene performance takes place in the center of town and Santa makes a special guest appearance at the celebration.

Another major venue of holiday fun in Ouray is the newly renovated Wright Opera House. Over the course of December, the opera house plays host to a variety of events, from *The Nutcracker Sweets* dance recital to performances of Dickens' *A Christmas Carol* and the Holiday Ice Dance, a mixer for the entire community with proceeds going back to the opera house.

Being the community-oriented town that it is, Ouray features plenty of holiday festivities great for the entire family. Gumdrops, frosting, and cookies make for a sweet combination at the Ouray Community Center during their annual gingerbread-house decorating day. The annual Craft Show at the Elks Lodge is another family-friendly activity. While there, let the kids help pick out gifts for family and friends—it will mean more and they'll have a great time doing it.

After a pleasant holiday surrounded by mountains, snow, and the people you love, spend the New Year in Ouray. The Elks Lodge sports a live band and serves breakfast after the midnight fireworks. The Ouray Community Center features live music, dancing, a fabulous buffet, and fireworks at midnight. If you're feeling ambitious, make the rounds and attend a third party—the New Year's Eve Gala at the Tundra Restaurant with more dancing, live music, and a splendid champagne toast to the New Year. The Tundra is a sure hot spot for the evening. The next day, nurse your dancing feet in the Ouray Hot Springs, a natural hot mineral pool surrounded by peaks that rival the Swiss Alps.

With the New Year chugging along, the Ouray Ice Festival rolls into town. Considered by many to be the best ice-climbing event in the world, the festival draws large and avid crowds. With other events such as snowshoe races and kids' climbing walls, it is sure to be a crowd-pleaser. After watching ice fly and crampons kick, take one last deep breath of mountain air and leave the quiet of Ouray, something you'll surely miss when you're back in the city.

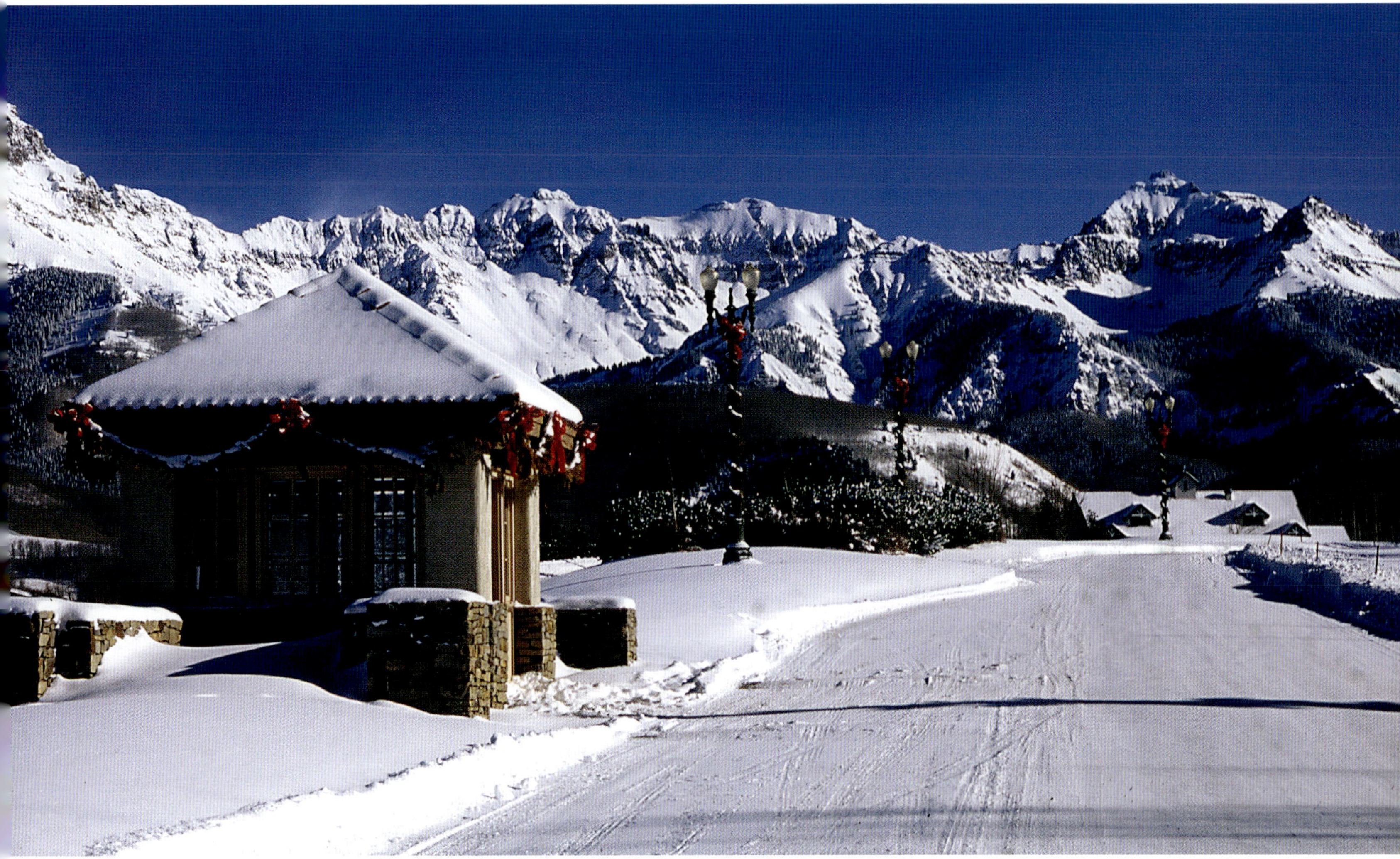

Above: The entrance to the town of Mountain Village, Colorado, near Telluride

Next page: Snowy willow swamp, off County Road 7, outside Ridgway, near Ouray

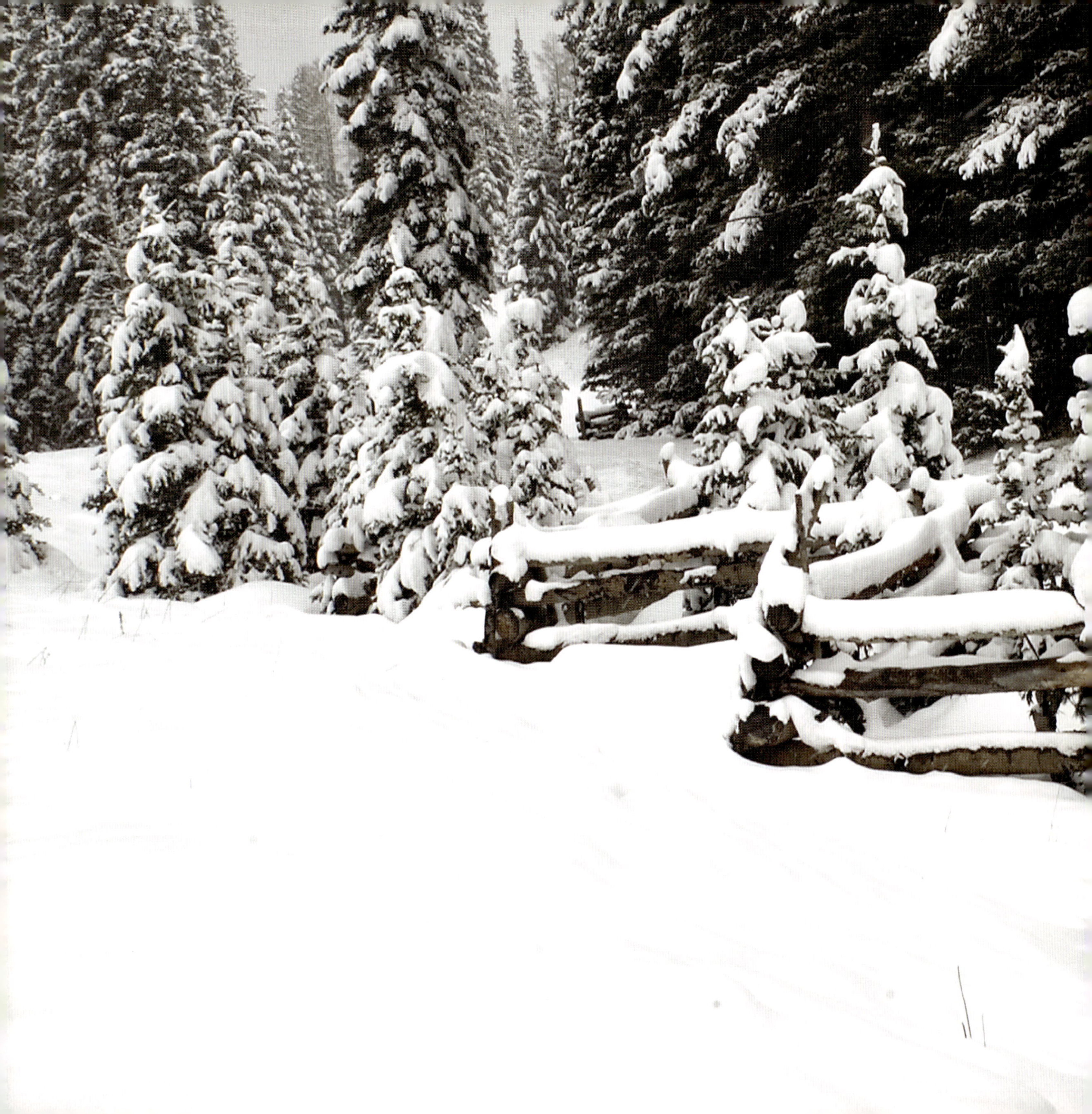

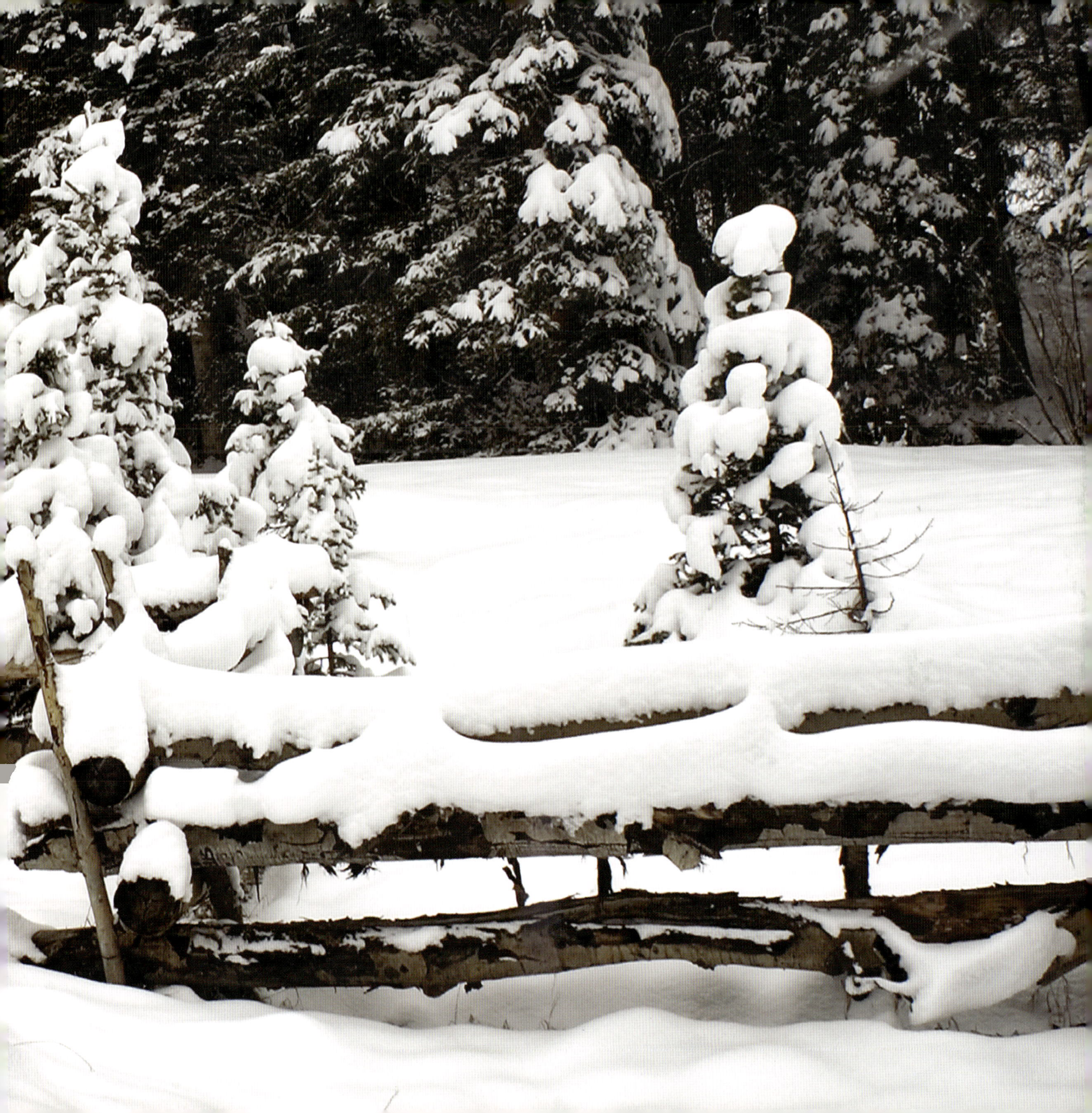

Vail

& BEAVER CREEK

Virginia:

"Please tell me the truth, is there a Santa Claus?"

Editor: *"Yes, Virginia, there is a Santa Claus. He exists as certainly as love and generosity and devotion exist...."*

—FRANCIS P. CHURCH,
THE NEW YORK SUN

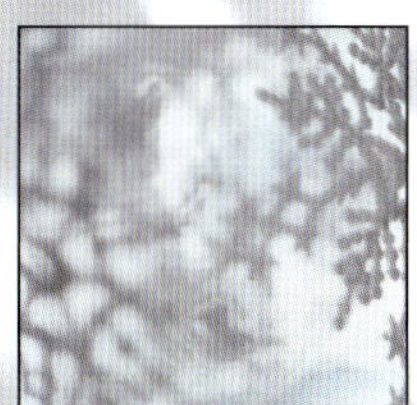

RANKED AS THE NO. 1 SKI RESORT in the country by *Ski Magazine,* Vail has the art of snow down pat. About 100 miles west of the Mile High City off I-70, this town is isolated enough for the perfect vacation, yet only a two-hour drive away from reality. Vail is within close proximity of Beaver Creek and Avon, so the holidays are three times the fun in this Colorado town.

Vail Valley, one of the most popular mountain destinations in Colorado, lights up with the buzz of shopping, snow, and Santa during the holiday season. A cultured night on the town is a grand affair in downtown Beaver Creek. With annual performances of the holiday classics *The Nutcracker* and *A Christmas Carol* at the Vilar Center, there is no shortage of holiday spirit or exciting performances. Paint the town red and green in the few days before Christmas in Lionshead and Vail Village during their holiday parades and tree lighting ceremonies.

Vail Village is a buzzing, bustling commercial holiday center during Snow Daze, a weeklong extravaganza of excitement in early December. The festival boasts one of the

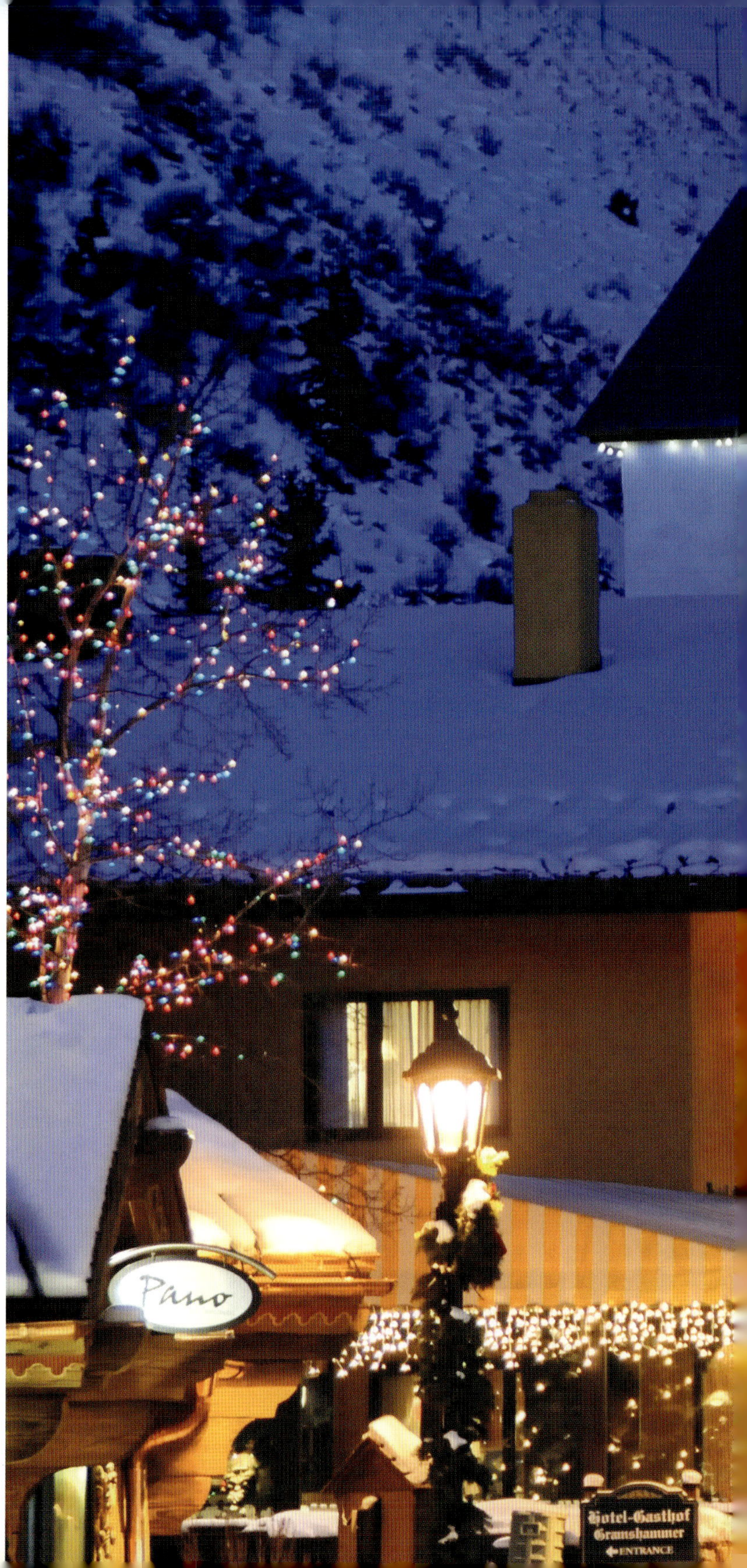

The Bavarian-style Vail Village, Vail

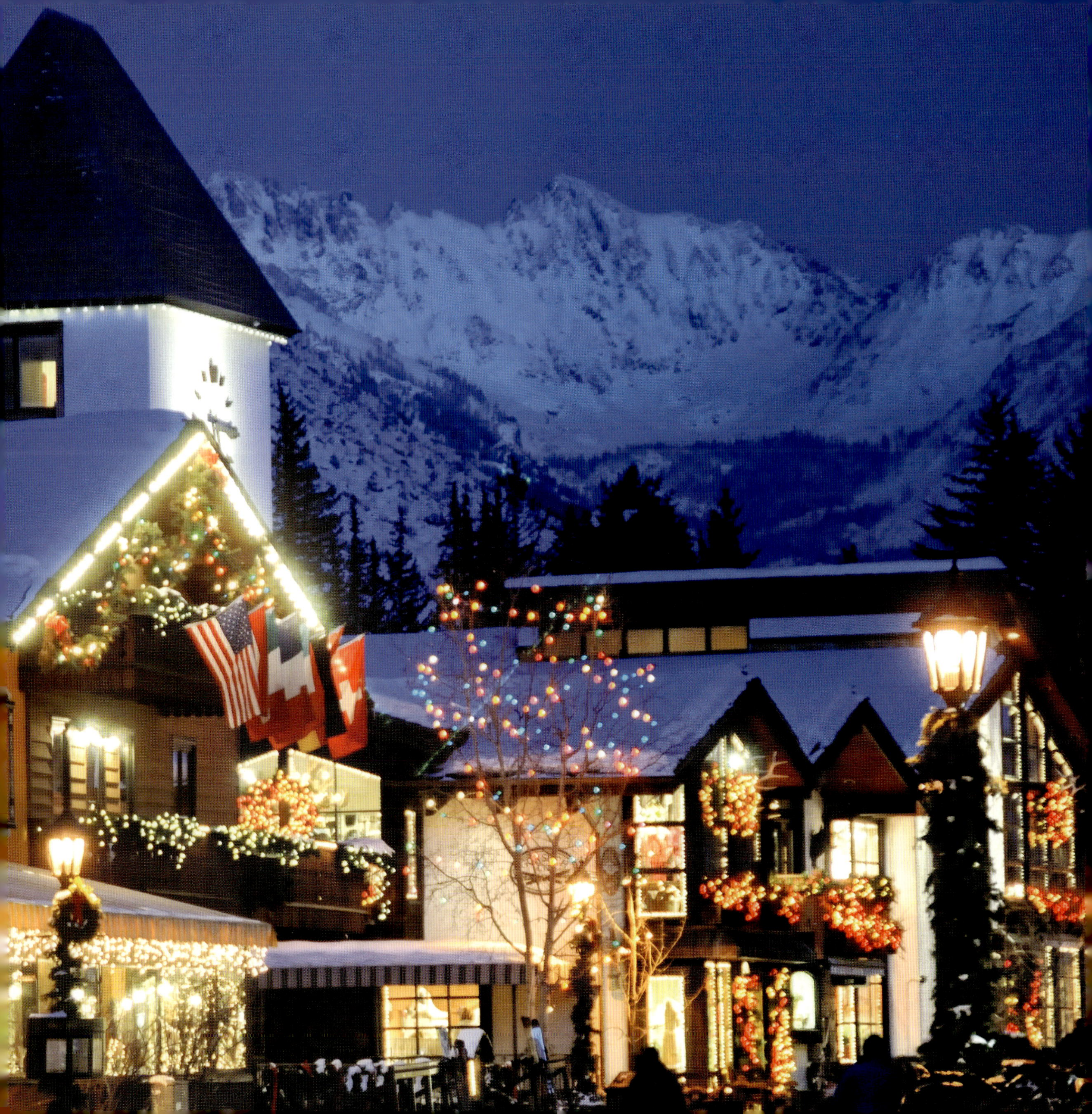

best ski parties in North America and is constantly flowing with activity. From street parties to expos and demos of the latest ski and snowboard equipment, Snow Daze is an excellent way to explore the town. All the excitement leads up to a highly anticipated headliner concert and fireworks on the final Saturday of the festival, an event you just can't miss.

You can't go to Vail without spending time on the mountain. So, take the gondola to the top of the mountain and dine at a five-star restaurant while gazing at unforgettable views of the valley below. Listen in on a Nature at Night chat presented by the Gore Range Natural Science School at the Eagle's Nest fire pit for an enlightening treat. Learn about everything from astronomy to nocturnal animals and gain an appreciation for the natural beauty of the mountains around you, all while gazing at the stars. If you opt to travel the peaks during the day, Adventure Ridge is a must. Tubing, ski biking, dogsledding, hut trips, kids' snowmobiling, snowshoeing, and trampolining all make this venue unbelievably fun.

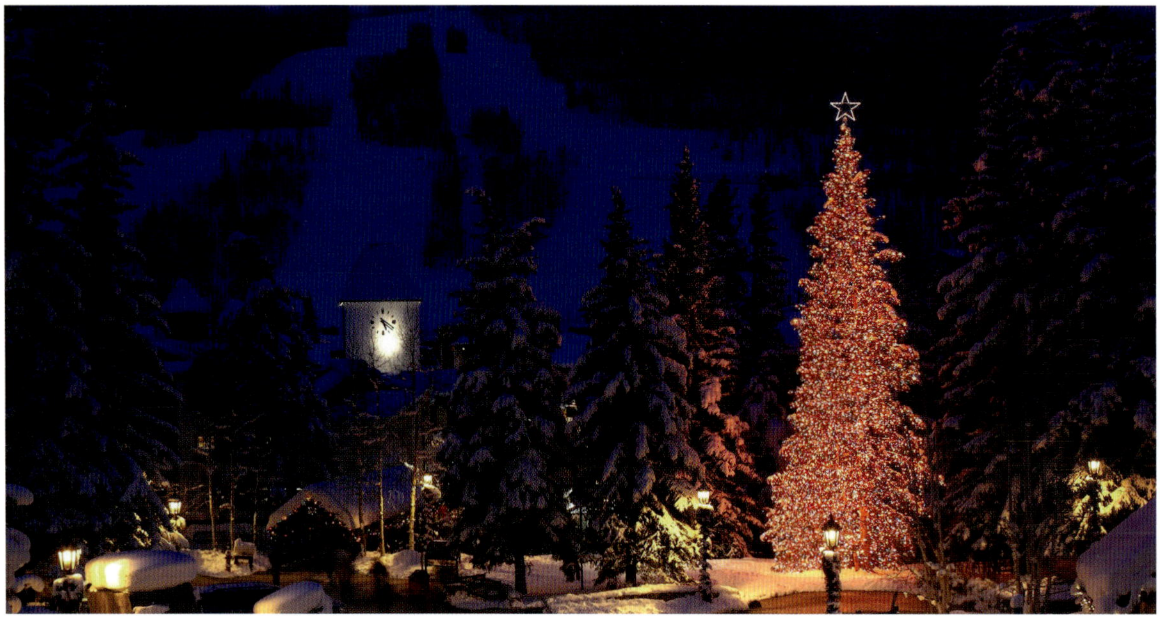

Above: Town tree and covered bridge, Vail
Right: Downtown shopping area, Vail

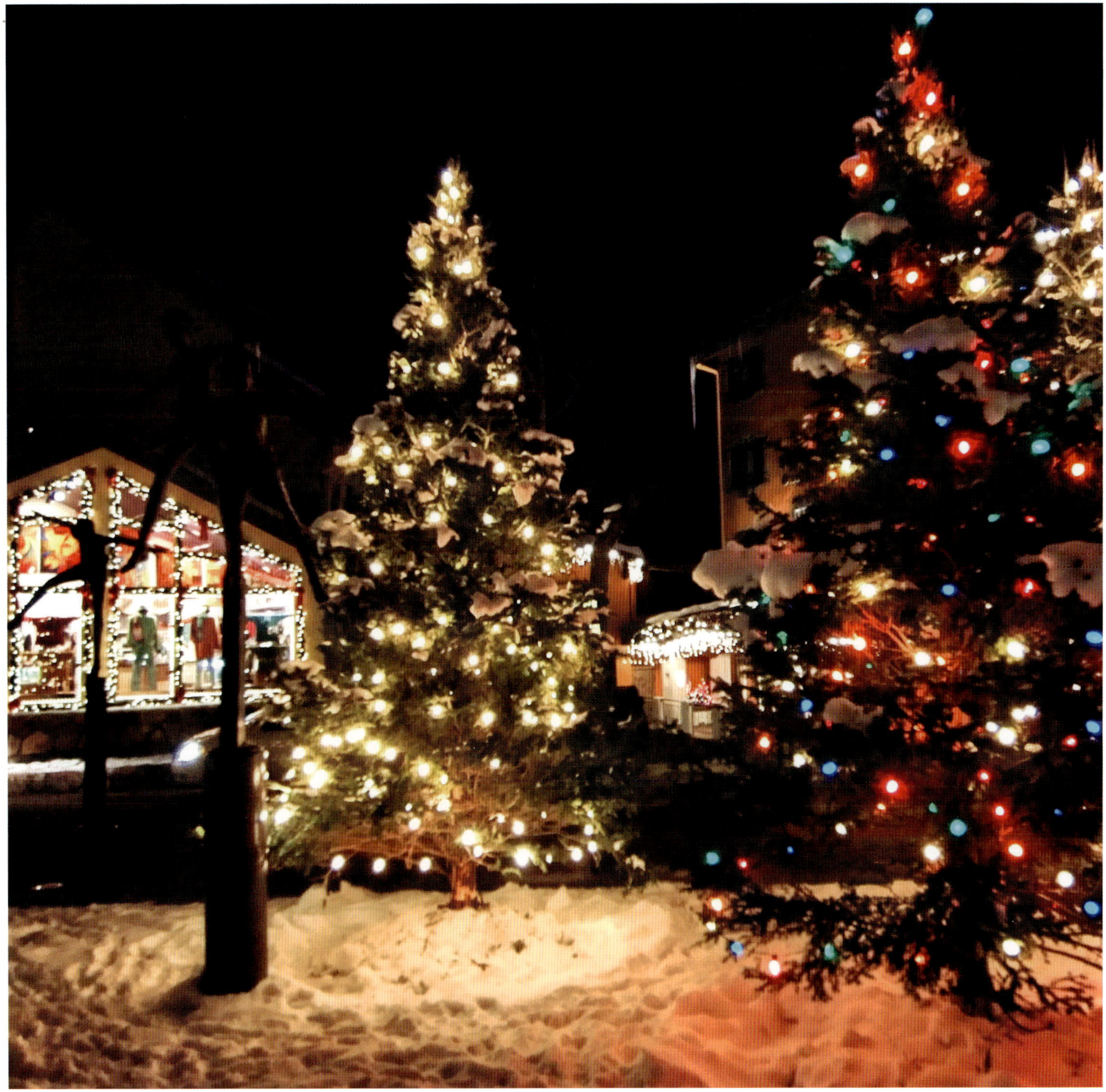

If you prefer to simply explore the slopes on your skis or snowboard, spend your time at the amazing Vail Resort ski area, sure to please all snow lovers.

Every year, members of the Figure Skating Club of Vail spend tireless hours at Dobson Arena preparing for one of the season's best holiday ice shows. A different theme every year draws a wide audience to the spectacular skating exhibition. In addition to club members, adorable beginners and some of the best skaters from around the country and Canada also participate in the holiday festivity.

Skiers spark a flame for the New Year during torchlight parades in both Vail and Beaver Creek. Celebrate in Beaver Creek with fireworks and in Vail with a ski down Golden Peak; fireworks and a street party follow the light show. No matter which show you decide to attend, the New Year is sure to be sweet in a setting this stunning.

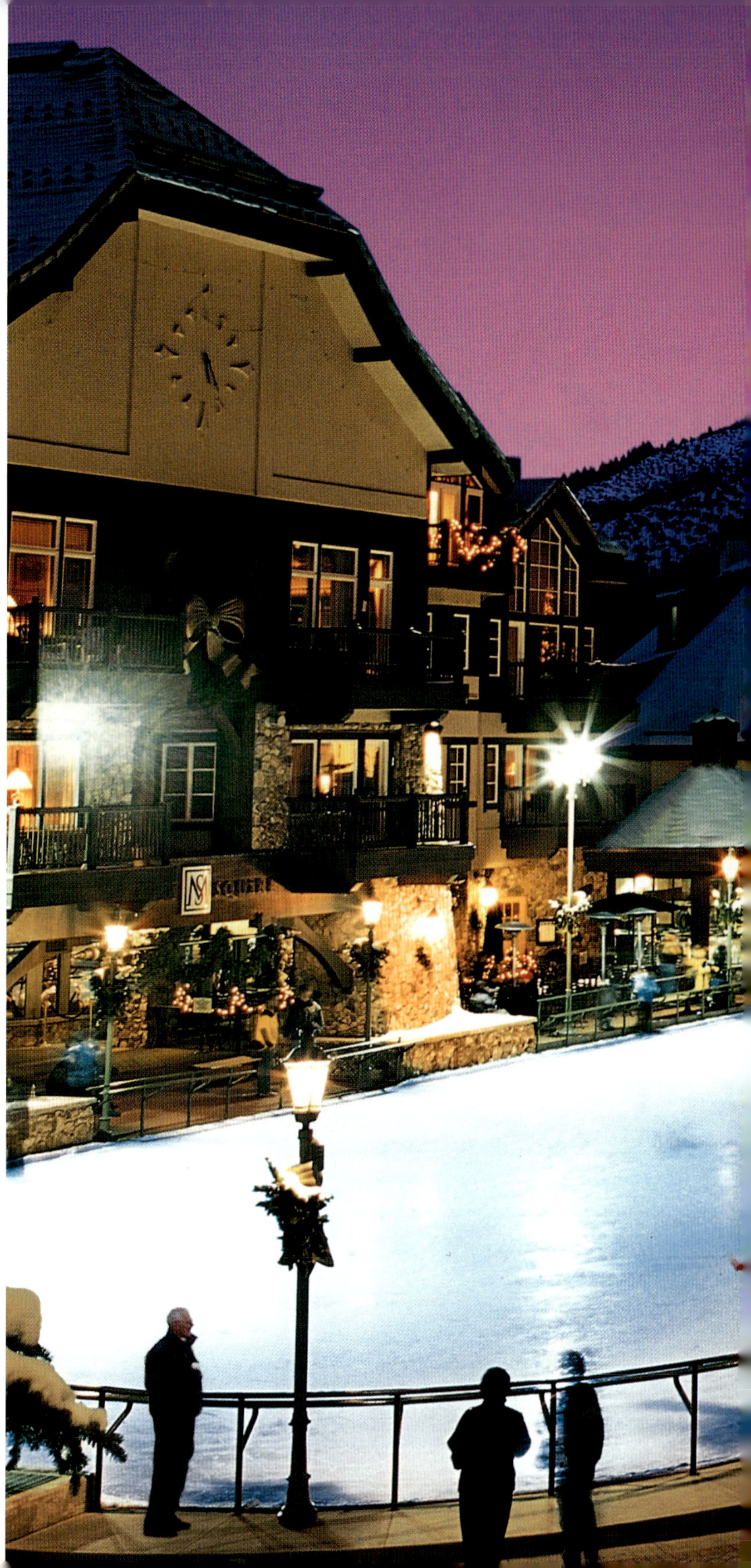

Right: Ice skating rink, Beaver Creek

Next page: Fireworks over the skating rink, Beaver Creek

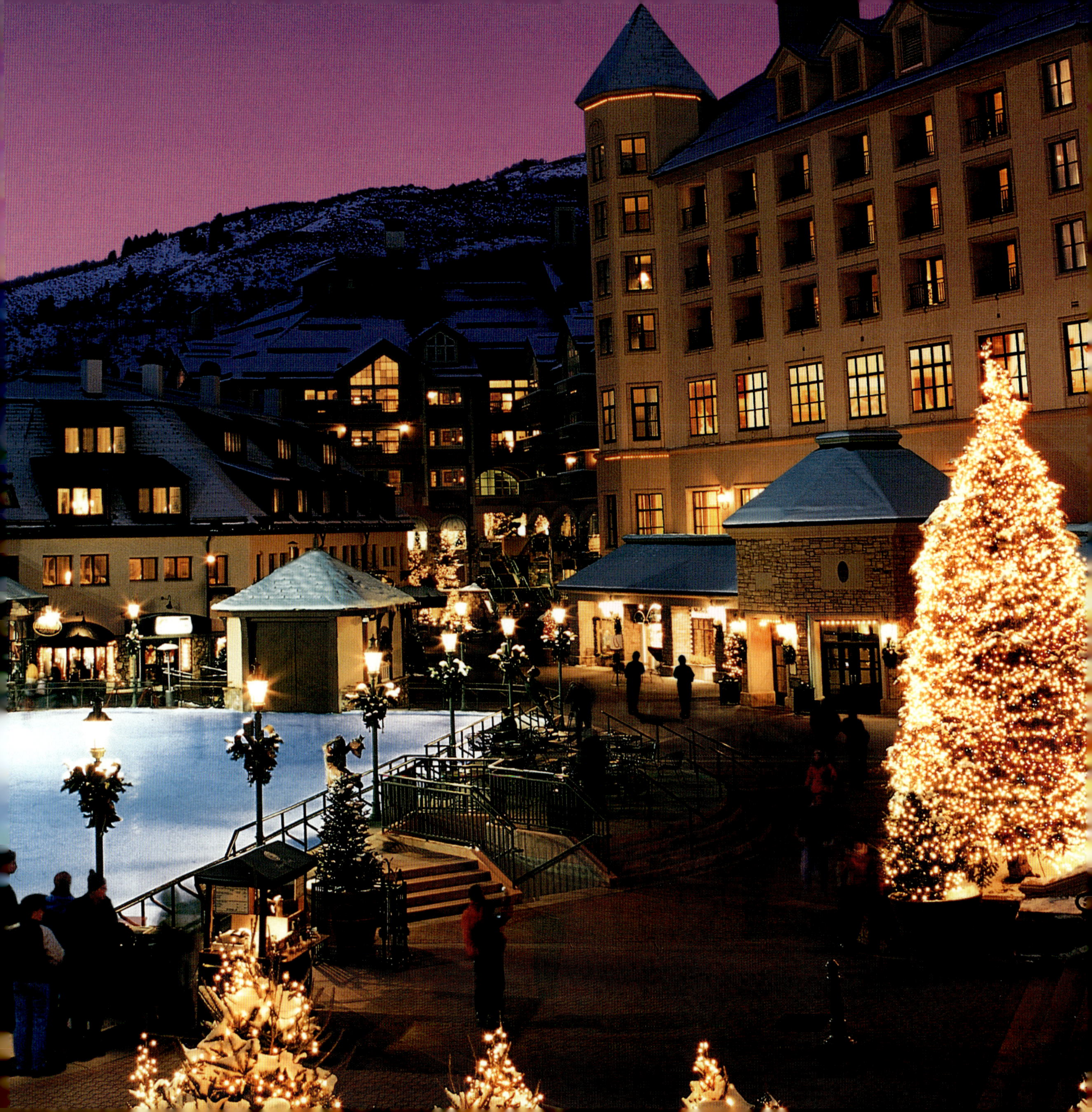

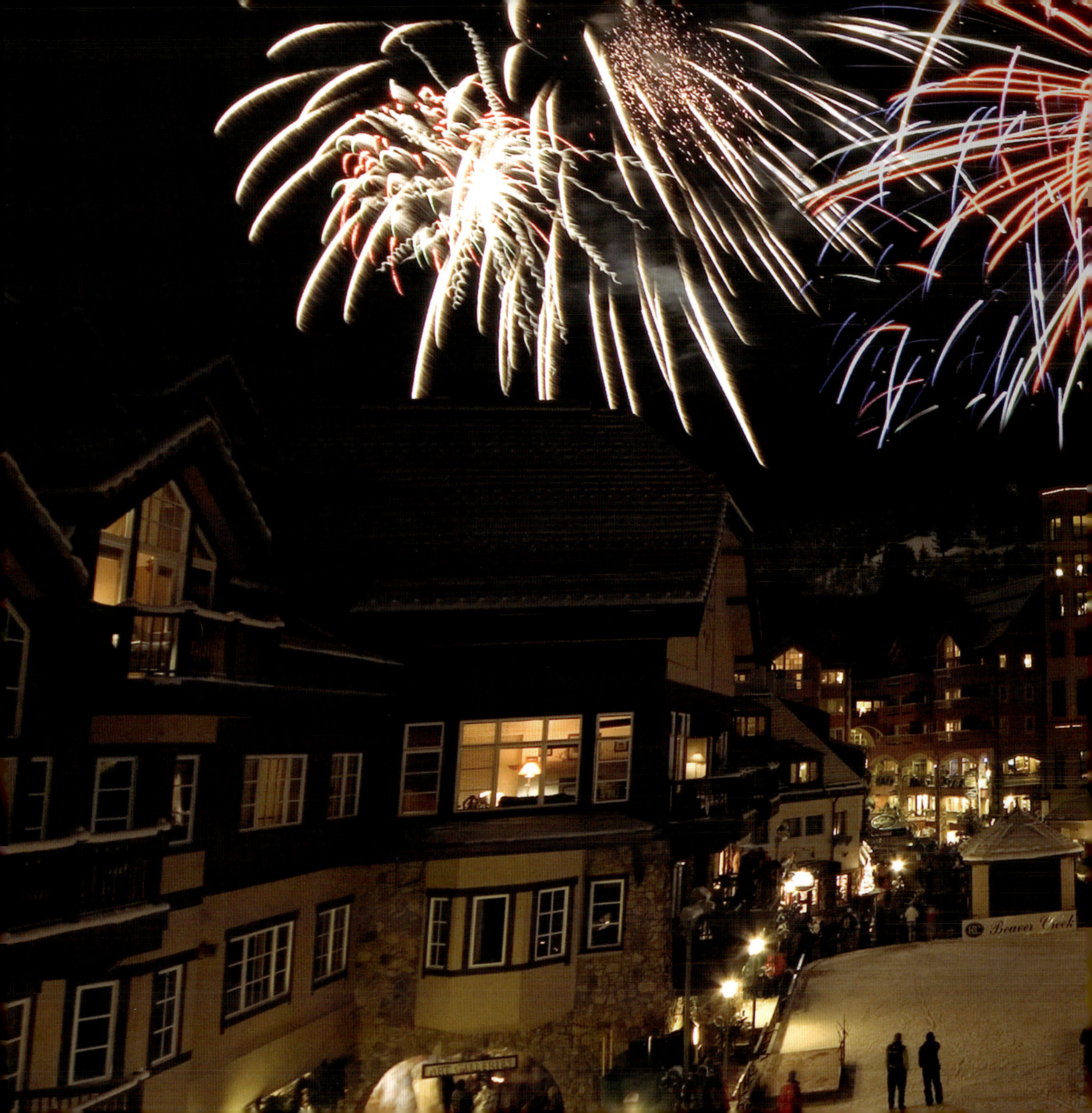
Beaver Creek
ART GALLERIES

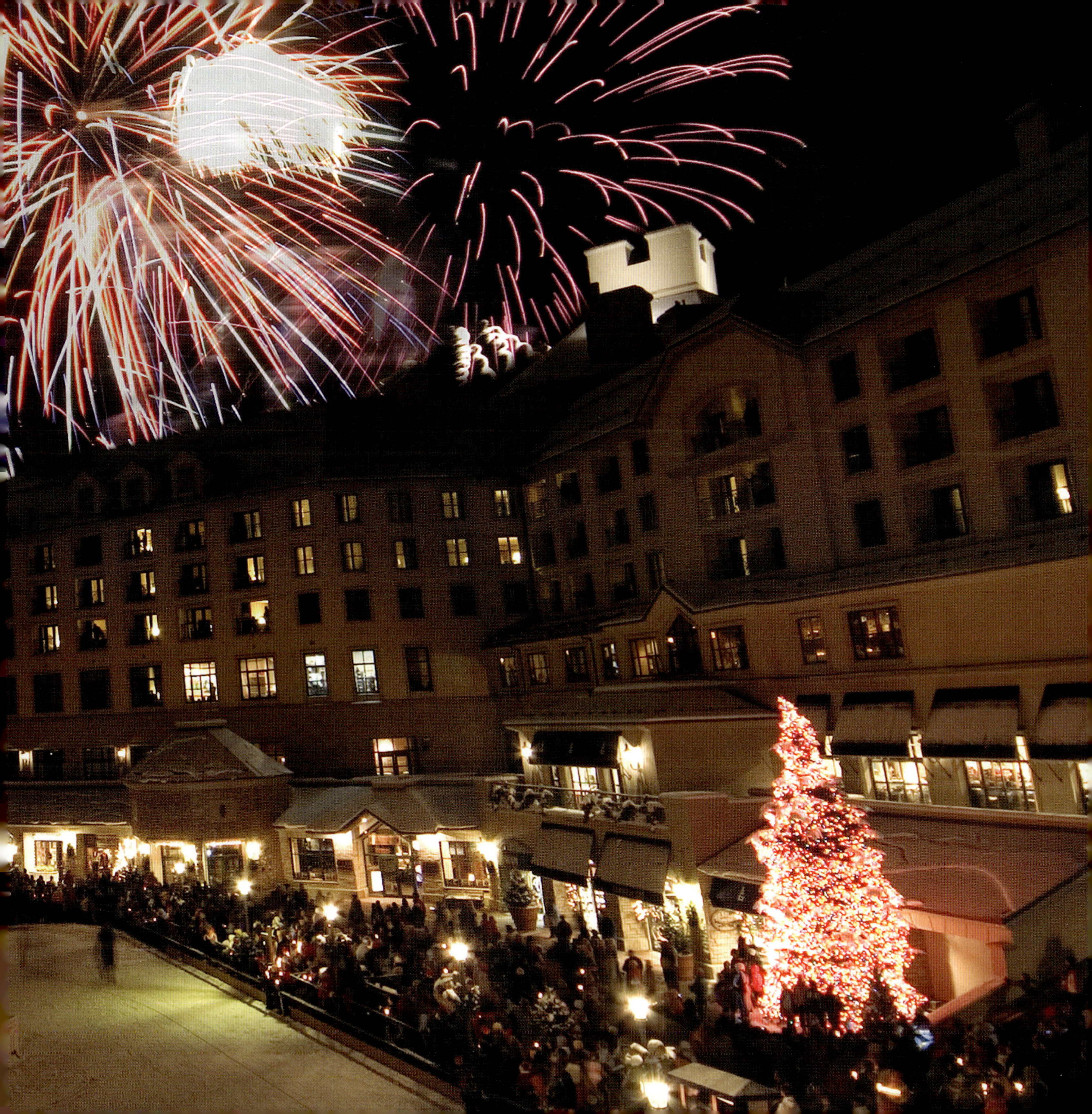

Photo Credits

Front cover Taimur Mahmood
Back cover (left) Steve Crecelius
Back cover (center) Susan Mosier
Back cover (right) Cathy Weaver/ City of Littleton
page 2–3 Ken Papaleo
page 4 Swingle Tree
page 6 Steve Crecelius
page 7 Steve Crecelius
page 10–11 Steve Crecelius
page 13 Steve Crecelius
page 14–15 Steve Crecelius
page 18–19 Steve Crecelius
page 20 Steve Crecelius
page 21 Chris Wyman
page 22 Daniel Bayer
page 23 Daniel Bayer
page 24–25 Biege Jones
page 26–27 Jason Dewey
page 28–29 Daniel Bayer
page 32–33 Marianne Martin Real Life Portraits
page 34 Alzheimer's Association of Colorado
page 35 Russell Dohrmann
page 36–37 Russell Dohrmann
page 38 Anne Barrett
page 39 Russell Dohrmann
page 40 Dan Bihn
page 41 Courtesy of Fort Collins DBA
page 42 Dan Bihn
page 43 Dan Bihn
page 46–47 Carl Scofield
page 48 Carl Scofield
page 49 Carl Scofield
page 50–51 Ken Papaleo
page 52 Steve Crecelius
page 53 Joe Kusumoto
page 54 Steve Crecelius
page 55 Steve Crecelius
page 58 Steve Crecelius
page 59 Courtesy of The Broadmoor
page 60–61 Steve Crecelius
page 62 Steve Crecelius
page 63 City of Colorado Springs
page 64 Steve Crecelius
page 66–67 Ben D'Andrea
page 70–71 Crested Butte Mountain Resort & Tom Stillo
page 72 Crested Butte Mountain Resort & Tom Stillo
page 73 Crested Butte Mountain Resort & Tom Stillo
page 74 Crested Butte Mountain Resort & Tom Stillo
page 75 Crested Butte Mountain Resort & Tom Stillo
page 76–77 Crested Butte Mountain Resort & Tom Stillo
page 80–81 Jackie Shumaker
page 82 Steve Crecelius
page 83 Steve Crecelius
page 84 Steve Crecelius
page 85 Terry Shapiro
page 86 Courtesy of St. John's Cathedral
page 87 Jackie Shumaker
page 88 Steve Crecelius
page 89 Steve Crecelius
page 90 Steve Crecelius
page 91 Steve Crecelius
page 92 Steve Crecelius
page 93 Steve Crecelius
page 94 Scott Dressel-Martin
page 95 Cathy Weaver/ City of Littleton
page 96–97 Steve Crecelius
page 100 Claude Steeleman
page 101 Claude Steeleman
page 102–103 Claude Steeleman
page 106–107 Susan Mosier
page 108 Susan Mosier
page 109 Courtsey of Ken Benson and the Grand Lake Area Chamber of Commerce
page 110–111 Steve Crecelius
page 112 Art Ferrari
page 113 Courtsey of Jeff Martin and the Grand Lake Area Chamber of Commerce
page 114–115 Steve Crecelius
page 118 Steve Crecelius
page 119 Steve Crecelius
page 120–121 Ken Papaleo
page 122 Courtesy of Synergy Photographics/Denver
page 123 Steve Crecelius
page 124–125 Bob Winsett
page 126 (top) Leisa Gibson
page 126 (bottom) Ric Stovall
page 127 Gary Haines
page 130 Glenwood Hot Springs
page 131 Kjell Mitchell, Glenwood Hot Springs
page 133 Vicky Nash, Resort Trends
page 134 Grand Junction Visitor & Convention Bureau
page 135 Courtesy of Hotel Colorado
page 138–139 Steve Sunday
page 140–141 Ken Papaleo
page 142–143 Courtesy of Ski Copper
page 146–147 Larry Pierce
page 148 Steve Crecelius
page 149 Corey Kopischke
page 150 Larry Pierce
page 154–155 Taimur Mahmood
page 156–157 Doug Berry
page 159 Doug Berry
page 161 Doug Berry
page 162–163 Taimur Mahmood
page 166–167 Steve Crecelius
page 168 Courtesy of Town of Vail
page 169 Steve Crecelius
page 170–171 Jack Affleck
page 172–173 Cody Downard
page 175 Steve Crecelius
last page Steve Crecelius

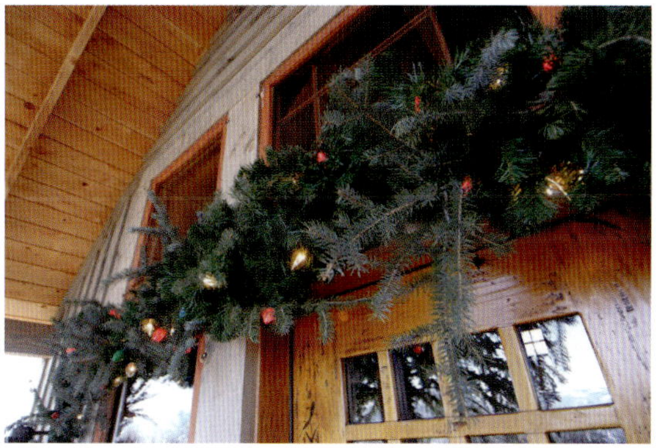

Published by
Colorado Expression magazine and
Westcliffe Publishers
a Big Earth Publishing company
3005 Center Green Drive, Suite 220
Boulder, Colorado 80301
www.bigearthpublishing.com

Printed in China, through World Print, Ltd.

Editor: Kelly Kordes Anton
Photo editors: Sarah Allen and Elizabeth Jones
Cover and interior design: Rebecca Finkel

International Standard Book Number: 978-1-56579-621-8

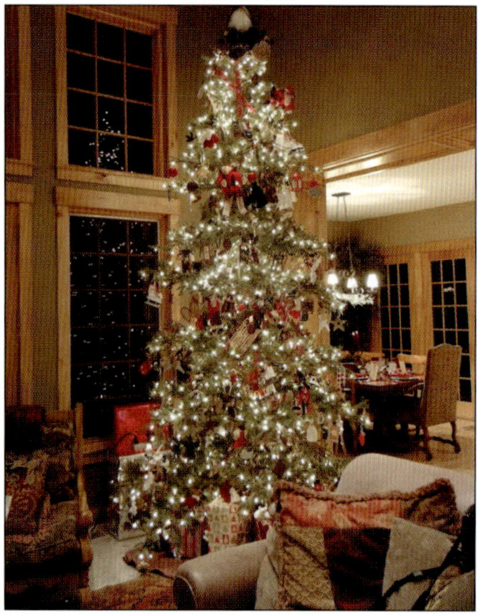

MERRY CHRISTMAS

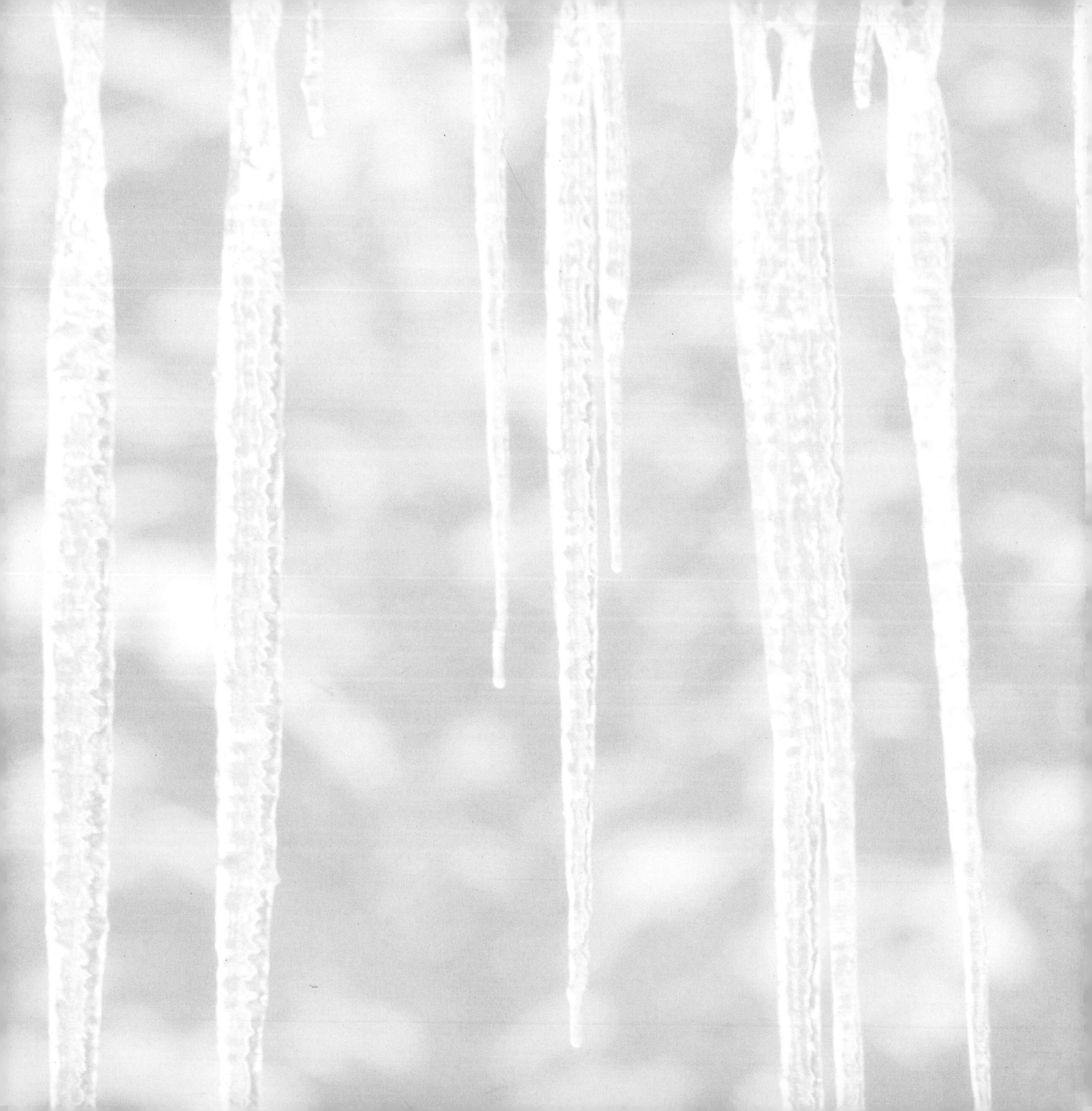